GLOBALIZATION
AND THE EVOLVING
WORLD SOCIETY

INTERNATIONAL STUDIES IN SOCIOLOGY AND SOCIAL ANTHROPOLOGY

Editor

S. ISHWARAN

VOLUME 71

PROSHANTA K. NANDI (ED.)
SHAHID M. SHAHIDULLAH (ED.)

GLOBALIZATION
AND THE EVOLVING
WORLD SOCIETY

GLOBALIZATION AND THE EVOLVING WORLD SOCIETY

EDITED BY

PROSHANTA K. NANDI

AND

SHAHID M. SHAHIDULLAH

BRILL
LEIDEN · BOSTON · KÖLN
1998

This book is printed on acid-free paper.

Library of Congress Cataloging-in-Publication Data

Globalization and the evolving world society / edited by Proshanta K.
Nandi and Shahid M. Shahidullah.
    p.   cm. — (International studies in sociology and social
anthropology, ISSN 0074-8684 ; v. 71)
    Includes bibliographical references and index.
    ISBN 9004112472 (pbk. : alk. paper)
    1. International economic integration.   2. Economic development.
I. Nandi, Proshanta K.   II. Shahidullah, Shahid M., 1950–
III. Series.
HF1418.5.G5818   1998
337—dc21   98–34821
                                                                          CIP

Die Deutsche Bibliothek - CIP-Einheitsaufnahme

Globalization and the evolving world society / ed. by Proshanta K.
Nandi and Shahid M. Shahidullah. – Leiden ; Boston ; Köln : Brill,
1998
    (International studies in sociology and social anthropology ; Vol. 71)
    ISBN 90–04–11247–2

ISSN 0074-8684
ISBN 90 04 11247 2

PRINTED IN THE NETHERLANDS

CONTENTS

Articles

Introduction
Globalization and Development: The Emerging Dynamics and Dilemmas

PROSHANTA K. NANDI* and SHAHID M. SHAHIDULLAH**

Discourses on globalization have recently begun in almost all areas of life and activities from industries to the Internet and music to the media. The collective actors and organizations of all walks of life today make reference to the emergence of a global society. The industrial and business leaders of the world firmly believe that globalization is a key to growth and survival. Percey Barnevik, Chairman and CEO of ABB, which has about 70,000 employees overseas, has nicely summarized the industrial discourses on globalization in his recent speech to the International Management Symposium held in Switzerland: "As we approach the new century, globalization is both a great business management challenge and an opportunity to spread prosperity around the world. To be successful, companies will have to be able to change as rapidly as their customers and the world economy. That means having a real presence in every part of the world, focusing on flexibility, tapping the strength of cultural diversity, rewarding cross-border collaboration, and accepting change as a way of life" (1996: 5).

The American auto giant, Ford Company, is now experimenting with the invention of a "world car" which can roam the global village. The discourses within the company is for the creation of a single automotive operation worldwide. The Korean electronic multinational giant, Samsung, professes that globalization is not a matter of choice, but survival. The Global Management Institute of Samsung leads the industrial globalization discourses in the Pacific-East. Similarly, in the northern hemisphere, there is now developing new discourses within the industrial and business community, following the examples of the EC, APEC, ASEAN and NAFTA, for the creation of FTAA (Free Trade Area of the Americas) by the year 2005, to cope with global challenges.

* Department of Sociology, University of Illinois, Springfield, Illinois, 62794, U.S.A.

** Department of Sociology and Social Work, Virginia State University, Petersburg, Virginia 23806, U.S.A.

The metaphors of globalization are also emerging at the center of contemporary political discourses, and they are different from the Cold War metaphors of containment, peaceful co-existence, mutually assured destruction, and détente. Many political observers and scholars believe that the G-7 is grossly unrepresentative, and that its structure should be enlarged to represent the global political society. The G-7 countries are exploring the possibility not only for the expansion of NATO (North Atlantic Treaty Organization) by including Russia and other East European countries, but also for the expansion of its political boundary by including China, India, Brazil and other industrial democracies of the world.

The discourses within the Internet industry is equally fascinating. The Internet industries now realize that out of the world's approximately 6 billion people, English is the language of only about 450 million people living in North America, Great Britain, Australia, and South Africa, although it is learned and spoken by millions in other countries. The concern for the industries now is the construction of a new global software operating system that can be used by people from different countries with different languages. A global system will ensure that the same document can be viewed by people from different languages and several languages can be used in a single document. The Web is globalizing the world, and it is now globalizing itself.

What these examples from the discourses in industrial, political, and the Internet communities suggest is that there have been emerging fundamentally new social forces and phenomena in the contemporary world of development. In fact, the following writing found on the wall of an American elementary school symbolizes the theme of contemporary globalization discourses: "We must study geography so that for us there is no foreign place. We must study humanity so that for us there is no foreign person" (Ping, 1982).

How are different societies, regions, and nations evolving in the context of globalization? What are the new possibilities, choices, and preferences for individuals and collective actors? What are the constraining issues and problems? How are different problems crossing the boundaries of time and space, and how are those, in turn, producing the need for new institutional designs and cultural models? How do the elites and the masses of different civilizations perceive the increasing globalization of the world? How is globalization impacting on development and change in the modern world, and what are the future problems and dilemmas of development? What sort of new challenges does globalization bring to the political governance of the modern world? And above all, what challenge does globalization bring to our understanding of the world from the perspective of social science? Scholarly discourses have explored and examined questions of these kinds, and the present special issue has addressed some of them.

The Problem of Globalization: Toward a Framework of Analysis

As a concept, globalization does not evoke a single image but rather an imagery of disparate meanings. While some see it as a highly positive force leading to economic liberalism, political democracy, and cultural universalism (Waters, 1995), some others see in its wake the rising power of transnational corporations, integration of international finance, diffusion of technological innovations, and the emergence of commodity culture around the world (Lie, 1996; Hirst and Thompson, 1995). There are some who view it suspiciously, for example, as harboring a blueprint of corporate layoffs (Gordon, 1996). And, there are those who see a dialectical relationship between the forces of globalization (greater integration and productivity) and those of counter-globalization (resistance), and stress the need for analyzing both of these forces together (Barber, 1995).

Many skeptics in the intellectual world believe that globalization is merely a social science metaphor. The nation-states will always remain as dominant social and political actors in the world arena. Political scientist Samuel Huntington claims that in the post-Cold War world, civilizations are becoming the key actors in the global arena, and the west and the rest will never be the same (1996). Globalization, of course, is a social science metaphor. The new world has been described by many terms such as "global village," "global neighborhood," "global community" and "global cyberspace." Such concepts as global company, global bazaar, global city, global quality (Greene, 1993), and global habit (Stares, 1996) have become a part of contemporary social and political discourses all around the world. These metaphors may be different, but they point to the emergence of a new series of social forces.

There are many skeptics in the world political arena as well. In western industrialized countries, many political conservatives are vehemently against the forces of globalization. They blame globalization for the declining economic productivity and increasing joblessness in the west. Recently, about 1,000 business leaders, political figures, and scholars from around the globe met at the annual World Economic Forum in Devos, Switzerland, where they focused on globalization. "While there was much to celebrate, there were also rising concerns about economic stress and social disintegration in the industrialized countries" (Gergen, 1996: 92). This has produced a public backlash against global integration and free-trade agreements. "The losers are now asserting themselves, embodied in the supporters of Pat Buchanan in America, the outbreak of labor unrest in France, or the chilling popularity of Gennadi Zyuganov, head of Russia's resurgent communist party" (Gergen, 1996: 92).

There are movements against globalization not only in western industrialized countries, but also in the developing world. In Mexico, politics has recently become very volatile because of the Zapatista peasant guerrillas, who are determined to oppose the progress of the NAFTA (North American Free Trade Agreement) and the expansion of free trade in Mexico. In the jungles of Southern Mexico, the Zapatista guerrillas recently held a convention titled "The Intercontinental Forum in Favor of Humanity and Against Neo-Liberalism." "The Zapatistas declared the biggest enemy of mankind to be the World Trade Organization in Geneva, which promotes global free trade" (Friedman, 1997). There are similar movements in almost all countries of the world and they focus on issues of poverty, environmental degradation, and cultural imperialism. The theme common to all these conservative-separatist believers is that globalization can be stopped.

There is no denying that contemporary globalization is bringing new problems and tensions, and is not evenly impacting on world societies. The western industrialized countries are being adversely affected because of global migration, and the loss of global market share. Many in the countries of the developing world believe that the massive invasion of foreign capital, culture, and technology is destroying their culture and the economy. But what all these impacts mean is that something is fundamentally changing in the modality of actions and organizations of contemporary world societies, and that we need serious understanding of the forces which shape and drive them.

One of the first and foremost ideas is that the traditional categories of describing the world societies in such terms as the "West and the Rest," "East and West," "North and South," "Developed and Underdeveloped," "First, Second, and Third World," and "Orient and Occident" should be revised. These categories help to locate a particular group of countries or a particular region, but they are not adequate to capture the multifaceted change and transformations that those countries and regions are experiencing and the way they respond and react to them as collective actors. The nation-states are still real. There are no visible signs of any immediate dissolution of the nation-states. But different nation-states themselves are deliberately becoming actors in the global arena. The cultures of the world are still very different, but intercultural diffusions and emulation are intensely growing. The old civilizational boundaries are still a matter of collective pride and heritage, but different civilizations today make continuous references to one another. Technology is still a local invention, but it is traveling swiftly across the world as do people with their competing values, beliefs and preferences.

There are emerging at present some significantly new kinds of economic, political, and cultural facts and events that are transnational, transcultural, and transcivilizational in nature. When Reebok takes a position of not buying soccer balls from Pakistan because they are stitched by children, it evokes a transcivilizational issue. Reebok chairman, Paul Fireman strongly believes that he can play a role in setting a new civilizational standard for child labor in Pakistan. He said: "We'd like to see everyone join with us, and although this will sound bizarre in the world of business, we'd rather see the world operate at a better level" (The Virginian-Pilot, 1997: A34). When the U.S. Department of Justice issues an order that women from all over the world, who can prove that they were victims of domestic violence, can legally apply for immigration to the United States, it evokes a new global dialogue on domestic violence and the equality of women in different world societies. In the same way, when the Chinese suggest that the western concept of human rights is not applicable in China, or the Japanese believe that the western concept of individualism is not applicable in Japan, they raise a new problem of relativity in modernization. What is needed is a serious understanding of the nature of these kinds of new transcultural and transcivilizational facts, the key processes through which they unfold, and the different ways societies respond and react to them. The processes of globalization cannot be stopped. It is irreversible.

There are many competing explanations of what globalization means. Outside the arena of scientific and intellectual discourses, globalization is perceived as an expansion of market economy. The business and industrial leaders of transnational companies, of course, are strongly in favor of globalization. One of the recent surveys shows that about seventy percent of the American companies believe that it is more likely that they will go overseas in the future (Bleakley, 1996). This is probably true of all transnationals from Japan, Germany, Italy, France, England, South Korea, India and other countries. The world financial market is being intensely globalized as more and more developing countries are opening their stocks and financial markets to international capital. Along with capital, technology also is in a process of massive globalization. The world's leading transnationals, who own about eighty percent of the world's leading technology, are aggressively becoming high-tech and global in scale.

The older strategies of foreign investment and the management of the transnationals are also changing. The transnationals overseas are increasingly employing local hires as a strategy of globalization. Foreign companies operating in the U.S. are increasingly hiring Americans, and American companies operating overseas are increasingly hiring native-born rather than U.S. expatriates. To access international capital, technology, and market share, as one American investment banker put it, "What you need at home are more people with international experience and what you need abroad are more people with home experience" (Bleakley, 1996). While such expansions are real and their impacts are multifaceted, globalization is more than the expansion of the market economy.

Globalization is also commonly described as a process of increasing cultural diffusion in world societies aided particularly by the Internet and the information superhighway. In this perspective, what is more observed is the globalization of the American pop culture. It is true that America's pop culture is globalizing, but cultural globalization is much deeper and pervasive.

Scholarly discourses on globalization do not negate common-sense explanations, but make them conceptually integrated and theoretically meaningful. There are two competing schools of explanations of globalization in social science. One is the perspective of world systems advanced by Immanuel Wallerstein and his think tank at the University of New York at Binghamton. This perspective states that globalization is basically an expansion of capitalism, commercialization, and commodification. In every age, societies are governed by a dominant global historical system. What is new in the contemporary phase of globalization is that it is being driven by the logic and necessities of the historical system of capitalism (Wallerstein, 1991). From the world systems perspective, the unit of analysis in the study of globalization is not a single nation or a group of nations. The unit of analysis is the historical system of capitalism which is bringing different nations into a vortex of change and transformations.

The world systems perspective helps to explain, for example, why Reebok went to Pakistan and Sears and Phillips to Bangladesh. But it does not help to explain why women working in Bangladeshi garment industries are breathing a new culture of independence and equality in controlling their life and income. The world systems perspective helps to explain why hundreds of Japanese companies operate inside the United States, but it cannot explain the rise of gender war in the management of the Japanese companies in America. Mitsubishi has recently settled a major sex harassment case, and has agreed to spend more than one hundred million dollars to address the issues of gender discriminations within the company in the future. The economic rise of the Pacific East can be understood from the world systems perspective, but it is limited to explaining the region's adherence to many values opposed to western liberalism.

Another school is the cultural paradigm of globalization. One variant of the cultural explanation is the exuberant theme of Fukuyama's End of History and the Last Man (1992). In this variant, globalization means the universalization of the design of western liberal society. As Fukuyama said: "What we may be witnessing is not just the end of the Cold War or the passing of a particular period of postwar history, but the end of history as such: that is, the end point of mankind's ideological evolution and the universalization of Western liberal democracy as the final form of human government" (1989: 4).

Another variant of the cultural theory of globalization is based on the theme of Benedict Anderson's "imagined communities" (1983), and Benjamin Nelson's intercivilizational encounters (1981). From this perspective, globalization is the spreading of a common human frame of action across the world societies—a frame of action which has been evolving since the beginning of the sixteenth century. Sociologist Roland Robertson of the University of Pittsburgh has been working on this perspective since the beginning of the 1980s, and it has generated a considerable amount of theoretical literature on both sides of the Atlantic (Robertson, 1992). The unit of analysis in this variant of thought is a global cultural frame of action. The world is being imagined as a new action space within which different countries and cultures conduct their affairs in divergent ways and styles, but always with reference to some common human goals and aspirations (Featherstone, 1990).

In both economic and cultural explanations, the unit of analysis is an "imagined totality"—a historical system for Wallerstien and a global action frame for the culturalists. In both, there are implicit assumptions that the emerging global social forces are being constructed and driven by those imagined totalities and trajectories. In these explanations, there are many intriguing insights about globalization as a structure of thought and action. But what is missing is an analysis of globalization as a process of societal and civilizational evolution of a special kind.

It seems that the enormous complexity of change and transformations resulting from globalization cannot be grappled within a single theoretical framework, either economic or cultural in nature. What is rather needed is the development of "middle-range theories" of the emerging forces. In the present study, globalization, therefore, is defined as a fundamentally new process of growth and development. It is a new developmental vision, a new adaptive strategy. It is not a structure, but more of a new strategy for growth and development, and the meaning of globalization is defined and construed by different individuals, societies, nations, and civilizations in varying ways.

In all ages, people lived within the bounds of their own communities, cities, regions, nations, and civilizations. In all ages, the lives of the people in one society were affected be developments and events in other societies and civilizations. Intersocietal and intercivilizational encounters are not entirely a phenomenon of the modern period. The rise of Christianity and its impact on Europe and the whole world was an irresistible global force for almost fifteen hundred years. The rise of the Islamic civilization was a pervasive global phenomenon for almost five hundred years. The American Revolution of 1776 was responsible for bringing revolutions against the feudal aristocracy in France, Holland, Belgium, and England in the late eighteenth century. The contemporary process of globalization, however, is qualitatively different. In the past, globalization was the result of war, invasion, and colonization, and it was a process for change and expansion of political boundaries.

Today, globalization is an evolutionary necessity, and it is an open and deliberate process of individual and collective choice for progress and development. Contemporary globalization is related to, but not an extension of, modernization. In different societies and civilizations including the west, there are strong oppositions to many facets of modernization (Escober, 1995; Wignaraja, 1993). Contemporary globalization is also related to, but not an extension, of westernization. The west itself is in an intense process of globalization. In the twentieth century, millions of people from the non-west migrated to the west for a better social and economic life. In the next Pacific Century, it is highly likely that millions of westerners will be permanently living in non-western societies for similar reasons, and their values and ideas will cross-fertilize many new cultural symbols and institutions.

There is also evolving a globalization of human love, blood, and genes. Westerners, particularly the Americans, are going to international match-making agencies in increasing numbers. Hundreds of thousands of women from the non-western countries also want to migrate to the west in search of new families. "Ever since the communism collapsed, tens of thousands of women in Russia, Ukraine, and other former soviet republics have signed up with matrimonial agencies and the mail-order-bride companies in the hope of finding a Prince Charming in the West" (The Virginian-Pilot, 1997: A29). This process and the hope, like all other processes of globalization, however, is not going without disillusionment. "For Russian women seeking an American Prince Charming, disillusionment is all too common" (The Virginian-Pilot, 1997: A29).

The authors in this special issue have addressed a number of development issues and dilemmas arising from globalization. Many important themes have emerged from their research. The first theme is that globalization does not mean the spread of unbounded economic prosperity around the world. The world society is still characterized by asymmetrical economic relations and widening inequality. The global social situation, finds Richard Estes in his research on "The World Situation: Development Prospect for a New Century," "is characterized by extraordinary disparities in social, political, and economic development." Bam Dev Sharda, George Miller, and Archibald Haller's paper on development indicators claims that the location and the national prominence of a country within the global economy is an important indicator of development.

The second is the theme of cultural globalization. Globalization is perceived by many in developing countries as a process of westernization and cultural imperialism. Winifred Poster's study on globalization, gender, and work in an American multinational company in India suggests that this issue is much more complex. Poster finds that American multinational company in India "brings together several cultures in one organization."

The third theme is about the problem of governing the global society. Globalization is not merely a process of the expansion of free-market economy; the multinational companies are the leading actors in the drama. One of the prominent questions in the literature on globalization is about the behavior of the multinational firms and their control and regulation by the nation-states. R.C. Frey's study on "The Export of Hazardous Industries to the Peripheral Zones of the World-System" reveals that many multinationals are exporting hazardous industries to developing countries where there are fewer controls and restrictions. He envisions that "until a global political authority exists" multinational companies will continue to "externalize their production costs on the periphery and contribute to the globalization of health, safety, and environmental risks."

The problem of the political governance of the emerging global issues has been further examined in Alessandro Bonanno and Douglas Constance's study on "Global Agri-Food Sector and the Case of the Tuna Industry" and J. Timmons Robert's study on "Emerging Global Environmental Standards: Prospects and Perils." Alessandro Bonanno and Douglas Constance claim that globalization is pervasive, and it cannot be stopped. The nation-states will have to be empowered to face the challenges of globalization. And one of the ways of empowerment is to create opportunities for democratic participation in decision-making. "The unity of the polity and the economy must be reconstructed" both at the national and international levels. This alternative would particularly "involve the creation of transnational polity forms which surrogate the functioning of the nation-state at the transnational level." Is globalization leading to the evolution of common international standards? J. Timmons Roberts finds that in the area of environmental governance, "global integration is bringing some level of international standardization."

The economic rise of East Asia within the span of a few decades is a puzzle in development and globalization literature. Alvin So and Stephen Chiu in their paper "Geo-Politics, Global Production, and the Three Paths of Development in East Asia" presented a thesis that the rise of East Asia is not a cultural puzzle. It is inextricably linked with the economics of global commodity production and the political dynamics of the Cold War.

The last but not the least important theme addressed in this special issue is about the challenge of understanding the emerging global society and the need for reform in social science. Shahid Shahidullah in his study on "The Nationality and Globality of Social Science: The Issues of Globalizing Sociology in America" argues that globalization is leading to the evolution of a new series of intercultural and intercivilizational facts and forces. These facts and forces are not dissolving the traditional boundaries of nations and civilizations, but are fundamentally transforming the nature and meaning of human actions, hopes, and dreams in contemporary global society. The individuals and nations within the global society are no longer constrained by the limitations of time and space. To explain and understand these dynamics of the emerging global society, social science, he believes, will need new paradigms.

REFERENCES

ANDERSON, B.
   1983   *Imagined Communities*. London: Verso.
BARBER, B.R.
   1995   *Jihad vs. McWorld*. New York: Times Books.
BARNEVIK, P.
   1996   *On Globalization*. Lecture Presented at the International Management Symposium, University of St. Gallen, Switzerland.
BLEAKLEY, F.B.
   1996   U.S. Firms Shift More Office Jobs Abroad. *Wall Street Journal*, April.

ESCOBER A.
   1995   *Encountering Development: The Making and Unmaking of the Third World.* Princeton, NJ: Princeton University Press.
FEATHERSTONE, M. (ed.)
   1990   *Global Culture: Nationalism, Globalization, and Modernity.* London: Sage.
FRIEDMAN, T.
   1997   Globalization: The Next Great Foreign Policy. *The Virginian-Pilot*, February.
FUKUYAMA, T.
   1992   *The End of History and the Last Man.* New York: Free Press.
FUKUYAMA, T.
   1989   The End of History? *The National Interest*, Summer: 3-18.
GERGEN, D.
   1996   Staying Ahead of the Lions. *US New and World Report* (Editorial), February.
GORDON, D.M.
   1996   *Fat and Mean.* New York: Free Press.
GREENE, R.T.
   1993   *Global Quality: A Synthesis of the World's Best Management Methods.* Milwaukee, WI: ASQC Quality Press.
HIRST, P., and THOMPSON, G.
   1995   *Globalization in Question: The International Economy and the Possibilities of Governance.* London: Polity Press.
HUNTINGTON, S.P.
   1996   *The Clash of Civilizations and the Remaking of the Word Order.* New York: Simon and Schuster.
LIE, J.
   1996   Globalization and Its Discontents. *Contemporary Sociology* 25: 585-587.
NELSON, B.
   1981   *On the Roads to Modernity: Conscience, Science, and Civilizations* [ed. by T.E. Huff]. Totowa, NJ: Rowman and Littlefield.
PING, C.J.
   1982   *International Education at Ohio University: The Search For International Community and Education for Interdependence.* Annual Convocation Address, Athens: Ohio.
ROBERTSON, R.
   1992   *Globalization: Social Theory and Global Culture.* London: Sage Publication.
STARES, P.B.
   1996   *Global Habit: The Drug Problem in a Boarderless World.* Washington, D.C.: Brooking Institution.
THE VIRGINIAN-PILOT
   1997   *Soccer-ball Child Labor Under Attack* (published from *New York Times*). February: A34.
THE VIRGINIAN-PILOT
   1997   *Mail-Order Match-Ups Often End in Heartbreak* (published from *New York Times*). February: A29.
WATERS, M.
   1995   *Globalization.* New York: Routledge.
WALLERSTEIN, I.
   1991   *Geo-Politics and Geo-Culture: Essays on the Changing World System.* Cambridge: Cambridge University Press.
WIGNARAJA, P.
   1993   *New Social Movements in the South: Empowering the People.* London: Zed Books.

Trends in World Social Development, 1970-1995

Development Challenges for a New Century[1]

RICHARD J. ESTES*

ABSTRACT

The world social situation is characterized by extraordinary disparities in social, political, and economic development. Between 1970 and 1995 economically advanced countries succeeded in advancing their development successes of earlier decades. Indeed, the highly advantaged development pattern observed for the majority of nations located in Northern and Western Europe, North America, Australia, New Zealand, and in selected countries of East Asia is unparalleled in human history. A substantial number of developing countries in Latin America and Southeast Asia also realized significant social gains between 1970 and 1995. Development trends occurring in Socially Least Developing Countries (SLDCs)—the majority of which are concentrated in the developing regions of Africa, Asia, and the successor states to the former Soviet Union—indicate that the majority of these countries are at risk of sinking into even deeper levels of poverty, despair, and human degradation. Rapid population growth, continuing high levels of military spending, chronic economic weaknesses, deepening poverty, diversity-related social conflict, weakened family structures, and the absence of adequate social welfare programs account for the negative development trends observed for many of the world's poorest developing countries.

Introduction

THE WORLD SOCIAL SITUATION is characterized by extraordinary contradictions. Despite impressive social progress for some countries since 1970 (Estes, 1995; 1996a; 1996b; 1997), much of the world's social landscape has been marred by recurrent wars (Brogan, 1990), civil conflicts (Boucher, 1987), chronic human rights violations (Amnesty International, 1997), corrupt governments (Freedom House, 1997), deepening poverty (UNDP, 1997), and growing numbers of political and economic refugees (UNHCR, 1995). Population growth continues to be rapid as is the rate of urban migration (World Bank, 1997). And the world's physical landscape

* School of Social Work, University of Pennsylvania, Philadelphia, PA 19104, U.S.A.

has been seriously compromised as well; today, people everywhere are struggling against the effects of deforestation, exhausted soil and animal resources, recurrent floods and other natural disasters, and the social consequences of depleted mineral and other natural resources (WRI, 1997).

The response of the world's governments to the current social situation reflects a more optimistic view of the future. Their priorities emphasize the need for: (1) a better balance between social and economic development (UN, 1995); (2) a renewed commitment to people and people's organizations as being at the center of the development process (UN/ESCAP, 1997); (3) the formulation of new development paradigms that better reflect the world's diverse cultures, traditions, and histories (Beverly and Sherraden, 1997; Estes, 1993); and (4) increased protection of the planet's fragile biodiversity and dwindling natural resources (WCED, 1992). Renewed attention also is being given to the special needs of historically disadvantaged population groups (USDOS, 1995; UN, 1990).

This paper assesses the extent to which the world's governments are succeeding in advancing the world's far-reaching social agenda. In particular, the paper reports the results of a comprehensive survey of worldwide social development trends for the 25-year period spanning 1970-1995. To that end, the paper:

1. Reports the results obtained through application of a statistically weighted version of the author's previously developed *Index of Social Progress* (WISP) to an analysis of world development trends since 1970;

2. Identifies the world's major 25-year social development successes and failures;

3. Identifies the world's social development leaders and socially least developing countries;

4. Compares the major social development trends taking place in major geo-political regions;

5. Identifies and briefly discusses the major social, political, and economic forces that are likely to influence further international development toward the year 2000 and beyond; and,

6. Provides baseline data against which future developments in the region may be assessed.

Methodology

The present study is the third in a series of analyses of worldwide social development trends (Estes, 1984; 1988). The purpose of all three studies has been to: (1) identify significant changes in "adequacy of social provision"[2] occurring throughout the world; and (2) assess national and international progress in providing more adequately for the basic social and material needs of the world's growing population.

Index of Social Progress (ISP)

The primary instrument used in this study is the author's extensively pre-tested "Index of Social Progress" (ISP). In its present form the ISP consists of 45 social indicators that have been subdivided into 10 subindexes: *Education; Health Status; Women Status; Defense Effort; Economic; Demographic; Geography; Political Participation; Cultural Diversity*; and *Welfare Effort* (Table 1). All of the ISP's indicators are known to be valid indicators of social development; indeed, the majority of the ISP's indicators are employed regularly by other scholars of socioeconomic development.

Weighted Index of Social Progress (WISP)

Owing to the volume of data gathered for this analysis only statistically-weighted subindex and index scores will be reported. The study's statistical weights were derived through a two-stage varimax factor analysis in which each indicator and subindex was analyzed for its relative contribution toward explaining the variance associated with changes in social progress over time. Standardized subindex scores were then multiplied by the factor loadings to create weighted subindex scores. Composite Weighted Index of Social Progress (WISP) scores were obtained through a summation of the weighted subindex scores.[3]

The WISP Versus Other Measures of Social Progress

The Index of Social Progress differs from other measures of social development in the number, range, and relevance of the indicators used in its construction. In all cases, the ISP is judged to be a more comprehensive instrument for assessing changes in social development *over time* than other indices of national and international progress (e.g., Gross National Product [GNP], Gross Domestic Product [GDP], the UNDP's "Human Development Index" [HDI], among others).

Data Sources

The majority of the data used in the analysis were obtained from annual reports supplied by individual countries to the United Nations, the World Bank, the Organization for Economic Cooperation and Development, the Office of Policy Studies of the U.S. Social Security Administration, and other international data collection organizations. Data for the *Political, Cultural* and *Geographic* subindexes were obtained from independent scholars and data gathering organizations (including Freedom House, Amnesty International, and others).

Table 1

Indicators on the Index of Social Progress (ISP95) by Subindex ($N = 45$)

I. Education subindex ($N = 4$)
      Combined 1st, 2nd and 3rd level school enrollment ratios (+)
      Percent of 1992 cohort reaching grade 5 (+)
      Public expenditure on education as % GNP (+)
      Percent adult literacy (+)

II. Health status subindex ($N = 8$)
      Life expectation at age 1 (+)
      Infant mortality rate per 1000 liveborn (−)
      Under 5 years of age child mortality rate (−)
      Calorie supply as % of requirement (+)
      Population in thousands per physician (−)
      Percent children immunized against DPT by age 1 (+)
      Percent children immunized against polio by age 1 (+)
      Percent of population with access to safe water (+)

III. Women status subindex ($N = 6$)
      Life expectancy of females as a % of males (+)
      Female adult literacy as % of males (+)
      Contraceptive prevalence among married women (+)
      Maternal mortality rate per 100,000 live births (−)
      Female primary school enrollment as % of males (+)
      Female secondary school enrollment as % of males (+)

IV. Defense effort subindex ($N = 1$)
      Military expenditures as % of GNP (−)

V. Economic subindex ($N = 5$)
      Per capita gross domestic product (+)
      Percent real growth in GDP (+)
      Average annual rate of inflation (−)
      Unemployment rate (−)
      External public debt as % of GNP (−)

VI. Demography subindex ($N = 6$)
      Total population (millions) (−)
      Crude birth rate per 1000 population (−)
      Crude death rate per 1000 population (−)
      Population annual growth rate (−)
      Percent of population aged 14 years and younger (−)
      Percent of population aged 65 years and older (+)

VII. Geography subindex ($N = 3$)
      Percent arable land mass (+)
      Average annual disaster deaths per 100,000 population (−)
      Average annual disaster injuries per 100,000 population (−)

Table 1

(Continued)

VIII. Social chaos subindex ($N = 4$)
    Violations of political rights ($-$)
    Violations of civil liberties ($-$)
    Internally/externally displaced persons per 100,000 pop. ($-$)
    Persons killed in armed conflicts per 100,000 population ($-$)

IX. Cultural diversity subindex ($N = 3$)
    Largest % sharing same or similar racial/ethnic origins ($+$)
    Largest % sharing same basic religious beliefs ($+$)
    Largest % sharing same mother tongue ($+$)

X. Welfare effort subindex ($N = 5$)
    Age first national law—old age, invalidity, death ($+$)
    Age first national law—sickness & maternity ($+$)
    Age first national law—work injury ($+$)
    Age first national law—unemployment ($+$)
    Age first national law—family allowances ($+$)

Country Selection

One hundred and sixty countries ($N = 160$) were selected for inclusion in the analysis using two criteria: (1) a 1970 population size larger than one million persons; and (2) the availability of timely, reliable, and comprehensive social indicator data. Countries with missing, inadequate, incomplete, or seriously distorted data were excluded from the analysis. When possible, however, estimates were made for missing data on selected indicators where such estimates where both possible and appropriate.

Time Frame

Index and subindex findings are reported separately for each of four time periods, i.e., 1970, 1980, 1990, and 1995; thus, the study provides a cross-sectional analysis of the "state" of world social development over a 25-year period.

Levels of Analysis

Data are reported for three levels of analysis: (1) worldwide development trends; (2) subregional variations; and (3) development trends occurring in each of the 160 countries included in the analysis.

World Social Development Trends

Figures 1 and 2 summarize the study's major findings on the WISP for all 160 countries included in the analysis. These time-series data cover the period 1970-1995 and reflect comparative WISP performance for the world's seven continental regions, i.e., North America, Australia-New Zealand, Europe, Latin America, Asia, Africa and, prior to its dissolution, the former Soviet Union.

- The world's most socially developed regions are Australia-New Zealand, Europe, and North America (Fig. 1). These regions had already attained the most favorable WISP ratings by 1970; further improvements on the index continued to accumulate for these regions between 1970-1980, 1980-1990.

- Despite their past accomplishments, significant WISP *losses* occurred in the world's three most socially advanced regions between 1990 and 1995: North America (−14%), Europe (−9%), and Australia-New Zealand (−8%). The losses appear to be associated with the severe economic problems that many countries in regions are experiencing; most of these problems predate 1990 but continued on through 1995. Even so, comparatively few differences characterize the development profiles of the highly advanced countries of North America (1995 WISP average = 79), Australia-New Zealand (1995 WISP average = 84), and Europe (1995 WISP average = 82).

- The world's least developed regions are Africa (1995 WISP average = 21) and Asia (1995 WISP average = 46). Scores for the African region were consistently lower relative to those achieved by other world regions during the entire 25-year period studied, albeit some modest improvement in WISP performance occurred between 1990-1995—the region's first positive WISP changes since 1970!

- As reported in Fig. 2, substantial 25-year gains occurred on the WISP for the Asian (+28.9%), Latin American (+11.2%), and African (+8.1%) regions. Important 25-year social gains also occurred for the North American (+6.6%), European (+4.5%) and Australia-New Zealand (+3.6%) regions.

- Asia is the world's most rapidly developing region, especially Asia's South Central (+56%), Western (+35%), and South East (+26%) subregions.

- Ironically, the world's slowest developing regions are the world's already most socially advanced regions: Australia-New Zealand (+4%), Europe (+5%), and North America (+7%). The comparative slow pace of development in these regions reflects their already advanced social status.

- By 1990 the political situation of the former USSR had deteriorated to levels significantly below 1970 levels. Today, of course, the former USSR no longer exists. The successor states to the former Soviet Union (FSU) have been distributed among two new subgroupings in this study: the Newly Independent States (NIS) and the countries of Central and Eastern Europe (CEE) (Table 2). Today, many of the countries contained in the two new groupings retain economic and military ties with one another through membership in the Commonwealth of Independent States (CIS).

- WISP scores for the reorganized countries of Central and Eastern Europe show a high level of social performance for the 11 countries included in this grouping, i.e., average WISP scores of 74, 69, 74, and 76 for 1970, 1980, 1990, and 1995, respectively (Fig. 3). Indeed, WISP scores for CEE countries for all four time periods compare favorably with those registered by the more socially advanced Developed Market Economy countries for the same period. WISP scores for CEE countries are significantly higher than those achieved by the group of 15 Newly Independent States for all time periods.

Table 2

Country List by Continent and Development Grouping, 1995 (N = 160)

	Developed Market Economies DME (N = 26)	Newly Independent States NIS (N = 15)	Central and Eastern Europe CEE (N = 11)	Developing Countries DC (N = 69)		Least Developing Countries LDC (N = 39)	
Africa (N = 49)	South Africa			Algeria	Libya	Angola*	Madagascar*
				Cameroon	Mauritius	Benin*	Malawi*
				Congo, P.R.	Morocco	Botswana*	Mali*
				Cote d'Ivoire	Namibia	Burkina-Faso*	Mauritania*
				Egypt, U.A.R.	Nigeria	Burundi*	Mozambique*
				Eritrea	Senegal	Central African Rep.*	Niger*
				Gabon	Swaziland	Chad*	Rwanda*
				Ghana	Tunisia	Comoros*	Sierra Leone*
				Kenya	Zimbabwe	Djibouti*	Somalia*
						Ethiopia*	Sudan*
						Gambia*	Tanzania*
						Guinea-Bissau*	Togo*
						Guinea*	Uganda*
						Lesotho*	Zaire*
						Liberia*	Zambia*
Asia (N = 45)	Israel	Armenia		Bahrain	Malaysia	Afghanistan*	
	Japan	Azerbaijan		China	Mongolia	Bangladesh*	
	Singapore	Georgia		Cyprus	Oman	Bhutan*	
		Kazakhstan		Hong Kong	Pakistan	Cambodia*	
		Kyrgyz Republic		India	Philippines	Lao P.D.R.*	
		Tajikistan		Indonesia	Qatar	Myanmar*	
		Turkmenistan		Iran	Saudi Arabia	Nepal*	
		Uzbekistan		Iraq	Sri Lanka	Yemen*	
				Jordan	Syrian Arab		
				Korea, P.D.R.	Taiwan		
				Korea, Republic of	Thailand		
				Kuwait	Turkey		
				Lebanon	Viet Nam		

Table 2
(Continued)

	Developed Market Economies DME ($N = 26$)	Newly Independent States NIS ($N = 15$)	Central and Eastern Europe CEE ($N = 11$)	Developing Countries DC ($N = 69$)		Least Developing Countries LDC ($N = 39$)
Latin America ($N = 24$)				Argentina	Guyana	Haiti*
				Bolivia	Honduras	
				Brazil	Jamaica	
				Chile	Mexico	
				Colombia	Nicaragua	
				Costa Rica	Panama	
				Cuba	Paraguay	
				Dominican	Peru	
				Republic	Suriname	
				Ecuador	Trinidad-Tobago	
				El Salvador	Uruguay	
				Guatemala	Venezuela	
North America ($N = 2$)	Canada United States					

Table 2

(Continued)

	Developed Market Economies DME ($N = 26$)	Newly Independent States NIS ($N = 15$)	Central and Eastern Europe CEE ($N = 11$)	Developing Countries DC ($N = 69$)	Least Developing Countries LDC ($N = 39$)
Oceania ($N = 4$)	Australia			Fiji	
	New Zeland			Papua-New Guinea	
Europe ($N = 36$)	Austria	Belarus	Albania		
	Belgium	Estonia	Bulgaria		
	Denmark	Latvia	Croatia		
	Finland	Lithuania	Czech Republic		
	France	Moldova	Hungary		
	Germany	Russian Federation	Macedonia, F.Y.R.		
	Greece	Ukraine	Poland		
	Iceland		Romania		
	Ireland		Slovak Republic		
	Italy		Slovenia		
	Luxembourg		Yugoslavia, F.R.		
	Netherlands				
	Norway				
	Portugal				
	Spain				
	Sweden				
	Switzerland				
	United Kingdom				

*Indicate countries officially identified by the United Nations as "Least Developing Country" (LDC).

 RICHARD J. ESTES

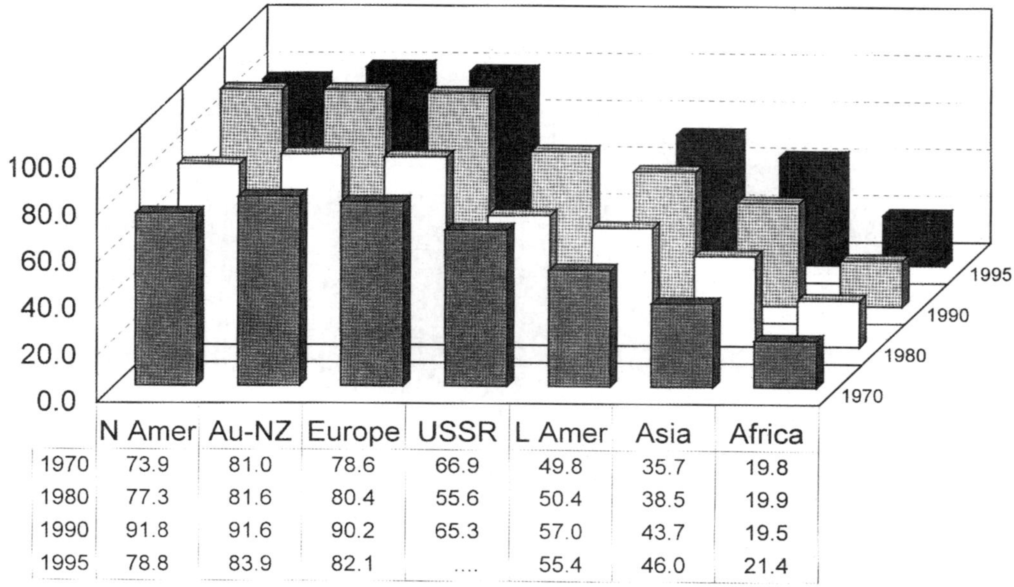

	N Amer	Au-NZ	Europe	USSR	L Amer	Asia	Africa
1970	73.9	81.0	78.6	66.9	49.8	35.7	19.8
1980	77.3	81.6	80.4	55.6	50.4	38.5	19.9
1990	91.8	91.6	90.2	65.3	57.0	43.7	19.5
1995	78.8	83.9	82.1	....	55.4	46.0	21.4

Figure 1. Average WISP scores by continent, 1970-1995.

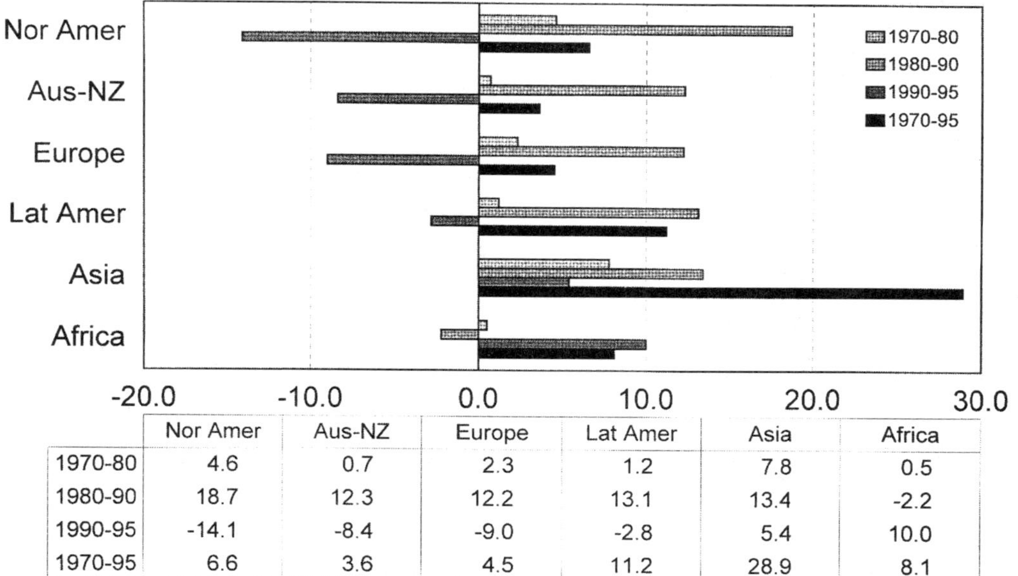

	Nor Amer	Aus-NZ	Europe	Lat Amer	Asia	Africa
1970-80	4.6	0.7	2.3	1.2	7.8	0.5
1980-90	18.7	12.3	12.2	13.1	13.4	-2.2
1990-95	-14.1	-8.4	-9.0	-2.8	5.4	10.0
1970-95	6.6	3.6	4.5	11.2	28.9	8.1

Figure 2. Percent change in average WISP scores by continent, 1970-1995.

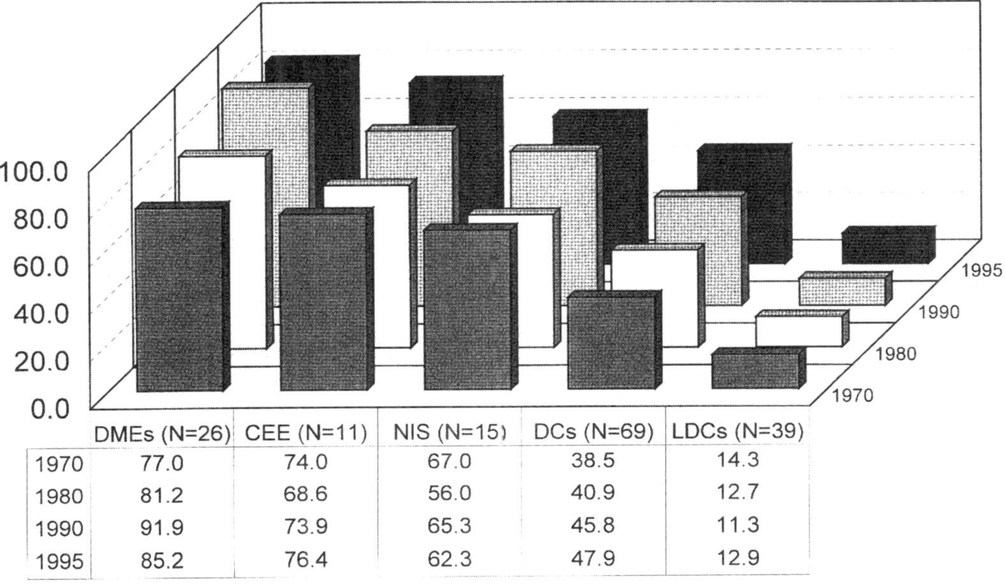

	DMEs (N=26)	CEE (N=11)	NIS (N=15)	DCs (N=69)	LDCs (N=39)
1970	77.0	74.0	67.0	38.5	14.3
1980	81.2	68.6	56.0	40.9	12.7
1990	91.9	73.9	65.3	45.8	11.3
1995	85.2	76.4	62.3	47.9	12.9

Figure 3. Average WISP scores by development groupings, 1970-1995 ($N = 160$).

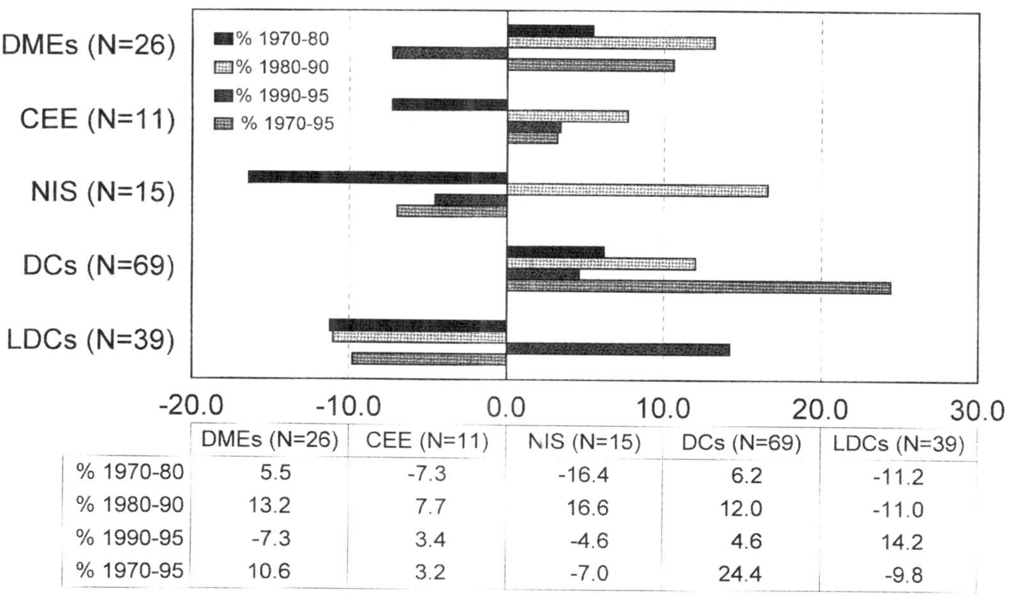

	DMEs (N=26)	CEE (N=11)	NIS (N=15)	DCs (N=69)	LDCs (N=39)
% 1970-80	5.5	-7.3	-16.4	6.2	-11.2
% 1980-90	13.2	7.7	16.6	12.0	-11.0
% 1990-95	-7.3	3.4	-4.6	4.6	14.2
% 1970-95	10.6	3.2	-7.0	24.4	-9.8

Figure 4. Percent change in average WISP subindex scores for developmental groupings, 1970-1995.

- Further, the WISP data summarized in Fig. 4 confirm that, despite their potentially explosive political situation, positive social changes continued to accrue for the majority of CEE countries between 1970 and 1995 (+3%).

- WISP ratings for the group of Newly Independent States, however, have tended to fluctuate dramatically since 1970, i.e., from a group average of 67 in 1970 to 56 in 1980, 65 in 1990 and 62 in 1995.

- In effect, average WISP scores for the NIS declined by −16% between 1970 and 1980 and, again, by −5% between 1990 and 1995. Important positive changes (+17%), however, occurred for NIS countries between 1980 and 1990. These positive social changes may have provided a certain measure of "social insurance" in helping NIS countries absorb some of the severe "social shocks" that followed their political and economic separation from the former Soviet Union in December, 1991.

- Despite the generally more positive social situation found in CEE countries relative to that observed for the NIS, the 1995 development profiles of both groupings more or less mirror their development status of 1970. Hence, the profound social, political and economic dislocations that resulted in the collapse of the former Soviet Union have all but eliminated the 25-year social gains that were achieved by NIS and CEE countries between 1970 and 1995.

The preceding patterns make clear that considerable variation exists in worldwide social development patterns. These differences are profound and, in all cases, have a significant impact on the lives of the people that reside in each of the study's major social development groupings. These patterns also confirm the high degree of interdependence that exists between a broad range of social, political, and economic forces that impact on the development profiles of entire world regions as well as on the world-as-a-whole. These factors, among others, include: (1) a region's past and recent social history; (2) type of polity; (3) type of economy; (4) availability of natural and other resources; (5) the level and quality of social investments in human capacity development; (6) the quality of the relationships between governments and their subjects and between national governments and neighboring states; as well as (7) the strength of national and regional commitment to social development goals and objectives.

Social Development Zones

In earlier studies WISP scores were used to place countries in one of five "Social Development Zones" (SDZs), i.e., non-geographic clusters of countries that share more or less comparable patterns of development (Estes, 1984; 1988). Figure 5 provides a graphic summary of the "distribution" of national, regional, and worldwide social development across the planet's major geographic regions in 1995.

World Social Leaders and Socially Least Developing Countries

Considerable variation also exists in the social development profiles of individual countries. These differences are reflected in the composite WISP scores and ranks reported separately for world "Social Leaders" (SLs), "Socially Least Developing

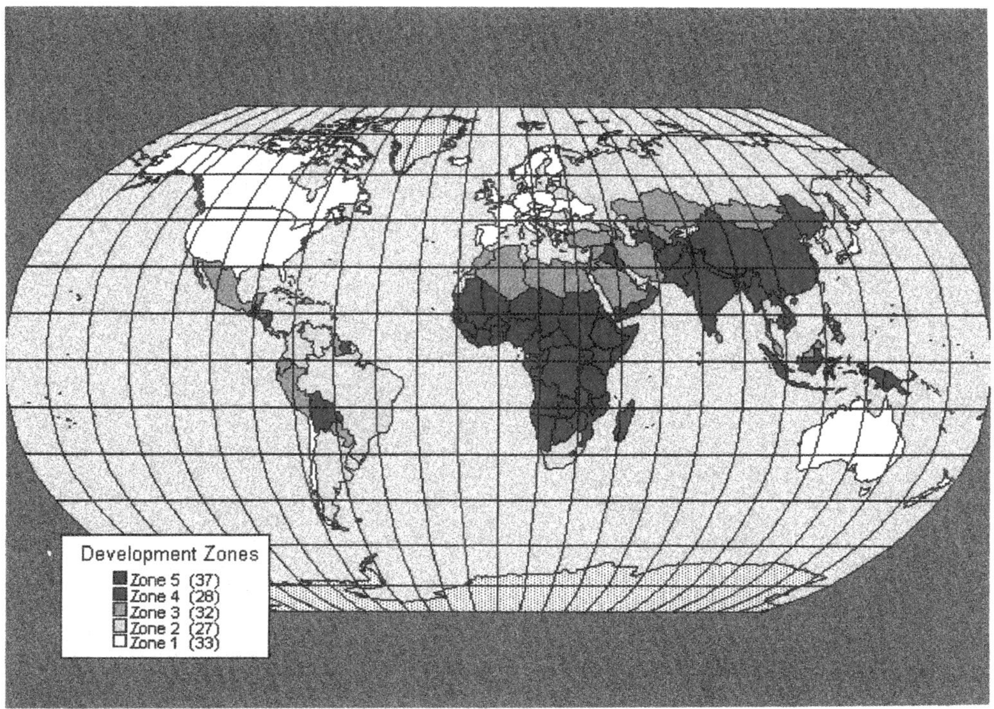

Figure 5.

Countries" (SLDCs), and "Middle Performing Countries" (MPCs) in Tables 3-5, respectively. The WISP rank positions reported in these tables identify the overall social development ranking of individual countries *relative to all 160 countries included in the study.*

World Social Development "Leaders" (SLs)

Table 3 identifies the 33 countries classified in this study as world "Social Leaders" (SLs). The majority of these countries are located in Europe ($N = 26/33$); many are comparatively small countries with national populations well under 25 million people (Median 10.1 million, SD = 50.4 million).

The majority of SLs ($N = 23/33$) also are classified as countries with Developed Market Economies (DMEs), i.e., countries which share highly advanced political and economic systems. Six SLs, however, are members of the Central and Eastern European development grouping, i.e., Bulgaria, Hungary, Poland, Slovenia, the Slovak Republic and the Czech Republic. An additional two SLs are among the successor states to the former Soviet Union (FSU) and, hence, are included in

RICHARD J. ESTES

Table 3

Country Rankings on the Weighted Index of Social Progress (WISP) by 1995 Rank: World Social Leaders (SLs), 1970-1995 (N = 33/160)

WISP95 score (base = 160)	WISP95 rank (base = 160)	Country	Position changes in WISP ranks 1970-1980 (base = 107)	Position changes in WISP ranks 1980-1990 (base = 124)	Position changes in WISP ranks 1990-1995 (base = 160)
98.4	1.0	Denmark	−1	2	0
95.6	2.0	Norway	−3	4	0
93.2	3.2	Austria	3	1	1
93.1	3.2	Sweden	−3	1	−1
91.9	5.0	France	3	1	1
90.7	6.2	Luxembourg	–	–	–
90.8	6.2	Finland	−1	6	3
89.1	8.0	Ireland	−4	−2	5
88.1	9.2	Germany	–	–	–
88.5	9.2	Poland	−8	0	16
87.2	11.4	Hungary	−7	0	8
87.5	11.4	Iceland	–	–	–
87.8	11.4	Netherlands	−5	4	−7
87.9	11.4	Italy	10	−6	−3
86.8	15.4	Belgium	3	−2	−6
86.9	15.4	Slovenia	–	–	–
86.4	15.4	United Kingdom	−7	0	−5
86.2	15.4	Portugal	5	3	5
85.5	19.3	Japan	12	−4	−6
85.3	19.3	New Zealand	−7	0	−5
85.8	19.3	Spain	7	−2	0
84.4	22.0	Czech Republic	–	–	–
83.1	23.0	Switzerland	7	2	−12
82.1	24.3	Greece	9	−1	−4
82.6	24.3	Australia	−1	−3	−7
82.0	24.3	Bulgaria	−5	−3	0
79.6	27.3	Slovak Republic	–	–	–
79.9	27.3	United States	4	1	−9
79.8	27.3	Estonia	–	–	–
78.1	30.0	Ukraine	–	–	–
77.7	31.2	Hong Kong	–	4	2
77.8	31.2	Canada	1	3	−16
76.7	33.0	Chile	−19	13	3
76.7	1.0	*Minimum*	−19.0	−6.0	−16.0
98.4	33.0	*Maximum*	12.0	13.0	16.0
86.0	16.5	*Average*	−0.3	0.9	−1.5

the group of Newly Independent States (NIS), i.e., Estonia and the Ukraine. With the exception of SLs classified as members of the NIS grouping, the majority of SLs have long histories as democratic countries with open-market economic systems. The Czech Republic, Hungary, and Poland were admitted to the Paris-based Organization for Economic Cooperation and Development (OECD)—the so-called "rich nations club"—as full members in 1995, 1996, and 1996, respectively. The remaining three non-DME Social Leaders currently are under review for admission to the OECD.

Economic conditions in the SLs are exceptionally favorable. As a group, these countries are characterized by comparatively high per capita GDPs (Median = $18,700), at least moderate rates of economic growth (Median = 3.0%), and low inflation (Median = 3.1%). SLs also have exceptionally high savings and investment rates with the result that SL national currencies tend to be highly stable and readily convertible. Further, external debt in most SL countries tends to be relatively low when compared with the public debt burdens of other development groupings (World Bank, 1997).

SLs also are characterized by slow rates of population increase (0.4%), low infant mortality levels (8/1000), and enjoy the world's longest average life expectation (79 years). Adult literacy levels in the SLs are high (98%) as are opportunities for pursuing advanced educational training. SLs also contain both a smaller percentage of age-dependent children (20%) and a higher proportion of elderly persons (14%).

One of the major features of social development in the SLs is the existence of extensive networks of social protection that help to offset the predictable income security risks to which people everywhere are exposed, i.e., work injury, sickness and disability, old age, pregnancy, unemployment, premature death, and solitary survivorship (USDHHS, 1997). As a result, spending patterns for domestic social programs are considerably higher in the SLs than in either MPCs or SLDCs (World Bank, 1997). On average, for example, European SLs devote some 46% of GNP to financing a broad spectrum of health and human services (OECD, 1996).

WISP scores for SLs averaged 79 in 1970, 81 in 1980 and 92 in 1990, a net increase of 17% over the 20-year period. In all, 17% of the world's population reside in the SLs, i.e., approximately, 972 million persons. The percentage of the world's population residing in SLs is expected to decline steadily to less than 15% by the year 2025; nearly all of which is accounted for by the high rate of population growth that is expected to continue between now and the first quarter of the next century in the world's poorer countries (UNDP, 1997).

Socially Least Developing Countries (SLDCs)

Thirty-eight countries emerged in the study as "Socially Least Developing Countries" (SLDCs). Three criteria were used to assign countries to this category: (1) con-

RICHARD J. ESTES

Table 4

Country Rankings on the Weighted Index of Social Progress (WISP) by 1995 Rank: Socially Least Developing Countries (SLDCs), 1970-1995 (N = 38/160)

WISP95 score (base = 160)	WISP95 rank (base = 160)	Country	Position changes in WISP ranks 1970-1980 (base = 107)	Position changes in WISP ranks 1980-1990 (base = 124)	Position changes in WISP ranks 1990-1995 (base = 160)
22.8	123.3	Haiti*	−17	6	−40
22.0	123.3	Tanzania*	2	−7	−23
22.4	123.3	Cameroon	−10	0	−32
21.8	126.3	Benin*	−13	−7	−14
21.0	126.3	Malawi*	−22	16	−24
21.1	126.3	Papua New Guinea	–	−2	−42
20.4	129.0	Pakistan	−18	15	−41
19.2	130.0	Cambodia*	−27	0	−22
18.2	131.0	Comoros*	–	–	–
17.5	132.2	Burundi*	−13	22	−38
17.6	132.2	Nepal*	−8	7	−35
16.5	134.2	Mali*	−20	0	−19
16.3	134.2	Sudan*	−12	−5	−30
15.5	136.0	Central African Rep.*	−10	−2	−25
14.6	137.0	Gambia*	–	–	–
13.4	138.0	Mauritania*	−33	7	−32
12.7	139.0	Bhutan*	–	–	–
11.8	140.0	Djibouti*	–	–	–
10.6	141.2	Yemen*	–	–	–
10.8	141.2	Nigeria	15	−23	−31
9.5	143.3	Cote d'Ivoire	−11	−9	−45
9.9	143.3	Zaire*	−3	−9	−40
9.5	143.3	Lao*	–	−5	−44
8.1	146.2	Guinea*	−24	−2	−27
8.5	146.2	Rwanda*	−13	9	−53
7.7	148.0	Uganda*	−14	0	−41
6.8	149.3	Guinea Bissau*	–	–	–
6.5	149.3	Burkina Faso*	−4	−2	−37
6.3	149.3	Eritrea	–	–	–
5.0	152.0	Niger*	−13	−1	−35
1.2	153.0	Ethiopia*	−19	0	−29
0.8	154.0	Chad*	−17	2	−33
−3.1	155.0	Mozambique*	–	−1	−32
−5.3	156.0	Liberia*	−19	−12	−47
−7.5	157.2	Sierra Leone*	−33	−8	−40

Table 4
(Continued)

WISP95 score (base = 160)	WISP95 rank (base = 160)	Country	Position changes in WISP ranks 1970-1980 (base = 107)	Position changes in WISP ranks 1980-1990 (base = 124)	Position changes in WISP ranks 1990-1995 (base = 160)
−7.4	157.2	Somalia*	−25	−7	−38
−10.8	159.0	Afghanistan*	–	5	−43
−24.7	160.0	Angola*	–	−3	−38
−24.7	123.3	*Minimum*	−33.0	−23.0	−53.0
22.8	160.0	*Maximum*	15.0	22.0	−14.0
9.7	141.2	*Average*	−14.7	−0.5	−34.5

sistent poor WISP performances; (2) net losses in WISP rank position between 1970 and 1995; and (3) recurrent high levels of social, political, and economic instability.

The majority of SLDCs are located in the developing regions of Africa ($N = 29$), Asia ($N = 7$) and Latin America ($N = 1$). Papua New Guinea is the only South Pacific SLDC included in the study (Table 4). Further, the majority of SLDCs already are officially classified by the United Nations as "Least Developing Countries" (LDCs) [$N = 32/38$]; the remaining six SLDCs are classified by the United Nations as Developing Countries (DCs): Cote d'Ivoire; Cameroon; Eritrea; Nigeria; Pakistan; and Papua New Guinea. In all cases, the desperate social situations that characterize all of this study's SLDCs justify their being considered for reclassification by the United Nations as LDCs and, with reclassification, assignment for preferential development assistance by the world community.

WISP scores for the SLDCs averaged only 15, 13, 10, and 10 for 1970, 1980, 1990, and 1995, respectively (Table 4). These scores reflect a pattern of steady social deterioration since at least 1970. Further, as a group SLDCs dropped an average of 49 WISP rank positions between 1970 and 1995, i.e., from a group average rank of 92 in 1970 to 141 in 1995!

Critical social indicators for the SLDCs reflect the extraordinary levels of social degradation that exist withn these countries. Life expectation in the SLDCs, for example, averages only 51 years. Infant (110/1000) and child mortality (177/1000) rates are the highest in the world as are the number of deaths from preventable infectious and communicable diseases (UNDP, 1997). Access to effective contraception remains uneven with the result that the SLDC rate of population increase is substantially higher than that found in the larger group of Developing Countries, i.e., 2.9% vs. 1.8%. The proportion of SLDC population under the age of 14 years averages 45%—the highest concentration of young people anywhere in the world.

Population migration also is a dominant feature of life in the SLDCs. Much of this migration originates in the search for improved economic opportunities but war, civil conflict and political instability also contribute to the process. In all cases, the social consequences of population migration can be devastating. In many of these countries, large-scale population migrations are contributing to: (1) the abandonment of children, old people and other non-economically productive family member in rural areas; (2) the weakening, often loss, of traditional kinship and family ties; (3) the loss of ancestoral lands, including those on which subsistence agriculture and other forms of economic activity are still possible; and (4) repeated exposure to poverty, malnutrition, and premature death for persons who are unable to satisfy the requirements of life and work in heavily congested and polluted urban areas. To date, no SLDC has been able to develop effective social programs for helping their citizens manage the devastating social problems associated with unplanned migration.

Unemployment also is widespread in the SLDCs. Official jobless rates average 20% in SLDCs but the actual jobless rate is known to be much higher. Unemployment is especially high among women, men over the age of 45, persons with disabilities, and illiterates. Schools in the SLDCs tend to be grossly inadequate with the result that relatively few people are prepared with the technical skills needed to succeed in the increasingly more competitive global marketplace. Opportunities for advanced technical training in the SLDCs is rare indeed.

SLDC per capita GDP averaged only $950 (SD = $508) in 1995. Private and public savings levels are exceptionally low while average public indebtedness levels are extraordinarily high. Most SLDC central governments depend on a combination of international loans, official development assistance, and private investment from outside of the country to finance even their rudimentary development efforts (World Bank, 1997). The dismal economic situation of most SLDCs is compounded by low-moderate economic growth rates ($< 3.0\%$), high inflation (37%), limited access to natural and other resources (including to transportation in the case of land-locked SLDCs), and the inability to compete as full partners in international markets.

Expenditures on public social programs in the SLDCs are minimal, albeit most SLDCs have enacted—but not implemented—ambitious social security schemes (USDHHS, 1997). Instead, SLDCs depend on a combination of traditional family- and community-centered self help and mutual aid systems to help their most desperately poor members. Ironically, defense spending in the SLDCs averages 4.6% of GNP, 50% higher than average expenditures for defense in Developing Countries.

Middle Performing Countries (MPCs)

The majority of the study's countries are classified as "Middle Performing Countries" (MPCs), i.e., as countries with WISP scores that fall within plus/minus one

Table 5

Country Rankings on the Weighted Index of Social Progress (WISP) by 1995 Rank, Middle Performing Countries (MPCs), 1970-1995 (N = 89/160)

WISP95 score (base = 160)	WISP95 rank (base = 160)	Country	Position changes in WISP ranks 1970-1980 (base = 107)	Position changes in WISP ranks 1980-1990 (base = 124)	Position changes in WISP ranks 1990-1995 (base = 160)
67.8	46.9	*High MPCs* (*N* = 28)	−1.2	0.1	−9.8
75.4	34.0	Lithuania	–	–	–
74.8	35.3	Cyprus	–	–	–
74.1	35.3	Yugoslav Republic	–	–	–
74.9	35.3	Romania	−6	−10	2
73.5	38.2	Latvia	–	–	–
73.7	38.2	Israel	5	0	−6
72.8	40.3	Korea, Republic	3	16	−10
72.1	40.3	Costa Rica	6	−1	−13
72.6	40.3	Taiwan	–	11	−13
71.2	43.2	Uruguay	−4	4	−16
71.2	43.2	Russian Federation	–	–	–
68.7	45.2	Croatia	–	–	–
68.1	45.2	Mauritius	–	6	−7
67.5	47.3	Armenia	–	–	–
67.6	47.3	Belarus	–	–	–
67.9	47.3	Argentina	−2	4	−16
66.0	50.0	Panama	−7	−3	−4
65.6	51.2	Moldova	–	–	–
65.1	51.2	Singapore	9	1	−17
63.8	53.0	Thailand	−1	6	−6
62.6	54.2	Cuba	−11	−4	−13
62.6	54.2	Colombia	4	−3	−12
61.8	56.5	Kyrgyz Republic	–	–	–
61.5	56.5	Venezuela	6	−11	−14
61.8	56.5	Tunisia	−3	5	−6
61.0	56.5	Jamaica	4	−4	−22
61.3	56.5	South Africa	−16	−12	12
60.0	61.0	Brazil	−6	−4	−16
52.6	77.3	*Moderate MPCs* (*N* = 33)	−2.9	0.3	−17.9
59.3	62.2	Trinidad & Tobago	−2	2	−22
59.0	62.2	Albania	−16	−6	−9
58.4	64.0	Paraguay	−2	−5	−9
57.9	65.2	Mexico	−8	6	−17
57.7	66.0	Uzbekistan	–	–	–
56.7	67.0	Ecuador	−4	−1	−15

Table 5
(Continued)

WISP95 score (base = 160)	WISP95 rank (base = 160)	Country	Position changes in WISP ranks 1970-1980 (base = 107)	Position changes in WISP ranks 1980-1990 (base = 124)	Position changes in WISP ranks 1990-1995 (base = 160)
55.5	68.5	El Salvador	−8	2	−13
55.0	68.5	Macedonia	−	−	−
55.3	68.5	Georgia	−	−	−
55.2	68.5	Lebanon	11	−38	−3
55.6	68.5	Jordan	5	5	−8
54.7	73.3	Kuwait	−	−	−
54.5	73.3	Malaysia	3	0	−17
54.3	73.3	Algeria	−13	15	−16
53.8	76.2	Dominican Republic	−1	2	−26
53.1	76.2	Honduras	−19	14	−16
52.1	78.4	Azerbaijan	−	−	−
52.4	78.4	Turkey	−1	2	−27
52.8	78.4	Sri Lanka	−5	−2	−30
52.8	78.4	Philippines	−6	3	−20
51.9	82.0	Peru	−11	5	−18
50.2	83.3	Fiji	−	−	−
50.3	83.3	Kazakhstan	−	−	−
50.8	83.3	Libya	22	−8	−13
49.1	86.3	Mongolia	−	−2	−16
49.2	86.3	Egypt	−6	3	−22
49.6	86.3	Bahrain	−	−	−
48.7	89.2	Guyana	−	−	−
48.3	89.2	Saudi Arabia	−	19	−27
46.6	91.0	Syria	0	−10	−17
45.3	92.3	Morocco	−1	5	−27
45.6	92.3	Qatar	−	−	−
45.5	92.3	Iran	1	−3	−24
34.3	108.3	*Low MPCs* (*N* = 28)	−8.6	−0.1	−28.6
44.3	95.0	Botswana*	−	−	−
43.3	96.2	Indonesia	41	−13	−24
43.3	96.2	Namibia	−	−	−
42.4	98.0	Bolivia	−4	−20	−11
41.4	99.0	Viet Nam	−4	−5	−17
40.9	100.3	Swaziland	−	−	−
40.1	100.3	Lesotho*	−	−8	−23
40.4	100.3	Tajikistan	−	−	−
39.2	103.2	Korea, PDR	−	−3	−38
39.8	103.2	Suriname	−	−	−

Table 5

(Continued)

WISP95 score (base = 160)	WISP95 rank (base = 160)	Country	Position changes in WISP ranks 1970-1980 (base = 107)	Position changes in WISP ranks 1980-1990 (base = 124)	Position changes in WISP ranks 1990-1995 (base = 160)
38.3	105.0	Turkmenistan	–	–	–
37.7	106.0	China	–	11	−44
35.7	107.0	Oman	–	–	–
33.5	108.2	Nicaragua	−21	3	−34
33.7	108.2	Guatemala	−12	3	−31
32.5	110.2	Zimbabwe	−16	5	−34
32.5	110.2	Iraq	−10	−4	−31
30.3	112.0	Myanmar*	−25	6	−34
29.3	113.2	India	1	4	−33
29.7	113.2	Bangladesh*	–	7	−19
28.6	115.2	Gabon	–	–	–
28.7	115.2	Congo	–	5	−29
27.8	117.0	Togo*	−6	10	−21
26.9	118.0	Madagascar*	−10	−12	−27
25.4	119.0	Zambia*	−12	4	−35
24.8	120.2	Ghana	−16	1	−23
24.9	120.2	Kenya	−12	−4	−30
23.8	122.0	Senegal	−23	9	−33
23.8	34.0	*Minimum*	−25.0	−38.0	−44.0
75.4	122.0	*Maximum*	41.0	19.0	12.0
51.5	77.8	*Average*	−4.1	0.1	−19.2

*Indicates countries officially classified by the United Nations as "Least Developing."

standard deviation of the average for all 160 countries included in the study (average = 49, SD = 28.4). The 89 countries that met this criteria were further divided into three subgroups, i.e., "High" ($N = 28$), "Moderate" ($N = 33$), and "Low" Performing MPCs ($N = 28$). Table 5 identifies the countries that were classified into these subgroupings.

As seen in Table 5, the majority of MPCs already are classified by the United Nations as Developing Countries (DCs). However, the MPCs also include 13 of the 15 Newly Independent States, five countries in the Central and Eastern European grouping (Romania, Yugoslav Republic, Croatia, Macedonia, Albania), three countries classified as Developed Market Economies (Israel, South Africa, Singapore), and seven countries classified by the United Nations as "Least Developing" (Zambia, Lesotho, Madagascar, Botswana, Togo, Bangladesh, Myanmar). With the exception of North America, MPCs are distributed across all of the world's major geographic

Table 6

Selected Characteristics of Middle Performing Countries (MPCs), 1995 (N = 89)

Social indicators	Hi MPC ($N = 28$)	Mod MPC ($N = 33$)	Low MPC ($N = 28$)	All MPC ($N = 89$)
I. Education				
Combined school enrollment ratios (+)	71.6	67.3	58.5	65.9
Public expenditure on education as % GNP (+)	4.7	4.5	5.0	4.7
Percent adult literacy (+)	92	83	72	82
II. Health status				
Life expectation at age 1 (+)	75	72	62	70
Infant mortality rate per 1000 liveborn (−)	21	33	65	39
Under 5 years of age child mortality rate (−)	26	40	92	52
Population in thousands per physician (−)	1000	1700	5909	2804
III. Women status				
Contraceptive use among married women (+)	63	50	35	49
Maternal mortality rate per 100,000 live births (−)	74	138	408	203
Female secondary school enrollment as % males (+)	105	143	83	94
IV. Defense effort				
Military expenditures as percent of GNP (−)	2.8	3.9	4.5	3.7
V. Economic				
Per capita gross domestic product (+)	$6,899	$5,322	$2,434	$4,910
Percent real growth in GDP (+)	2.2	1.5	3.2	2.3
Average annual rate of inflation (−)	57.1	50.0	106.7	70.0
Unemployment rate (−)	9.0	13.9	16.4	13.1
External public debt as percent of GNP (−)	31	47	112	62
VI. Demography				
Total population (millions) (−)	24.2	18.8	99.3	45.8
Population annual growth rate (−)	0.9	1.8	2.6	1.8
Percent of population aged 14 years and younger (−)	27	36	41	35
Percent of population aged 65 years and older (+)	8	5	4	6
VII. Geography				
Average annual disaster deaths per 100,000 (−)	0.6	1.6	5.0	2.3
Average annual disaster injuries per 100,000 (−)	166	791	2185	1150
VIII. Social chaos				
Violations of political rights (−)	3.0	4.6	4.9	4.2
Violations of civil liberties (−)	3.4	4.6	5.0	4.4
Displaced persons per 100,000 population (−)	369	71	236	216
Persons killed in armed conflicts per 100,000 (−)	0.3	0.6	0.0	0.3
IX. Cultural diversity				
Percent sharing similar racial/ethnic origins (+)	77	74	69	74
Percent sharing similar religious beliefs (+)	74	79	63	72
Percent sharing same mother tongue (+)	82	74	64	73

Table 6

(Continued)

Social indicators	Hi MPC ($N = 28$)	Mod MPC ($N = 33$)	Low MPC ($N = 28$)	All MPC ($N = 89$)
X. Welfare effort				
Age first national law—old age, invalidity, death (+)	55	36	22	38
Age first national law—sickness and maternity (+)	47	27	25	33
Age first national law—work injury (+)	61	46	42	49
Age first national law—unemployment (+)	27	5	3	11
Age first national law—family allowances (+)	27	7	8	14
WISP95 score	67.8	52.7	34.3	51.6

regions with very heavy concentrations of countries in Asia and Latin America: Asia ($N = 36$), Latin America ($N = 22$), Africa ($N = 20$), Europe ($N = 10$), and Oceania ($N = 1$).

Modal social development profiles vary considerably within the three groups of MPCs. The data reported in Table 6 confirm, for example, that MPCs include countries that already possess many of the "social ingredients" needed to emerge as countries with fully developed market economies over the near-term (High MPCs), i.e., stable political systems, dynamic economies, access to critical natural resources (especially energy), and good quality health, education, and welfare systems. Countries classified as "High MPCs" are moving forward at a steady pace and, as a result, their social indicator trends reflect more favorable patterns than those observed for other clusters of MPCs, i.e., 56, 58, 67, and 68 for 1970, 1980, 1990, and 1995, respectively.

As a group, though, the MPCs also include countries whose development patterns place them at considerable risk of further social deterioration, i.e., the Low MPCs. The comparatively poor performance of the majority of MPCs on the leading social indicators reported in Table 6 suggest that the recent development gains of many of these countries are fragile indeed. In many situations, their comparative recent social gains of some Low MPCs actually overlap the more negative development trends taking place in the lower ranking SLDCs. WISP scores for the Low MPCs averaged 27, 29, 32, and 34 in 1970, 1980, 1990, and 1995, respectively. These patterns are especially worrisome inasmuch as some 2.8 billion people reside in the Low MPCs including in the world's two population giants—China and India.

Threats to World Development: The Unfinished Agenda

The world's nations have arrived at a critical crossroads. Substantial progress has been made in achieving at least some of the planet's social goals. But much more remains to be done. The situation is especially critical in the world's poorest developing countries, especially those 38 countries identified in this study as "Socially Least Developing" (SLDCs). Poverty in the majority of SLDCs continues to persist at desperate levels with the rsult that many SLDCs are located in the vortex of national, regional and international instability. Thoughtful action must be taken if the social tragedies that have occurred in the SLDCs over the last 25 years are to averted as a new century unfolds. Certainly, renewed attention must be given to the following "threats" to future worldwide social development.

1. *World Population Threats*

Though lower than in the past, the world's overall rate of population increase averaged 1.7% in 1995. At the current growth rate, the worldwide population is expected to reach approximately 6.1 billion persons by the year 2000, 7.0 billion by the year 2010, and 8.2 billion persons by the year 2025. By the year 2025 the population growth rate is expected to drop to 1.0%; at the same time, population doubling time (PDT) is expected to slow to every 60 years rather than every 45 years which is currently the case.

Eighty percent of the world's population growth since 1960 has been concentrated in the planet's poorest regions; ninety-five percent of this increase has occurred in the poorest countries in these regions. At the same time, the proportion of the world's population living in "more developed" regions has declined from 31% in 1960 to 23% in 1990. These demographic trends are expected to continue until at least the year 2025 when less than 20% of the world's populations will reside in "more developed" regions. Under even the most optimistic of scenarios the majority of the world's governments are likely to experience severe challenges to their ability to provide for even the basic needs of so many people.

2. *Global Weapons Threats*

Despite the end to the Cold War, weapons and the international trade in weapons remain serious threats to world peace and security. In the main, the source of these threats are three-fold: (a) the continued existence, even proliferation, of nuclear weapons and weapons-grade nuclear materials; (b) the continuing, in some cases expanded, international trade in conventional armaments; and (c) the continued existence and illegal international trade in chemical, biological and other weapons of mass destruction.

3. *World Economic Threats*

The major economic threats to further world development include: (a) unemployment and underemployment; (b) the persistence of meaningless work; (c) the absence of adequate occupational health and safety standards; (d) continuing high levels of external indebtedness; (e) widening world poverty; and (f) "aid fatigue" as reflected in the reduced flow of official development assistance from more developed to less developed countries. The precise nature of each of these threats to world economic development have been described elsewhere and are only noted here (UNDP, 1997; World Bank, 1997).

The persistence of these patterns confirms that the majority of the world's poorest countries are expected "to achieve more with less." As a result, more stringent controls are being placed on the choices available to national governments in their efforts to respond to local realities. Official Development Assistance (ODA) already has been reduced significantly and, ODA funds that are available, are being more "conditioned" than in the past. Similarly, donor demands for "structural adjustment" and other macro-level economic reforms are likely to intensify. Hence, a broader mix of development "partners," including more private sector partners, is needed.

4. *Deepening Global Poverty*

Along with continuing high rates of population growth, poverty remains a dominant feature of world social development. In a comprehensive study of global poverty, the World Bank estimated that at least 1,200 million persons worldwide live in poverty. Of this number, approximately half of the world's poor were living under conditions of absolute poverty, i.e., not possessing the basic material resources required to sustain dignified human life. Further, the study confirmed that: (a) worldwide, approximately 1 : 5 persons lives in poverty; (b) poverty exists in all regions of the world; (c) poverty is unevenly concentrated in Asia and Sub-Saharan Africa; and (d) the incidence of poverty is on the increase.

In Africa, poverty is concentrated in resource-rich Nigeria and Ethiopia and within many smaller, land-locked, countries. The majority of these countries have only recently obtained their political independence from European colonial powers. In Asia, poverty is concentrated primarily in the South and East Asian subregions. In South Asia most of the absolute poor are to be found in Bangladesh, India, Indonesia, Pakistan, and the Philippines. In East Asia the largest portion of the poor are concentrated in Central and Western China, and Viet Nam.

The UNDP estimates that over two thirds of the world's poor live in just 10 African and Asian countries: Bangladesh, Brazil, China, Ethiopia, India, Indonesia, Nigeria, Pakistan, the Philippines, and Viet Nam (UN/DPI, 1996: 3). Further, the majority of the world's poor are women and children most of whom reside in rural communities. The situation is especially acute among rural households headed by women whose husbands have migrated to urban centers in search of paid employment.

A more recent study undertaken by United Nations Children's Fund concluded that the number of the world's *absolute poor* increased to more than one billion persons by 1993—this despite a seven-fold increase in the wealth of nations over the past half century (Unicef, 1997). The transnational nature of contemporary poverty was poignantly summarized by the United Nations Development Programme when it concluded that,

> Poverty is no longer contained within national boundaries. It has become globalized. It travels across borders, without a passport, in the form of drugs, diseases, pollution, migration, terrorism and political instability (UNDP, 1994).

5. *Diversity-Related Social Conflicts*

Diversity-related social conflict remains a central challenge at the top of the world's social agenda. The most enduring of these conflicts are associated with: (a) *plurality*; (b) *race*; (c) *religion*; (d) *ethnicity*; (e) *language* and *accent*; (f) *caste*; and (g) *social class*. In all cases the diversity-related social conflicts result from asymmetric power relationships between members of more powerful and less powerful groups. The intensity of such is accentuated during periods of economic downturn and political uncertainty.

Today, serious diversity-related social conflicts can be found in virtually every country. These conflicts contribute directly to the rapidly increasing levels of crime and personal violence that exists in the majority of the world's cities and other population centers. The situation is made worse during periods of economic recession and in situations where opportunities for individual and collective advancement are remote. In all cases, diversity-related social conflicts are intense, dehumanizing, and pernicious; always, they deprive the world's peoples of the very human and material resources that are needed to bring such conflicts to an end.

6. *Weakened Family and Kinship Systems*

Traditional family and kinship systems are undergoing profound changes everywhere in the world. In the main, these changes are being driven by *economic* forces, e.g., repeated failures in subsistence agricultural, the availability of "high" paying jobs in urban factories, new economic opportunities in neighboring and distant countries. But *social* and *political* forces figure centrally in the changes that are affecting traditional family forms as well, e.g., continuing high rates of population increase, population aging, the need for increasingly numbers of women to pursue careers outside the home, recurrent wars and civil conflict, among others.

Nearly all of these changes have occurred in the absence of adequate social welfare and other supportive programs (e.g., unemployment and housing schemes, job training, income support during periods of work injury or illness support, child care assistance, services for the dependent aged, etc.). In the absence of such programs, the world's smaller and increasingly urbanized families have become more vulnerable than in the past. Consequently, millions of persons have drifted into poverty and find themselves unable to draw on the traditional family systems that offered social and economic assistance in the past.

Comparatively few of the world's poorer countries are able to absorb the economic and social costs associated with the loss of traditional family and kinship systems. Poor countries simply lack the resources to implement the types of "social safety nets" which residents of more developed countries take for granted. Any yet the need for such programs exists and grows more urgent each day.

Prospects for the Future

Following decades of only modest social improvement, once again, the majority of the world's countries are strengthening their capacity to meet at least the basic needs of their growing populations. Many developing countries are begining to achieve their development objectives at a rapid pace indeed; in time, some can be expected to join the group of so-called "more developed" countries. Other developing countries, though, remain outside the range of social progress. For them, the pace of social progress is exceedingly slow, even backward relative to the development accomplishments of earlier decades. More common in these countries are intractable problems of poverty, ill health, high population growth, inadequate housing, unstable governments, civil conflict, economic uncertainty, and substantially weakened traditional family and kinship systems.

At the outset of a new century, the need is apparent for new, more dramatic, initiatives that will transform *all* of the world's nations into more caring and socially productive societies. At a minimum, these initiatives must promote: (1) the elimination of absolute poverty everywhere; (2) enhanced popular participation at all levels of social organization; and (3) a more equitable sharing of the planet's abundant resources.

The social changes implied by these goals are complex and they will not yield easily to quick or simple solutions. Rather, sustained investments will be required over the long-term to reverse the social, political, and economic conditions that have trapped such a large portion of the world's population in grinding poverty. At the heart of these change efforts, though, must be a commitment to strengthening the capacity of local people to provide for their basic social and material needs within the realities of their own cultures and environments. No other approach to social development can hope to help the world's poorest countries rid themselves of the deeply entrenched patterns of mal-development that have held their populations hostage for more than four decades.

NOTES

1 An earlier version of this paper was presented at the 27th Asia and Pacific Regional Conference of the International Council on Social Welfare held in Jakarta, Indonesia, September 2-6, 1997.

2 "Adequacy of social provision" refers to the changing capacity of governments to provide for the basic social and material needs of the people living within their borders, e.g., for food, clothing, shelter, and access to at least basic health, education, and social services (Estes, 1984).

3 The following factor loadings and formulae were used as statistical weights in calculating composite WISP scores for individual countries:

WISP95 = {[(Factor 1) $*$ .697)] + [(Factor 2) $*$ .163)] + [(Factor 3) $*$ .140]} where:

Factor 1 = [(Hlth $*$ .93) + (Educ $*$ .91) + (Welfare $*$ .92) + (Woman $*$ .91) + (Political $*$ .84) + (Econ $*$ .71) + (Diversity $*$ .64)],

Factor 2 = [(Defense Effort $*$ .93)],

Factor 3 = [(Geographic $*$ .98)].

REFERENCES

AMNESTY INTERNATIONAL
1997 *Country Reports* (series). London: Amnesty International.

BEVERLY, Sondra G. and Michael SHERRADEN
1997 Investment in human development as a social development strategy. *Social Development Issues* 19 (1), 1-18.

BRANDT COMMISSION
1980 *North-South: A Programme For Survival.* London: Pan Books.

BROGAN, Patrick
1990 *The Fighting Never Stopped.* New York: Vintage Press.

BOUCHER, Jerry et al.
1987 *Ethnic Conflict: International Perspectives.* Newbury Park CA: Sage Publications.

ESTES, Richard J.
1984 *The Social Progress of Nations.* New York: Praeger.

ESTES, Richard J.
1988 *Trends in World Social Development.* New York: Praeger.

ESTES, Richard J.
1993 Toward sustainable development: from theory to praxis. *Social Development Issues* 15 (3), 1-29.

ESTES, Richard J.
1995 Social development trends in Africa. *Social Development Issues* 17 (1), 18-47.

ESTES, Richard J.
1996a Social development trends in Asia. *Social Indicators Research* 37 (2), 119-148.

ESTES, Richard J.
1996b Social development trends in Central and South America. *Social Development Issues* 18 (1), 25-52.

ESTES, Richard J.
1997 Trends in European social development: development prospects for the new Europe. *Social Indicators Research* 42, 1-19.

FREEDOM HOUSE
1997 *Freedom in the World, 1996-1997.* New York: Freedom House.

UNITED NATIONS CHILDREN'S FUND (UNICEF)
1997 *The State of the World's Children, 1997.* New York: Oxford University Press.
UNITED NATIONS DEPARTMENT OF PUBLIC INFORMATION (UN/DPI)
1996 The geography of poverty [URL http://www.un.org/dpcsd/dspd/dpi1782e.htm].
UNITED NATIONS DEVELOPMENT PROGRAMME (UNDP)
1997 *Human Development Report, 1997.* New York: Oxford University Press.
UNITED NATIONS ECONOMIC AND SOCIAL COMMISSION FOR ASIA AND THE PACIFIC (UN/ESCAP)
1997 *Report of the Fifth Asian and Pacific Ministerial Conference on Social Welfare and Social Development.* Bangkok: UN/ESCAP.
UNITED NATIONS HIGH COMMISSIONER FOR REFUGEES (UNHCR)
1995 *The State of the World's Refugees, 1995: In Search of Solutions.* New York: Oxford University Press.
UNITED NATIONS
1990 *World Declaration on the Survival, Protection, and Development of Children: The Plan of Action.* New York: United Nations.
UNITED STATES DEPARTMENT OF HEALTH AND HUMAN SERVICES (USDHHS)
1997 *Social Security Programs Throughout the World, 1997.* Washington: Social Security Administration.
U.S. DEPARTMENT OF STATE (USDOS)
1995 *The World Social Summit: The Copenhagen Declaration and Programme of Action.* Washington: U.S. Department of State.
WORLD BANK
1997 *World Development Report, 1997.* Washington: World Bank.
WORLD COMMISSION ON ENVIRONMENT AND DEVELOPMENT
1992 *Agenda 21: Plan of Action of the World Conference on Environment and Development.* New York: WCED.
WORLD RESOURCES INSTITUTE
1997 *World Resources, 1997-1998.* New York: Oxford University Press.

Globalization, Gender, and the Workplace

Women and Men in an American Multinational Corporation in India[1]

WINIFRED R. POSTER*

ABSTRACT

This paper examines what happens to workplace gender relations when an American high-tech multinational corporation opens a subsidiary in India. It argues that the literature on globalization fails to incorporate an understanding of the gendering of work in a cross-cultural context. Therefore, it outlines a set of theoretical models characterizing gender relations in India and the U.S.—"confinement control" and "normative control," respectively. It then presents findings from interviews with 60 women and men in the organization. It is argued that this company exhibits a hybrid of the two cultural patterns, such that gender relations among employees *inside* the organization more closely resemble normative control, whereas gender relations with clients and officials *outside* the organization more closely resemble confinement control. The final section discusses the negotiations and tensions that are associated with this coexistence of gender patterns.

MULTINATIONAL CORPORATIONS have become a compelling focal point of the globalization process. As dominant figures in the world economy, they have a tremendous role in the movement of technology, resources, and information from one region of the globe to another. In this process, they also transfer practices and ideologies regarding *relations between women and men*. Yet, within the dialogue and research on globalization, the "gendering" of this process is often overlooked. Few theoretical models explain how gender is constructed in a cultural manner, and fewer still explain what happens when gender ideologies are transferred by organizations to different places in the world.

The purpose of this article is to elucidate these issues by examining the cultural character of gender relations in a multinational corporation. It asks the following questions: Do multinationals import gender ideologies from their home countries

* Sociology Department, Stanford University, Stanford, CA 94305-2047, U.S.A.
E-mail: poster@leland.stanford.edu.

when transplanting operations overseas? Do they adopt the gender ideologies of the host countries? Or, do they mix the gender ideologies from home with those from host countries? Thus, this paper hopes to demonstrate how gender is intrinsic to the exportation of organizations overseas, and therefore, fundamental to the globalization process.

This study is based on observation and interview analysis of an American multinational computer company located in New Delhi, India. This company provides an interesting context for such an analysis given that it has *American* ownership, management, and policies, but also has a full *Indian* staff and is located in an *Indian* environment. The question then becomes, which set of gender relations becomes dominant in the organization—that of India or that of the United States?

The following will describe how both Indian and American ideologies of gender are negotiated in this single organization. First, this paper reviews the literature on multinationals and gender in the globalization process. Second, it develops theoretical models of gender relations in India and the United States—"confinement control" and "normative control," respectively. It then describes how, on one hand, both sets of ideologies exist concurrently in the company, but on the other hand, each applies to different types of social relations. Finally, it will discuss how this coexistence of ideologies came about, and what tensions arise because of it.

Research on Globalization, Multinationals, and Gender

The study of multinationals and gender in the globalization process has emerged from two different fields: industrial relations and feminist studies. Each one provides different insights on the dynamics of labor relations in the global economy. The first approach documents variations of the labor process in different national contexts, but without recognizing gender as an integral factor. The second approach focuses more attentively on the role of women in multinationals, but does not take into account the variability and flexibility of the gender ideologies organizing those work relations.

Within the field of comparative industrial relations, the debate on labor patterns in multinationals has involved two conflicting viewpoints (Belanger et al., 1994). One argument is that there has been a *convergence* of work structures among multinationals world wide (Frenkel, 1994). Through the process of transferring operations overseas, multinationals export their labor policies along with their capital and technology. Some argue that this happens in an ethnocentric manner (Florida and Kenney, 1991), and others in an exploitative manner (Frobel et al., 1980); in either case, the result is a homogenization of the labor process. In contrast, the second view points to a *divergence* process among multinationals. Because the organizations themselves are "embedded" in the social environments where they are situated (Granovetter, 1985), work relations will vary greatly. Diversity among multinationals is governed by such factors as regional industrial networks (Saxenian, 1994), the state (Burawoy, 1985), cultural beliefs and practices (Hofstede, 1991), and labor resistance patterns (Belanger et al., 1994).

This literature has broadened our understanding of what happens to the labor process during globalization. A crucial limitation of these studies, however, is that they assume these labor processes are *gender neutral* (Lee, 1995). Therefore, a parallel line of research on multinationals has been conducted by feminist scholars. These analyses reveal the central role of gender in globalization. They demonstrate how multinationals have hired millions of women workers throughout the world (Lim, 1985; Ward, 1990). In fact, within export processing zones, multinationals often hire women *exclusively* for their workforce. What is striking is that women are being recruited most heavily in industries which are internationalizing the fastest—indicating how women are at the forefront of the globalization process. The drawback is that these industries are also characterized by poor working conditions and low pay (Green, 1983).

Aside from documenting the *extent* of women's incorporation in the global economy, feminist scholars have also developed theoretical models explaining *why and how* this has occurred. They offer perspectives from a wide range of fields, such as "development" theory which emphasizes the masculinization of the development process (Boserup, 1970), to "world system theory" which emphasizes the structure of international capitalism (Ward, 1984), to the "international gender division of labor" which emphasizes the intersection of global capitalism with patriarchy (Nash and Fernandez-Kelly, 1983). Despite the variation in their explanations of why the global economy is gendered, these theories have in common a crucial underlying assumption: gender enters the globalization process in *multiple* ways. In other words, the "gendering" of the global economy involves not simply the inclusion of women as workers in multinationals. Rather, the multinationals themselves embody gendered principles, through their ideologies, practices, and policies.

These studies, however, have been less successful in explaining why gender relations transform when multinationals resituate to different local, national, and regional contexts. One reason is that they have neglected the cultural and ethnic meanings of gender in those contexts. Yet, several recent studies have alluded to the importance of this point. Cross-national studies show that cultural gender ideologies impact women's rates of labor force participation (Clark et al., 1991), and levels of occupational sex segregation (Charles, 1992). And in a revealing case study, Lee (1995) demonstrates how two multinationals in different regions of Asia—even though owned by the same parent company—develop different styles of gender relations due to the existence of locally-specific labor markets and ideologies.

Thus, there is evidence that gender relations are socially constructed in a cultural manner. What needs to be addressed at this point, is how such gender relations are reconfigured in cross-cultural settings. Multinationals provide an ideal context for this type of study, since they contain *several* cultural influences within a *single* setting—that of the host country, and that of the country of origin. Therefore, we need to ask what happens to relations between women and men when there are two sets of gender ideologies within one organization? Which one becomes dominant? And how are they negotiated? Given the lack of theoretical models explaining how gender relations are culturally-generated, we first need a model of how gender is constructed in India and the United States.

Theorizing Gender Relations in the Workplace Cross-Culturally

A primary objective of this project is to understand how and why gender relations in the workplace should vary cross-culturally. To do so, this study draws from a theory called the "social control of women," which focuses on the way that power over women is conceptualized and exercised in different cultural settings. In particular, I will ague that the dominant set of gender relations in India resembles a system of *confinement control*, whereas the dominant set in the United States resembles a system of *normative control* (Fox, 1977). The basic difference in these two systems has to do with what is being controlled, and how the control is carried out (see Table 1).

To begin with, confinement control (as it exists in India) is focused upon separating women from men (Afshar and Agarwal, 1989; Papanek and Minault, 1982). The belief is that most men—but particularly the non-familial ones—have a polluting influence on women (Mandelbaum, 1988). The primary objective of this system, therefore, is to protect women from the harmful effects of such men. This goal

Table 1

Social Control of Women in the Workplace in the United States and India

	The American pattern: normative control	The Indian pattern: confinement control
Purpose of control	Relegation of women to low-level positions	Separation of women from (unsafe) men
Focus of control	*Content* of women's activities	*Boundaries* of women's activities
Method of control	Internally-administered: encouraging women to adopt low-status behaviors	Externally-administered: seclusion of women to designated spaces, schedules, and relations
Types of restrictions upon women's activities	Scope and nature of work (what tasks they can do) Access to events and information (what resources they have) Extent of recognition and advancement (how well their work is accepted)	Extent of social interaction with men (with whom they can work) Extent of physical mobility (where they can work) Extent of temporal mobility (when they can work)

is achieved by "confining" them, or more specifically, by segregating them in the workplace to limit their contact with men. In contrast, normative control (as it exists in the United States) is focused upon restricting women's access to privileged male domains within organizations. The objective of this system is to suppress women's achievements so that they remain in low-level positions.

Since each of these systems has a different *purpose*, each also has a different *method* of control. Normative control works (in part) by encouraging women to adopt low-status behaviors. This is illustrated by studies such as Kanter's (1977) in which women internalize norms involving low self-esteem, ambitions, and aspirations. Within such a system, women regulate *their own* actions (Bordo, 1993), specifically by refraining from pursuing men's jobs. This is opposite to confinement control, which operates by the direct imposition of rules *by others*, through means of secluding women to designated spaces, schedules, and relations within the organization (Liddle and Joshi, 1986; Mies, 1979).

The key factor distinguishing these two systems then is the *focus* of control: normative control is aimed at the *content* of women's activities in organizations, whereas confinement control is aimed at the *boundaries* of women's activities. While the first is concerned with *what* women are doing at work and *how* they are doing it, the second is concerned with *where* they are doing their work, *when* they are doing it, and most importantly *with whom* they are doing it.

Below, the analysis will illustrate how these cultural rules influence gender relations in the setting of a multinational corporation. But first, two points should be noted about this conceptual scheme. For one, these forms of social control are not necessarily comprehensive within each society. Their effects may vary in different contexts (according to region, institution, etc.) and among different groups (according to age, caste, religion, etc.). Second, these forms of social control are not mutually exclusive. In fact, they may exist simultaneously (to greater or lesser degrees) within the same society. The point instead is to conceive of them as the *dominant* forms of social control in each context, in order to reveal the fundamental differences in their gender relations.

The Setting, Methodology, and Participants

The analysis is based on a case study of a major multinational computer company, that will be referred to as American Technical. American Technical is a subsidiary of an American company, operating in India since 1989. Its operations involve administration, sales, marketing, and the manufacture and assembly of computer components. At the time of the study, there were approximately 200 employees in the organization nation-wide. On-site field work for the project was conducted at American Technical's corporate office in New Delhi, and its factory in Bangalore.

The study was conducted over a period of four months, from September 1995 to January 1996. The methodologies include: 60 semi-formal interviews, document analysis, and observation. Interviews were conducted in English, and lasted 30 to 90 minutes. In order to acquire an interview sample that would allow comparisons across different groups within the organization, respondents were selected through a stratified random sample according to gender, department, and occupational level. Thirty-five of the respondents were from the corporate office, and twenty-five were from the company's factory.

The sample had the following characteristics. Most were young (an average age of 32) and married (67%). That most of the respondents were Hindu (83%) is a common characteristic for the Indian population. However, the fact that the proportion of people from single versus joint families was high (58%), and from cities versus villages was high (90%), may be attributed to the fact that this is an urban, educated sample.

Within this setting, the question was posed: what is the outcome of the confrontation of American and Indian gender relations, especially considering that they are so distinct? The answer, as shown below, is that both systems are evident. Each cultural model influences a different sphere of relations within the organization: normative control guides relations *among employees*, while confinement control guides relations *between employees and their external contacts*. In other words, one is more prominent *within the company*, and the other is more prominent *outside the company*. This is evident in the fact that the employees—both male and female—report completely different types of restrictions on women's behavior in each realm. The next sections describe these dynamics, first within the organization, and then outside. This is followed by a discussion of how the coexistence of these gender ideologies came about.

Gender Relations Intra-Organizationally: Normative Control

American gender ideologies are clearly reflected in the internal relations of American Technical. Here, restrictions on women's behaviors are geared towards what tasks women can do, and how women can do them. The employees described three types of constraints in particular, those relating to the scope and nature of their jobs, the extent of access to organizational resources, and the amount of recognition for their work. In this way, normative control targets the *content* of their jobs. It works by undermining women's abilities to carry out the same tasks as men, and consequently their abilities to compete with men in the same jobs. As a result, women remain in low status positions, and abstain from threatening male domains of power at the top of the organizational hierarchy. Below is a description of the three types of restrictions, as documented in the experiences and attitudes of both male and female employees.

Restrictions on the Scope and Nature of Work

One restriction on women's intra-organizational relations has to do with the *kind of work* they are assigned. This happens because normative control inhibits women from performing their jobs on an equal level with men. It is done by *undermining women's qualifications* for their jobs, or in other words, by attempting to prove that women are not good at their tasks. Many times this attack on women's skills is achieved by sex-typing their jobs as "masculine." Thus, women are labeled unfit workers by virtue of the fact that their "natural" skills do not match their job tasks. Then, this is used as an excuse to prevent women from doing certain types of work.

An example of these restrictions involves activities using physical labor. Female employees report that they are forbidden from doing anything strenuous, since this is labeled "men's work." A female employee in the technical repair department explains:

> If I have to lift up a monitor, which is almost 35 kilograms, my boss says, "Why are you doing it? You are a female." I say, "Why can't I do it? You weigh 45 kilograms, and are of a certain age. I am also 45 kilograms, and of the same age. So what is the difference between us? I can also lift it." If I have to shift this thing from here to there, I will do it myself, whereas everybody else will object to it.

As this worker points out so astutely, the labeling of tasks as masculine or feminine has little to do with the *actual* skills of the worker, since women are often capable of doing these activities as proficiently as their male coworkers. Still, women are not allowed to do them because the tasks are not "feminine." What is striking is that this rule is imposed upon female employees even though physical labor is necessary for completing the tasks (i.e., one has to lift and turn computers in order to fix them). This illustrates the power of these restrictions: it is more important to maintain the limitations on women's jobs than it is to get the work done.

Another woman in the sales department describes how this sex-typing is used to underrate women's qualifications:

> I hear people saying that if a boy was there, he would have been more capable of doing this job. [We are] running throughout the day to take the laser printers inside the service center, and sometimes we carry the equipment ourselves. I think we [women] have been very successful in our profession, but still people say that a male could have done a better job because we have to lift the equipment.

Thus, even if a woman is doing a job well, someone will argue that a man could do it better. Attitudes like these have detrimental effects on women's careers, by deflating their self-confidence, and moreover, deflating the confidence of others (like their supervisors) regarding women's abilities. The implication here is that men are considered better suited at physical work, and this justifies giving them the job.

In this way, normative control seeks to exclude women from certain tasks and jobs, on the basis that women are not capable of doing them. This process of restricting the scope of women's work has important implications for organizational stratification. If women are not doing the same tasks as men, they will not be evaluated in the same manner. Ultimately, this can be used to justify limiting their rewards as well. It is also important to note how this feature of normative control differs from that of confinement control (as outlined in detail later on). In that situation, the *content* of the work (in terms of *what* women are doing) is completely irrelevant for restricting women's jobs. Instead, limitations are placed on the *boundaries* of the job (in terms of where, when and with whom work is done).

Restrictions on Access to Events and Information

Another type of constraint on women's work has to do with access to organizational resources. These resources are in the forms of job feedback, communication between employees, and participation in networks and meetings. The workers in American Technical report that these resources are crucial for doing their jobs. Yet, women workers find that their male colleagues have much greater access to them. This is another way that normative control limits women's abilities to carry out their work effectively.

As an example, many female employees describe how they are excluded from important events which directly involve their work. A female marketing executive on her way to a meeting had the following experience:

> One of our dealers was here, and they have a large organization. He was just passing by in the corridor and he said to me, "You are joining us for a marketing meeting?" And my account manager with him said, "Don't be ridiculous. Before inviting people like her, you should ask me whether we require people like this. Come on, do you think she should be there in a meeting like this?" The dealer is an external person who respects me—or respected me till that time—for what I was doing for the organization, and he just turned around and said, "Oh! I didn't know that this person is so inconsequential."

A woman in sales describes a similar situation:

> Let's say marketing or somebody is organizing an event, and you are supposed to be there. The other guy—who's a boy—is formally informed about the event. He'll be invited. At the same time, you won't even be invited. But it will be [communicated] to your bosses, that so and so persons have reached the event, and so and so other person has been irresponsible.

These quotes demonstrate how women are excluded from events to which men in contrast have complete access. They also indicate how women's low status is enforced in the process. In one case, a woman's role in a project is trivialized, and she is humiliated in front of a client. In the other case, a woman is made to look unreliable in the eyes of a superior. In both cases, women's performance records are defiled, and their careers are jeopardized. But in addition, their professional identities and senses of self-worth are undermined. This is a characteristic feature of the normalization process—making women feel inadequate at their jobs.

As a second example of restricted access to resources, female employees report difficulty in obtaining information about their jobs. For instance, employers provide instruction and training more frequently to male employees than to females. A woman executive explained how her supervisors would refuse to assist her in her work. Then, after her work was completed, they would criticize it and tell her she should have asked for guidance beforehand:

> If I am making a decision on how an event has to be held, I request their [i.e., supervisors'] help. It would be like, "I don't have the time for this thing. You spend your time on this rubbish anyway, so just go out and do whatever you want to." And the moment I make a decision and I implement it, I get feedback saying, "How the hell could you take that decision? This is such a stupid way of doing it. All you could have done is ask me about it." And when the event is taking place, the [supervisor] comes and makes a lot of noise about, "It is such a disaster" and so on. So, (a) you didn't have the feedback which may have been important in the first place, and (b) you feel very de-motivated when you have gone ahead and done something at that point, and somebody is telling you, "This is a disaster."

When women are ignored in this manner, they feel unsure about the quality of their work. This subsequently causes them to question their own abilities. Moreover, in cases like this one, the lack of information about this employee's work directly hinders her ability to complete the task effectively. Thus, reduced access to resources is another way that normative control operates to restrict women's organizational careers.

Restrictions on Recognition and Advancement

A third type of constraint women describe has to do with the recognition they receive for their work. Female employees experience a great deal of difficulty gaining acceptance for their achievements. In some cases, male employees express subtle scepticism about the competency of females as coworkers in the same jobs. In more extreme cases, men express overt hostility when women excel in their work. Both types of behaviors have tangible effects on women's career advancements, as demonstrated below.

One obstacle to recognition for women has to do with the fact that their work is not evaluated in the same manner as men's. Rather, *different standards* are used to assess their work. A female technician describes: "In the beginning when I joined American Technical, I didn't feel I was getting the same type of appreciation [as men] in the job, which I should get from all the department people and all other engineers with whom I work. I did not feel that the working atmosphere was very cordial or helpful." Similarly, a female factory worker explains:

> I feel that I did a good job in my work. I've been very innovative, and got new methods. But I feel I have had to earn respect for it. I don't feel it just came. Whereas, if a guy comes from the same kind of background, and he knows his job right away, then he gets all the respect. He doesn't really have to work all that hard to earn it.

These sentiments are summarized by a woman in marketing: "A woman has to do her job a few times better than a man to be able to get some acceptance and recognition in the same area or field. The expectation of a woman is much more as compared to a man." In all, these quotes reveal how the standards for quality in women's work are much higher than in men's work. Both the acceptance of equivalent work, as well as the recognition for superior work, are difficult to come by for women employees. The result is that women find they must work harder in their jobs or else wait later in their careers to receive equal amounts of recognition as their male colleagues.

This difference in standards has direct effects on women's career paths in the organization. It is particularly apparent when it comes to promotions. In one case, a female employee experienced a barrier to job advancement early in her career at American Technical. Like most new recruits, she joined the organization under a "temporary" status. However, she was then denied a promotion to the "permanent" status since, as a female, she was expected to quit. This case demonstrates how women can be subjected to completely different review processes than men. Specifically, the decision about this woman's job was guided by evaluations of behaviors *of her gender*, rather than by her qualifications *as an individual*. Moreover, such evaluations were based on *assumed* behaviors (i.e., that women have higher turnover rates), whether or not they are true in reality. The end result is that women face a glass ceiling in the organization.

Another obstacle to the recognition of women's work is a tendency by male coworkers and superiors to *discredit* and *disparage* women's achievements. This means that female employees experience not only a shortage of positive feedback, but a plethora of negative reactions to their successes. A female executive recounts: "Inside the department, male colleagues feel threatened with your being a lady out there. If you are successful, they just attribute it to 'because you are a woman, so you got it'." This statement suggests that women's accomplishments are undeserved, and that women attain high positions in the organization through quotas rather than merit. Such resistance is even more pronounced when women equal or even surpass men's achievements. "They [the male coworkers] never thought they would be sitting with a woman across the table as an equal. Most of them have not got a promotion themselves in the first year. And if you [as a woman] start doing okay, and if you get a promotion, they cannot take it nice." In the sales department, a similar experience is reported: "At heart, it is very difficult [for men] to accept a girl at the same level. It is very difficult. It takes a lot. They would not show it, but it comes indirectly. If it is below their level, it is fine. They don't have any problem. If at the same level, the acceptance takes more time than it would take otherwise."

These incidences reveal two underlying themes of normative control. First, they indicate how the *source* of these restrictions has to do with the protection of male domains of power in the organization. This is evident in the fact that male workers begin to resist women's accomplishments *just at the point when women reach men's levels in the job hierarchy*. When women's status is lower than men's, male employees do not object to women's presence in their departments. However, once women compete with men at their level, the male employees feel threatened and then actively obstruct women's progress. This is a characteristic feature of normative control—placing limitations on *how* women do their work, so that they remain in low levels within the organization.

In addition, these incidences reveal an important point about the *process* of normative control in American Technical. Normalization involves an element of internalization on the part of the women themselves. Several female workers recount how the above tactics caused them to doubt their competence in their jobs. One training specialist explains her response to the lack of feedback from her superior: "[As] a woman, we think, 'Is what I'm doing right? Have I actually done it, or should I keep on doing it?'" This experience is reiterated by a communications specialist who talks about the effect of being excluded from male events:

> It is not a very healthy, positive kind of relationship which confirms you as an individual, that "Yes, you are doing a good job, and I'm here to help you and make life simple for you." *It is an attempt to keep bring down you mentally: "You are incompetent, you are unable to do this."* There seems to be some sort of a glee that: "You haven't done this, so you are screwed up," which, if it gets to you, can really bring you down. *So, you start questioning your own ability, your being a good professional.*

As a result of the negative feedback, women begin to accept that they are not good at their jobs, and become discouraged from excelling in their work. This complacency then keeps them in their low status jobs. In sum, this is how women become *normalized*: they internalize norms restricting their behaviors, and subsequently act out those restrictions themselves.

To conclude, this section has sought to describe how the American form of gender relations has become dominant *inside* the organization, among employees.

Specifically, it illustrates how the restrictions on women's behavior are heavily influenced by normative control. Here, the focus of control is on the content of women's jobs. It operates in three ways—by limiting *what they can do* in their jobs, *what they can know* about their jobs, and *how much recognition* they get for their efforts. The principle of this system is to circumscribe how women do their work, in order to limit their achievements and their mobility within the organization. This is very different from the gender relations between employees and their contacts *outside* the organization. As shown in the next section, those follow a pattern more closely approximating the Indian social control of women.

Gender Relations Extra-Organizationally: Confinement Control

When it comes to their relations with people *outside* of the organization, women in American Technical face an entirely different set of constraints on their work roles. The primary form of social control in this context is *confinement*. The focus of this system—as influenced by Indian gender ideologies—is the boundaries of women's work. The purpose is to keep female employees separated from men in the public sphere. So, in order to prevent women's contact with these men, the organization develops several types of restrictions on women's jobs: those regarding women's social interaction with men, their physical mobility, and their temporal mobility.

Restricting Women's Interaction with Men

One type of restriction is on the *types of people* with whom women may interact. This arises because the confinement control system prohibits women from interacting with unfamiliar men in the public sphere. In particular, female employees in American Technical are discouraged from having contact with *men outside of the organization*. This includes all the people a woman might talk to or meet in her daily routine: clients, messengers, vendors, government officials, etc. Thus, the restrictions on social interaction apply across class lines, whether the man is a "laborer" or the "elite of hotels."

Why is this kind of interaction considered so problematic? Answers are provided by *both* male and female employees in the organization. To begin with, women report that men outside react unfavorably to the fact that they are female. A woman in sales talks about dealing with male clients: "Customers can be very hostile. That is a job hazard being in sales. You have to witness all kinds of people. You can't say, 'I don't want to meet this man because he is not nice to talk to, because he is so arrogant, because he is so hostile.' Your orders are that you got to meet him." Similarly, a woman training specialist recounts: "In my profession there are hardly any women. In an event, I meet fifty resellers, and about three are women. And the men are shocked to see that I'm a woman. They get put off. [They say to themselves:] 'We may not get what we want'." Thus, one reason that these men do not want to work with women is that they are unable to take advantage of male-bonding to get special favors. In such ways, female employees in American Technical experience a great deal of resistance from men outside the company.

Male employees have different concerns about these social interactions. They fear that women will not be able to conduct their work effectively if they have to interact with external men. A male general manager explains: "There are certain jobs where the employee has to go to customs or clearance, where there is a lot of rough and tough. You have to go and negotiate or maybe raise your voice. There, it is just possible that a woman may not be able to achieve good results." This sentiment is repeated by a male administrative coordinator:

> With government officials, if lady goes and asks, she will not get the full information. Naturally. There is a law: like poles repel, and unlike poles attract. The officials will just answer your question. They will not go into whether you have got the help. They will not bother. Whereas in multinationals, it is not like that—you will get the full information.

The belief is that—unlike men within multinational corporations—men outside are very difficult to handle. This "naturally" impedes women's ability to get their work done, according to these male employees.

As a result of these types of attitudes, women's jobs in American Technical are altered in a number of ways. Sometimes this means *adapting the job* in order to help women cope with resistance from external men. When I asked one female administrator if there were any such changes in her job, she replied:

> In fact, that is one of the reasons why we suggested a designation change while dealing with outside customers. Normally my boss is traveling and I have to sign letters on his behalf, quotations are sent on his behalf. So, if I say I am the secretary working for him, they say, "Okay, but we still would like to have your boss's signature." Therefore, a designation change makes a big difference. For an outsider, when you say you are a "marketing coordinator" it carries a lot more weight than saying I am a "secretary to XYZ."

In this situation, upgrading a woman's job title was necessary to counteract the lack of respect (at least partially on account of her gender) she received from male clients.

Other times, this transformation of jobs involves *redirecting the tasks* which demand contacting male clients. For example, one female secretary recruits male coworkers in the office to do chores that require associating with external men: "Sometimes I feel that I have to take people's help—like in my department, I take my boss's help—to get certain things from customs. [When *I* talk to them,] they may not realize that there is an urgency. But, if *my boss* goes and talks to them, then definitely it is urgent." Moreover, this rearrangement of tasks by gender can be so extensive that—even within the *same job title*—women's and men's jobs can involve completely different sets of activities. A male imports administrator in the factory explains:

> If you have to do my job, you need to have a lot of patience. You have to go and face lot of *people outside*. You have to go and stand in some queue to meet some government official. You have to wait for hours to transport a customs official. Those things, I don't think ladies will be able to do. A lady is here in the same department, but she is doing more office work, like ordering. I look after the outside work, customs and all that.

Here, the assignment of tasks to employees is guided entirely by restrictions on social interaction (i.e., whether the work deals with people internal or external to the organization). The female employee takes the desk job (interacting with American Technical employees), whereas the male takes the field job (interacting with outside clients). In this way, confinement control generates a division of labor by gender *within occupations* based on with whom one interacts.

Finally, another adaption of jobs is *reserving occupations for men* that deal with interactions outside. One employee talks about why a man rather than a woman should do "facilities" work:

> These kind of jobs, I feel that men should do because they have to interact with a lot of people of different levels *outside*. In India, you may have to deal with a plumber who is going to come and fix a problem, or deal with a senior executive who is going to come. You could end up talking to a sweeper who is cleaning your office. I would call him a lower level in that sense. So, since they are all different levels of people, I would feel more safe if a man is handling the job rather than a woman.

Thus, contact with men outside—of any status level—merits exclusion of women from the job, in his eyes. It is in this manner that confinement control influences workers' attitudes on the sex segregation of occupations.

In sum, each of these restrictions on women's jobs reveals the influence of confinement control in the company. Each involves a constraint upon women's social interaction with men. Thus, unlike the patterns of normative control that were discussed in the previous section, the focus of control here is on the boundaries rather than the content of the job. In other words, it concerns *with whom* one interacts, instead of *what* one is doing in the job. These restrictions also differ from those of the previous section in that they are clearly designated to relations with people *outside* rather than *inside* the company.

Restrictions on Physical Mobility

A second feature of the externally-based gender relations involves restrictions on *where* women do their work. In particular, these restrictions target women's movements outside of the company. The idea is to prevent women from going places where they will encounter the types of men described above—men in the public world, who are neither family members nor coworkers. Since such encounters may occur anywhere outside the boundaries of the organization, restrictions are placed on women's jobs so that they stay inside the company.

As an example, one type of restriction prevents women from doing any *tasks* in their jobs that involve going outside the organization. In this sense, a male district manager described activities forbidden to female employees: "Lots of nights-out, and traveling. Traveling is not easy, as far as India is concerned, especially when you are traveling in trains. You may not get confirmed tickets, and it is not so safe. Things are getting better, but if you make a comparison, guys are better for it." Indeed, female employees confirm that such attitudes affect their jobs. A female administrator explains that her boss "is orthodox about sending me out on traveling matters for trainings and all. He says, 'You are a girl, so how are you going to stay in hotels?' Since I am a girl, it may cause problems for me if I travel and stay alone." This reference to women traveling alone reveals an important underlying theme in these physical mobility restrictions. The primary concern among American Technical employees is that, when unaccompanied by "safe" men (i.e., male coworkers), women who go out in the public world are highly susceptible to the dangers of "unsafe" men (i.e., all others). For this reason, women's jobs are circumscribed to limit activities in which they would be alone and unprotected.

A second type of restriction is that women are excluded from *all-male activities* (in cases where they are actually allowed to do work out of the office). This is illustrated in the experience of a female training specialist who was forced out of a post-meeting gathering:

> We were traveling, and we were all going for dinner. So my Indian regional manager said, "You must be tired. Why don't you just go back to your room and rest." I said, "No, I'm not tired." I didn't understand what he was trying to say. He actually had to take me aside and say, "What are you doing? Go back to your room and have dinner there. Don't mix with bad company."

Here, the rules on physical mobility are eased to permit a woman to travel outside. But as this example shows, such rules are never completely eliminated. This woman was not allowed to join her colleagues because the setting for the activity was outside the perimeter of the organization, where she might come in contact other types of men (referred to as "bad company" in this quote). In this way, the boundaries of women's movements in male circles are rigidly enforced.

A more extreme example of these restrictions is the exclusion of women from *entire jobs* which require traveling (as opposed to excluding women from one or two tasks *within a job*). This is done by categorizing those occupations which involve field work as "masculine," and those involving office work as "feminine." This justification is then used to prohibit women from jobs which send employees out of the office. A male manager provides some examples of such jobs: "In sales, marketing, and support, their customers are around the country. So it requires that we go and meet them, and sell to them, and service their machines which we have supplied. You can't do that remotely from the office." Thus, while it is appropriate for men to do work that is mobile, it is not appropriate for women. Instead, women must hold jobs that can be done from "the office."

This opinion is reiterated by a male employee, who also labels as masculine the job of "... fields sales, because it involves a lot of traveling. And occasionally you have to go to real weird places where you just can't find any accommodation." Finally, a third employee agrees:

> Typically a sales or support job, which is primarily externally-focused, and takes an employee outside the office, or outside the city, or outside the country. In this kind of a job, people have to travel long distances. Some of it is very rough travel, given the transport link conditions in India. Sometimes it can become troublesome for a lady to travel during work.

In these examples, traveling is consistently seen as a masculine activity. This categorization merits the exclusion of women from a wide range of jobs—sales, support, and marketing. Furthermore, this last comment reveals how the *range of travel* for women is not the issue. Whether the travel is local, domestic or international, it is forbidden to women because it requires leaving the realm of the organization.

These incidences demonstrate how confinement control limits the physical mobility of female employees. In particular, strategies are developed to restrict women's movements outside the organization. These commentaries also demonstrate how different confinement control is from normative control. Here, the focus of the control is on the *boundaries* of the job rather than the *content*. In other words, the reason for restricting women's jobs has to do with where women go in their jobs, instead of how well they can do the work. A manager in sales explains:

> Once you are in the job, I don't think there is any difference—a lady can do a job as well as a man. But it is the other external conditions of travel—living in some hotels in some towns—which may not suit some of the ladies. If you look at all these jobs which are in the office, it doesn't involve too much travel outside, and doesn't involve staying overnight outside. These jobs definitely suit women.

This shows how *it is assumed* that women and men are equally competent at performing their tasks. Instead, it is the "external conditions" which necessitate limitations on women's work. Similarly, a male general manager reiterates the importance of job boundaries when he was asked which criteria are more important for selecting women's work: "I won't say job content, but extensive traveling. Most of our engineers or managers do quite extensive traveling, and it could be sporadic. It is not planned traveling. I think in today's social context in India, perhaps it is more convenient for men to do such jobs than women." So, as guided by the ideologies of the culture, physical mobility rules are more concerned with the places women go rather than what they are doing in their jobs.

Restrictions on Temporal Mobility

A third restriction on externally-based gender relations has to do with *when* women do their work. These rules are established to limit the amount of time women spend in the organization. The reason is that, under confinement control, it is considered unsafe for women to work after normal daytime hours. Nighttime is a period when women are more susceptible to the influences of outside men—primarily because women's male coworkers are not present in the office to act as guardians. Therefore, strict limitations are placed on women's working hours so that they are not alone in the office. As described by one personnel executive: "If you are a female employee, she is not supposed to work beyond 7:00 p.m. in the evening." The result of such attitudes is that women's work hours are rigidly fixed. By contrast, men have great freedom in their schedules.

Restrictions on women's temporal mobility considerably inhibit their ability to work when they need to. But in addition, these rules have many secondary repercussions for women's jobs. In particular, the lack of flexibility in women's schedules is used as a reason to exclude them from many occupations. A male accountant in the corporate office describes how this happened in one of his recruiting sessions:

> I remember when we had a vacancy in accounting, this point was brought out: "Why not take a woman?" Frankly, a woman was never in contention for the job, because you would not expect a woman to go home at twelve at night. You cannot do that kind of thing. It is unsafe for women basically.

Because of the temporal mobility restrictions, women are not even considered for these jobs. This type of occupational sex segregation is also evident in American Technical's factory. The manager explains why she prefers male workers on the production line:

> Many of the women that work here don't have their own transportation. And if I keep one of my women after dark or late at night, it becomes my responsibility to make sure that they get home okay. That becomes a hassle in some cases, and you begin to wonder if you would have been better off with a male, where you don't have to worry about these things.

Like the previous example, men are selected for jobs because they are unaffected by temporal mobility rules, and therefore can work at any time.

This employee also points out some important features of temporal mobility in the confinement control system. First, she explains how the *protection* of women from outside men is key to the confinement control process. She implies that rules forbidding women to work after hours can be circumvented—as long as a guardian is available to chaperon them. This indicates that the fundamental issue for temporal mobility is not actually *when* women work, but with *whom* they are working—and most importantly, whether they are alone or accompanied by coworkers. Second, she reveals how temporal mobility restrictions can intersect with those of physical mobility. Transportation in particular links the two processes, since women who work late must travel home alone as well as stay in the office alone. Although these are two different physical settings, the common feature is that in both women may encounter unfamiliar men. The confinement control solution for this situation, as the manager explains, is for bosses or male coworkers to act as escorts both inside the organization, and outside in their commutes.

A final point about these rules is how they differ from those of normative control. As with the physical mobility restrictions above, the basis for temporal mobility rules has nothing to do with the content of women's jobs (in terms of their abilities to perform the tasks). Rather, the focus is on the boundaries of women's activities (in terms of when they work). This is confirmed by several employees. A male general manager at the corporate office says: "Among our engineers and managers, I really feel any qualified, skilled female would be able to do the job as good as a male. It is the other restrictions that keep them away from such jobs, compared to what we see as a desk job, which is 9-to-5." This same attitude is repeated by a female factory manager:

A male or female can do any job. But what happens here is that some jobs require a person doing that job to stay very late. And in this culture, in this society, what happens is that it is very difficult for a woman to do that. [The managers] may prefer to get a male for it because they know that they can rely on that person to stay late or stay overnight. I used to vehemently disagree when somebody used to say, "No, I need a man, I need a guy. I am not going to hire a woman for this job." And I would argue and fight all the time about it, until I realized that there are some restrictions—society, culture, infrastructure, and so on—that cause limitations.

Thus, confinement control does not assign jobs according to whether men or women are better qualified to accomplish the tasks—it assigns jobs according to the hours required for the work. This focus on job boundaries over job content is also evident in the range of jobs listed in these quotes. From managerial work, to professional work, to production work, confinement control puts greater emphasis on *when* the work takes place than *what* type of work is done.

Both of these comments reveal a second crucial difference between confinement and normative control. It has to do with the *method* of social control, in terms of how the restrictions are enforced. Normative control is enforced *within the individual,*

as women internalize low status attitudes and behaviors, and then limit their own
actions. However, as the quotes above illustrate, confinement control is enforced
externally, from constraints *in the outside world*. In other words, while women
under normative control restrict themselves, women under confinement control are
restricted by others. Based on this contrast in methods of control, workers give
different reasons for excluding women from male jobs. While normative control
focuses on women's deficiency of skills, confinement control focuses on "restrictions
from society, culture. . ." regarding when it is acceptable for women to work.

Thus, under the influence of Indian gender ideologies, women are literally "confined" within the boundaries of American Technical. The idea of this confinement
system is to prevent female employees from having contact with men outside the
company. Consequently, several restrictions are placed on women's jobs, regarding
their social interactions, physical mobility, and temporal mobility. This is in sharp
contrast to the dynamics of normative control, which guides women's relations with
their male colleagues within the organization. The next section will discuss how this
hybrid system of gender relations was generated.

Discussion

This analysis has attempted to demonstrate how gender relations in an American
multinational corporation in India are influenced by social control systems of both
the United States and India. The meeting of two cultures in this setting yields a
dual structure of gender relations. This structure is characterized by separate realms
of influence for each culture within the organization. Regarding relations *inside* the
organization, normative control predominates; here, women experience restrictions
on the content of their work. However, regarding relations *outside* the organization,
confinement control reigns and women experience restrictions on the boundaries of
their work.

The next section will attempt to make some sense about how this unique situation
arose, and how it is maintained. It will ask: How did the coexistence of two cultures
in the same organization come about? What effect does this hybrid structure have
on the organization's members—do they accept or reject the two cultures? And on
the whole, do the cultures exist in a compatible or conflicting manner? These issues
will be addressed as I examine the negotiations and tensions between American and
Indian gender ideologies.

Negotiation of the Cultures

The negotiation of cultures in American Technical has involved a twofold process. On one hand, the dominant presence of Indian gender ideologies in the *external*
relations of the employees can be attributed to the broader cultural environment outside the organization. It is not surprising that Indian practices and beliefs influence

the extra-organizational gender relations, given that the social context for this setting is Indian. Indeed, regardless of how employees treat each other inside the company's walls, they feel a need to adopt Indian relations when interacting with people in the rest of the world. The main reason is a belief—held by both male and female employees—that there are people in the public world who pose a particular danger to women, and that precautions are needed to shield women from those groups. Confinement control, therefore, is strictly enforced in externally-based relations.

On the other hand, the negotiation of cultures is also affected by a second, counterveiling process. The strong presence of American gender ideologies *inside* the company has been a result (at least in part) of the corporate culture. Company policies have *implicitly* influenced gender relations through a broader emphasis on informality and openness in the workplace. These policies involve democratic decision-making, free communication, and teamwork. They also attempt to break down hierarchical relations between employees (such as those between managers and subordinates) in the context of everyday interactions. This feature of American Technical policies has resulted in a "Westernization" of the workplace. And, in a secondary manner, it has resulted in a Westernization of gender relations as well. By encouraging *interaction* between women and men (as normative control entails), rather than encouraging *distance* between women and men (as confinement control entails), the company supports American styles of gender relations. (It should be noted, however, that the "freedom" of interaction granted by American gender relations is also accompanied by many constraints, as the previous discussion has attempted to demonstrate.)

In addition, the company addresses gender relations among the workers in an *explicit* manner. For example, managers organize formal training sessions on diversity issues (which include gender). Such programs are highly influenced by American ideologies, since they are often developed by the parent company in the U.S., and then introduced directly to employees in the subsidiary. In this sense, the company policies contribute to the dissemination of American beliefs and practices regarding gender.

The question that remains is how have these American gender ideologies become so widely accepted within the organization, especially given that the staff is entirely Indian? Furthermore, what has enabled Indian workers to adopt norms for their internal relations that are opposite to those used in their external relations? In other words, how do they resolve the contradiction that it is *acceptable* for women to interact with male *colleagues*, but *unacceptable* to interact with male *clients*?

The answer is that American Technical policies weaken the influence of confinement control within the company. They do this by undermining Indian rules regarding social interaction. In particular, it involves a reconceptualization of the categories of "safe" versus "unsafe" men. Within the wider society of India, the range of men considered to be "safe" is very narrow—it only includes men inside the *household*. However, American Technical expands this category to include those inside the *organization* as well. This new definition enables women to interact with their male employees, while it simultaneously maintains the justification for women to avoid other males.

The result is a clearly-defined—and (for the most part) comfortable—separation of spheres of relations. This is reflected in the comments about gender relations outside and inside the company. Outside the organization: "In an Indian environment, you don't treat women and men as equals. There is always a distance maintained." Whereas within the organization: "The environment is free and friendly here. The American Technical company policy is instilled in everyone, so that communication between men and women is not a barrier. There is an openness whether the person is below you or above you, whether it is a man or a woman. Definitely, women will feel free." These comments reveal the strong effect of American gender ideologies upon the internal relations of the company. They provide an opportunity for women to interact with men inside that does not exist in their interactions outside. In this way, the company policies are able to mitigate the intensity of confinement control within the organization.

However, the influence of confinement control is not eliminated completely. This is due to the fact that normative control varies within the organization. Specifically, there is *spatial* variation in the implementation of normative control which is related to the "top-down" structure of the corporate policy. What happens is that normative control becomes most intense in relations which are closest to the "top" of the company (i.e., the president). The president has become the primary advocate of American culture because: (1) he has the most familiarity with American norms, as the only American expatriate in the company; and (2) he also has the most power to disseminate these norms, through his dominant position in the organizational hierarchy. So, as one moves physically further and further away from his office, the visibility of normative control becomes weaker and weaker. The attitudes of the employees become less American as their desks are located further away from the President's office, as their offices are placed further down the floors of the building, and as the buildings are placed further away from the corporate office in the country—leading ultimately to the factory, where the attitudes are the most Indian. This pattern illustrates the variability of American gender ideologies within the company, and the significance of the corporate policy in disseminating them.

Tensions Between the Cultures

The result of this negotiation process is that Indian and American cultures operate fairly harmoniously within the same organization. Because each one influences different sets of social relations, they come in contact with each other only infrequently. Nonetheless, there are some instances when the two intersect, and consequently, when tensions are generated between them.

One tension arises from male grievances that the American gender relations are *over-implemented* within the company. These men resist normative control because it conflicts with the gender relations to which they are accustomed—those of confinement control. In particular, they object to its failure to maintain the barriers between men and women. They find the freedom of interaction between the genders under normative control to be uncomfortable and unacceptable. A sales manager vocalizes this idea when asked how American culture affects the company:

> ... in the sense that they have tried to inculcate certain norms. For example, in no Indian company would people dare to call each other by their first names. I find it very difficult to see that happen. I guess I do it *within the office*. But when it comes *outside*—especially if she is of my age or if she is senior—I find it very difficult to call her by her first name in front of an outside person.

This worker feels uncomfortable calling a woman by her first name because such an act defies Indian social customs. Within these customs, formality of social interaction is imperative, because it serves as a primary way of keeping barriers between men and women. Informalness, on the other hand, oversteps such barriers. It is for this reason that male workers experience a clash between the casualness of the American company policies and the restraint of Indian customs.

Another male employee who is a marketing manager expresses a similar opposition to American gender relations. He talks about this in his recommendations for improving work relations in the company:

> I would make this environment little bit more local. In this country, there are certain social norms and modes about male-female interaction that we tend to follow in our everyday lives which are very conservative. We greet each other this way [he gestures by putting the palms of his hands together]—we don't shake hands or hug. Some of the female and male employees do subscribe to these views. They don't feel very comfortable in these environments which encourage free mixing, body touching, things like that. People would do it for good dynamic sales, but I think personally I will not be very comfortable. This company comes across more as an American company—in terms of the kinds of events we have, and in terms of the social interaction that we encourage through the official part. I would make the company a little closer to local norms and the local socio-behavior, and let it evolve as the local social pattern evolves.

This employee adheres to American customs under obligations to his job, but otherwise, he feels the American gender relations are inappropriate and overly-utilized. The American customs involve too much physical contact—"mixing, touching, and shaking hands." In this way, normative patterns transgress the social separation between women and men. Therefore, he suggests that the "local" patterns—characterized by confinement control—should be adopted instead.

In direct contrast to these views, female employees complain that American policies are *under-implemented*. Referring to the company's management, a female communications specialist argues:

> They need to recognize diversity, and they need to translate that into hard realities, and therefore make life a little better for female workers. Because I have seen a lot of cases where there are messages from the U.S., or from our President, and in our own division, people take it so lightly. I think, very seriously speaking, they need to educate a lot of our coworkers on the women in the organization, in terms of how to respect them, and translate it into every work area.

Women like this object when the American policies are not executed fully. Although the American system of normative control has definite disadvantages for these women, it offers one advantage in that it weakens some of the restrictions of confinement control. Most importantly, normative control dismantles the barriers to social interaction. Therefore, when company policies are not enforced, such barriers are slow to break down. One female operations administrator provides an example: "It takes time for men to accept the fact that, if somebody [female] touches you unintentionally, there is nothing wrong in it. They are never used to it, because it is in the background in which they have been brought up. It takes time to adjust and understand this particular American attitude." Under confinement control, female workers feel they do not have enough latitude to interact with men inside the organization. And without the institutional support for change, they find their male coworkers unwilling to adopt American customs.

Finally, a third tension has to do with women's objections to confinement control in extra-organizational relations. They resist limitations on their temporal and physical mobility. One female executive contests her lack of freedom to conduct work outside the office, such as from her own home:

> There is a lot of talk about, "If you need to work from home, and you want some equipment etc., you can do that. We supply you books, and take this home and work from home." But people are not committed to that. You can see that the person doesn't care, and he is not being serious about it, the moment somebody makes a comment about, "You're here in the office for only four hours. It does not look as if you are doing your hourly work."

Because this woman attempted to work in a different location—and consequently defied the rules of physical mobility—her coworkers chastised her for spending too many hours outside the office. In this way, female employees find the confinement system excessively restrictive. Moreover, their frustration is exacerbated by the difficulty of juggling two systems of social control simultaneously. They find it especially problematic to reconcile the *mobility* they experience within the organization, with the *immobility* they experience outside. The fact that the same types of behaviors are restricted in one realm, and permitted in another, generates a great deal of confusion and discomfort for the women workers. In this sense, tensions are endemic features of the coexistence of the two cultural systems.

Conclusion

In sum, the case of American Technical illustrates how gender is directly implicated in the globalization process. Here, gender relations based upon *American* ideologies and practices are imported to a work setting which is entrenched in the customs and beliefs of *Indian* society. In the process, the multinational corporation becomes a global arena, as it brings together several different cultures in one organization. The case of American Technical reveals one type of outcome of this convergence—a coexistence of two sets of gender relations, each with its own sphere of influence.

Thus, this study provides new insights to the literature on globalization. For industrial relations, it demonstrates the potential for multinationals to be affected by two labor processes at one time—these organizations can be both embedded in local cultures, as well as influenced by international pressures. For feminist studies, it demonstrates the importance of distinguishing and characterizing the gender relations of different cultures, and in addition, the importance of recognizing the malleability of these gender systems, such that multiple systems can exist in the same organization simultaneously.

NOTES

1 An earlier version of this article was presented at the American Sociological Association meetings, August 1996. This research was conducted with the support of the National Science Foundation (Grant #SBR-9625604), and the University of California at Berkeley Professional Studies Abroad in India Program. I am grateful to the participants of the study for their generous offerings of time and knowledge, as well as to Szonja Szelenyi, Cecilia Ridgeway, and Michael Burawoy for their excellent comments. The opinions expressed herein are those of the author alone.

REFERENCES

AFSHAR, H. and B. AGARWAL
    1989 *Women, Poverty, and Ideology in Asia: Contradictory Pressures, Uneasy Resolutions.* London: The MacMillan Press, Ltd.
BELANGER, J., P.K. EDWARDS and L. HAIVEN
    1994 *Workplace Industrial Relations and the Global Challenge.* Ithaca: ILR Press.
BORDO, S.
    1993 Feminism, foucault and the politics of the body. In: C. Ramazanoglu (Ed.), *Up Against Foucault: Explorations of Some Tensions Between Foucault and Feminism,* pp. 179-202. London: Routledge.

BOSERUP, E.
   1970 *Women's Role in Economic Development*. London: Aleen and Unwin.
BURAWOY, M.
   1985 *The Politics of Production*. London: Verso.
CHARLES, M.
   1992 Cross-national variation in occupational sex segregation. *American Sociological Review* August 57, 483-502.
CLARK, R., T.W. RAMSBEY and E.S. ADLER
   1991 Culture, Gender and labor force participation: a cross-national study. *Gender and Society* 5, 47-66.
CONNELL, R.W.
   1987 *Gender and Power: Society, the Person and Sexual Politics*. Stanford: Stanford University Press.
FLORIDA, R. and M. KENNEY
   1991 Transplanted organizations: the transfer of Japanese industrial organization to the U.S. *American Sociological Review* 56, 381-398.
FOX, G.L.
   1977 'Nice girl': Social control of women through a value construct. *Signs* 2, 805-817.
FRENKEL, Stephen
   1994 Patterns of workplace relations in the global corporation: toward convergence. In: J. Belanger, P.K. Edwards and L. Haiven (Eds.), *Workplace Industrial Relations and the Global Challenge*, pp. 240-274. Ithaca: ILR Press.
FROBEL, F., J. HEINRICHS and O. KREYE
   1980 *The New International Division of Labour: Structural Unemployment in Industrialised Countries and Industrialisation in Developing Counties*. Cambridge: Cambridge University Press.
GRANOVETTER, M.
   1985 Economic action and social structure: the problem of embeddedness. *American Journal of Sociology* 91 (3), 481-510.
GREEN, S.
   1983 Silicon valley's women workers: a theoretical analysis of sex-segregation in the electronics industry labor market. In: J. Nash and M.P. Fernandez-Kelly (Eds.), *Women, Men, and the International Division of Labor*, pp. 273-331. Albany, NY: Suny Press.
HARRISON, B.
   1994 *Lean and Mean: The Changing Landscape of Corporate Power in the Age of Flexibility*. New York: Basic Books.
HOFSTEDE, G.
   1991 *Cultures and Organizations: Software of the Mind*. London: McGraw-Hill Book Company.
KANTER, R.M.
   1977 *Men and Women of the Corporation*. New York: Basic Books.
LEE, C.K.
   1995 Engendering the worlds of labor in China: women workers, labor markets, and production politics in the South China economic miracle. *American Sociological Review* 60, 378-397.
LIDDLE, J. and R. JOSHI
   1986 *Daughters of Independence: Gender, Caste and Class in India*. London: Zed Books Ltd.
LIM, L.
   1985 *Women Workers in Multinational Enterprises in Developing Countries*. Geneva: International Labour Organisation.

MANDELBAUM, D.
1988 *Women's Seclusion and Men's Honor: Sex Roles in North India.* Tucson: University of Arizona Press.

MIES, M.
1979 *Indian Women and Patriarchy: Conflicts and Dilemmas of Students and Working Women.* New Delhi: Concept Publishing Company.

NASH, J. and M.P. FERNANDEZ-KELLY (Eds.)
1983 *Women, Men, and the International Division of Labor.* Albany, NY: Suny Press.

PAPANEK, H. and G. MINAULT (Eds.)
1982 *Separate Worlds: Studies of Purdah in South Asia.* Delhi: Chanakya Publications.

SAXENIAN, A.
1994 *Regional Advantage: Culture and Competition in Silicon Valley and Route 128.* Cambridge: Harvard University Press.

WARD, K.
1984 *Women in the World-System: Its Impact on Status and Fertility.* New York: Praeger.

WARD, K.
1990 *Women Workers and Global Restructuring.* Ithaca, NY: ILR Press.

The Export of Hazardous Industries to the Peripheral Zones of the World-System

R. SCOTT FREY*

ABSTRACT

The export of hazardous industries to the peripheral zones of the world-system is explored. The nature of the problem is first examined. Political-economic forces driving the transfer of hazardous industries to the periphery are outlined. The extent to which this transfer has adverse consequences for peripheral countries is discussed. The results of an approximate assessment of the costs and benefits associated with the transfer of hazardous industries to the periphery are presented. The paper concludes with a brief discussion of what needs to be done to curb the problem.

Introduction

SOME OF THE CORE'S hazardous production processes, products, and wastes are transferred to the peripheral zones of the world-system by transnational corporations (TNCs) (e.g., Barnett and Cavangh, 1995: 184-207; Brown et al., 1993; Castleman and Navarro, 1987; Covello and Frey, 1990; Frey, 1995, 1997; Leonard, 1988; Pearson, 1987).[1] Since few peripheral countries have the ability to adequately assess and manage the risks associated with hazards, the transfer of core hazards to the periphery increases the health, safety, and environmental risks facing the peripheral countries (Covello and Frey, 1990). TNC export practices are therefore contributing to the globalization of health, safety, and environmental risks (Beck, 1992).

The globalization of the risk problem is discussed in terms of the transfer of hazardous industries from the core to the periphery. The scope and nature of the problem is first examined. Political-economic forces driving the transfer of hazardous industries to the periphery are then outlined. The extent to which this transfer has adverse health, safety, environmental, economic, and social consequences for

* Department of Sociology, Anthropology, and Social Work, Kansas State University, Manhattan, KS 66506, U.S.A. (abcde@ksu.edu).

peripheral countries is reviewed. The results of an approximate assessment of the costs and benefits associated with the transfer of hazardous industries to the periphery are presented. The paper concludes with a brief discussion of what needs to be done to curb the problem.

The Problem

Industrial activity in the periphery has grown dramatically in the past four decades (Froebel et al., 1980; Leonard, 1988; Ross and Trachete, 1990). The periphery's share of the total manufactured goods produced in the world-system grew from 4% in 1955 to 19% in 1989, and it continues to grow (French, 1993: 30; also see Ross and Trachete, 1990: Chapter 6). Much of this activitiy has been sponsored by the TNCs (Jenkins, 1987). The United Nations Environment Programme (1984: 30) and the United Nations Centre on Transnational Corporations (1988) have reported that over 60% of all industrial investments in the periphery during the 1980s was made by TNCs.

The transfer of industrial operations in record numbers to the periphery has increased the production of hazardous materials and wastes, air and water pollution, and the risk of large-scale industrial accidents there (Covello and Frey, 1990). The growth rate of hazardous production processes has been greater than that of the overall industrial growth rate in the periphery and it has been far greater than the growth rate of hazardous industries in the core (Low and Yeats, 1992; Lucas et al., 1992). It is not possible to estimate the full scope of the problem because reliable and valid comparative data are not readily available, but there is a growing body of evidence from Africa, Asia, and Latin America indicating that the problem is serious (see, e.g., Barry, 1994; Bello and Rosenfeld, 1992; Bogard, 1989; Castleman, 1985a; 1985b; Leonard, 1988; Pearson, 1987; Sanchez, 1990; 1991; Sklair, 1993). (See Table 1.) Selected cases (Bhopal in India, the maquiladoras of northern Mexico, and the export manufacturing zones of East and Southeast Asia) are discussed throughout the paper.

The Political Economy of the Export of Hazardous Industries

Political and economic forces characterizing relations within and between countries of the world-system promote the transfer of hazardous industries to the periphery. In an effort to expand markets and curb production costs, many core-based TNCs have moved industrial production facilities to sites located in the periphery and many peripheral states have pursued export-oriented industrial policies to attract core industry.

Table 1

Selected Examples of the Transfer of Hazardous Industries to the Periphery

Industry	Location	Type of hazard	Multinational affiliation	Type of affiliation
Asbestos milling	South Africa	Children with asbestosis	Cape Asbestos (UK)	Subsidiary mining operation
Asbestos textile manufacture	Juarez, Mexico	Not informing workers and neighborhood of pollution	Amatex (U.S.)	Subsidiary
Asbestos insulation manufacture	Brazil	Failure to affix product warnings, failure to reformulate products to eliminate asbestos	Johns-Manville (U.S.)	Subsidiary
Asbestos friction product and textile manufacture	Bombay, India	Workplace hazards uncontrolled, failure to inform workers and tell them of medical exam findings	Turner & Newall (UK)	74% ownership
Asbestos cement manufacture	Ahmedabad, India	Water pollution, solid waste dumping, no warnings on products	Johns-Manville (U.S.)	Minority ownership, marketing of exports, raw material sales, plant design and construction supervision
Asbestos brake manufacture	Madras, India	Solid waste dumping	Cape Industries (UK)	25% ownership

Table 1
(Continued)

Industry	Location	Type of hazard	Multinational affiliation	Type of affiliation
Asbestos brake shoe manufacture	South Korea	Substandard working conditions	Not known	—
Battery manufacture	Indonesia	Hundreds of workers with kidney disease, pollution of drinking water with mercury	Union Carbide (U.S.)	Subsidiary
Chromate and diochromate	Lecheria, Mexico	Waste dumping, workplace exposures producing nasal septum perforation	Bayer (Germany)	Partial ownership
Dye manufacture	Bombay, India	Water pollution	Montedison (Italy)	Partial ownership
Steelmaking	Malaysia	Air pollution, workplace hazards	Nippon Steel (Japan)	Minority ownership and plant design
Polyvinyl chloride manufacture	Malaysia	High worker exposure to vinyl	Japanese companies	Partial ownership
Arsenical pesticide production	Malaysia	Arsenic poisoning in workers	Diamond Shamrock (U.S.)	Subsidiary
Pesticide manufacture	Bhopal, India	Unsafe plant operation. History of injurious exposure preceding 1984 accident	Union Carbide (U.S.)	51% ownership

Adapted from Barry (1994), Castleman (1985a), and Castleman and Navarro (1987).

Problems in the Core

Scientific and public concern with the health and environmental risks of industrial production emerged as an important issue during the 1970s in many core countries (Brickman et al., 1985; Hays, 1987). This concern gave rise to a host of health, safety, and environmental regulations (Brickman et al., 1985; Fiorino, 1995).[2] Such regulations increased industrial production costs in the core and pushed hazardous industries to the periphery (Castleman, 1985a; Castleman and Navarro, 1987; Leonard, 1988).

The effect of such regulations on the spatial dispersion of hazardous industries to the periphery is a subject of some debate (e.g., Castleman, 1985a; 1985b; Jaffe et al., 1995; Levenstein and Eller, 1985; Low and Yeats, 1992; Tobey, 1990). And several researchers report that it has been exaggerated (Jaffe et al., 1995: 143-150; Leonard, 1988; Tobey, 1990). Leonard (1988), for instance, reports that there is little evidence to support the claim that increased regulation has led to the large-scale transfer of hazardous industries to so-called "pollution havens" located in the periphery; rather, only certain aging and economically marginal processes have been exported: benzidine-based dye production, arsenic production, asbestos processing, lead refining, battery manufacturing, and pesticide production. On the other hand, results of a survey of U.S. companies operating in Mexicali, Mexico indicate that lax environmental regulations influenced the decision of 25% of those companies surveyed to locate in Mexico and a 1991 U.S. Government Accounting Office study found that many Los Angeles furniture manufacturers relocated to Mexico after the establishment of stringent air pollution restrictions in California (French, 1992: 30-31; Sanchez, 1990).

Factors other than environmental regulation have contributed to the movement of hazardous industries to the periphery. These include international economic conditions such as exchange rate conditions and comparative resource endowments; labor, energy, and transportation costs; and business investment conditions. The spatial dispersion of hazardous industry also reflects a much larger trend in economic globalization processes.

Whatever the relative importance of these interrelated forces, the point is that core-based TNCs have found it economically advantageous to transfer hazardous industrial activities to the periphery through a variety of subsidiary, licensing, and joint venture arrangements. Production costs are considerably less in the periphery because of low wages, cheap resources and energy, low taxes and other subsidies, and limited state control of the environment and the health, safety, and well-being of its citizens. Reduced costs in the periphery enhance the competitiveness of TNCs and promote capital accumulation in the core. In other words, capital flows to those peripheral countries having an absolute advantage in industrial production.

Problems in the Periphery

Confronted with poverty and the resulting political pressures, debt, low agricultural and mineral commodity prices, and a world system that does not allow them to participate fully in economic production and exchange, many peripheral states have pursued export-oriented policies (including deregulation of the economy, removal of trade restrictions, and liberalization of controls on captal movement) in an effort to attract industrial production processes from the core. In fact, many peripheral countries are so anxious to industrialize that they are willing to take almost any industry offered: hazardous or otherwise. Nowhere is this pattern more pervasive than in countries like India (Bogard, 1989; Bowonder, 1987) and the export-processing zones of Mexico (Barry, 1994; Sanchez, 1990; 1991) and the newly industrializing countries of East and Southeast Asia (Bello, 1996; Bello and Rosenfeld, 1992).

The Indian government has offered financial incentives to core-based industries for decades in an effort to encourage industrialization, provide jobs, and foster technology transfer. The Indian state of Madhya Pradesh lured the Agricultural Products Division of Union Carbide to build a pesticide plant at Bhopal, the capital of the state, in the 1970s. The plant was welcomed as a source of jobs and the pesticides produced at the plant were viewed as a cheap input for boosting local food production and increasing food sufficiency. Production began in 1979, but the factory never did live up to employment and production expectations and it proved to be financially unprofitable for Union Carbide. The plant operated at partial capacity until an accident on 3 December, 1984 when 40 tons of methyl isocyanate and other chemicals were released into the city's air.

More than 2,000 factories (employing over 500,000 workers and stretching along the 2,000 mile border from Tijuana on the Pacific Coast to Matamoros on the Gulf of Mexico) operate under the maquiladora program in northern Mexico (Barry, 1994; Kochan, 1989; Sklair, 1993). The program was established in 1965 by the Mexican state to combat economic problems along the border by encouraging regional industrialization, employment, and new technology imports and management practices (Lerner, 1993; Scramstadt, 1991). Cheap labor, lax regulations, generous tax incentives, and close proximity to the U.S. consumer market are regularly used by the Mexican state to attract TNC investment. Plant owners include a "Who's Who" of international capital: Chrysler, IBM, RCA, ITT, DuPont, Eastman Kodak, Zenith, Xerox, Sony, Ford, United Technologies, Hitachi, and other lesser known U.S., Canadian, European, and Japanese TNCs. Various consumer products are produced for export to the U.S., including furniture for several U.S. companies, auto parts for Chrysler, high-tech electronic components and computer disks for Sony, Foster Grant sunglasses, hospital gowns for Kimberly Clark, and garage door openers for Sears. Maquila plants also produce hazardous wastes and other substances that are not managed effectively and contaminate the air, water, and soil. This exposes

workers and the inhabitants of surrounding squatter settlements to a host of technological hazards and increases the risk of large-scale industrial accidents (Barry,
1994; Kochan, 1989; Multinational Monitor, 1995; Sanchez, 1990; 1991).

Export-oriented industrialization based on foreign assembly began in East and
Southeast Asia in the 1950s (Bello and Rosenfeld, 1992; Brohman, 1996: Chapter 3).
State-directed development of the export industry first emerged in Hong Kong in the
early 1950s. It spread to Taiwan, South Korea, Singapore, and the Philippines by the
1960s, surfaced in Indonesia and Sri Lanka in the 1970s, and became a dominant
force in China by the late 1980s. Hundreds of assembly plants (controlled by TNCs
based in the U.S., Japan, and Europe) produce electronics, textiles, toys, apparel,
and footwear for export but do not pay duties on imported components. Asian
states have used these plants in an effort to generate foreign exchange, alleviate
unemployment, and introduce new production techniques and management practices.
Industrial activity in these zones is sheltered from trade unions and stringent health,
safety, and environmental regulations (Bello, 1996; Bello and Rosenfeld, 1992).
The pollution-intensive nature of the imported production processes and lax state
regulation have contributed to a number of undesirable consequences (Bello and
Rosenfeld, 1992; Brohman, 1996: 123-131; Pearce et al., 1994).

Vulnerabilities and Risks in the Periphery

Industrial production can damage the environment and adversely affect human
health through occupational exposure and environmental dispersion of hazardous
wastes and substances in the soil, water, and air, or large-scale system failures such
as explosions and fires (Bogard, 1989; Covello and Frey, 1990; Pearce et al., 1994).
There are also a number of undesirable social and economic consequences associated
with the transfer of hazardous industries, including staggering economic costs and
the unequal distribution of costs and benefits.

Peripheral countries are particularly vulnerable to the risks posed by hazardous
industries because of a poorly-trained, undernourished, and unhealthy workforce
that is uninformed about industrial hazards. There is limited public awareness of
technological risks, weak labor unions and politically unresponsive state agencies,
and inadequate risk assessment and management capabilities (Covello and Frey,
1990; Michaels et al., 1985; Pearce et al., 1994). The problem is compounded
by the fact that hazardous industries are often located in rapidly growing cities
faced with many health, safety, and environmental risks (Pearce et al., 1994; World
Resources, 1996: 1-156).

Environmental Risks

Emissions of toxic substances, the improper disposal of hazardous wastes and
materials, and large-scale system failures contribute to the risk of environmental

damage. Environmental damage takes several different forms: soil contamination, groundwater pollution, biodiversity loss, contamination of rivers and coastal regions, air pollution, and threats to plant and animal health. Most research examining the environmental effects of hazardous industries is limited to the temperate climates of the core countries, but the adverse environmental effects of hazardous industries in the tropical regions of the periphery may be very different and far more severe (Logan, 1991). Since reliable data do not exist on the full breadth and nature of the problem, it is not possible to estimate the extent of environmental damage. But such damage is a potentially important problem because it could deplete important natural resources, threaten the stability of larger ecosystems, and threaten human health.

The environmental effects of the Bhopal accident are not well understood, but the long-term effects include damage to vegetation, animal, and fish species (Bowonder, 1987). The maquilas of northern Mexico have contributed to water pollution on both sides of the border and threaten fish and wildlife (Barry, 1994; Kochan, 1989). Similar problems exist throughout the export-processing zones of East and Southeast Asia (Bello and Rosenfeld, 1992).

Human Health Risks

Estimates of occupational and environmental exposure to the hazards posed by imported industries and the attendant health consequences are not fully known (Pearce et al., 1994). Given the experiences of the core countries and reports from peripheral countries (Barry, 1994; Castleman, 1985a; Michaels et al., 1985), hazardous industries pose a serious threat. Those exposed are at substantially increased risk of death, disease, and disability because of their increased susceptibility to various site-specific cancers, skin irritation, respiratory problems, neurobehavioral problems, birth defects and miscarriages, genetic changes and damage to the immune system, and acute and chronic damage to specific body organs. In addition those living near hazardous facilities and waste disposal sites are at increased risk of death and injury from fires and explosions.

Since reliable data do not exist on the occupational and environmental exposure to the routine, fugitive, and accidental emissions of hazardous substances, it is not possible to estimate the actual number of deaths or cases of disease and injury that can be attributed to them. (The United Nations estimates that there are at least 6,000,000 cases of environmental and occupational disease each year and most of these cases occur in the periphery (LaDou, 1992: 224).) One thing is clear: the populations of peripheral countries are at far greater risk of death, disease, and disability from hazardous industries than their core counterparts (Reich and Okubo, 1992).

Consider the industrial accident at Bhopal in December 1984. The death toll is estimated to have been somewhere between 6,000 and 20,000 humans. Deaths were disproportionately concentrated among children and infants. Several hundred thousand more suffered from the exposure, but the long-term effects of such exposure are uncertain (Bowonder, 1987; Bowonder et al., 1985; Melius, 1992).

The human health problems linked to the maquila plants in northern Mexico are pervasive. Air pollution and groundwater and surface water contamination have been documented at many points along the border (Barry, 1994; Kochan, 1989). Hazardous waste management is also a severe problem, for many plants dump and store hazardous wastes in a haphazard fashion (Sanchez, 1990; 1991).[3] Industrial accidents and adverse health conditions among maquila workers and the inhabitants of areas surrounding the plants are high (Barry, 1994; Kochan, 1989; Sanchez, 1991). Numerous incidents have been reported, but none more dramatic than the cluster of 50 anencephalic babies born in the Brownsville, Texas-Matamoros, Mexico area (19 in Brownsville and 31 in Matamoros) in the early 1990s (Suro, 1992). The health problems caused by the maquiladora plants are so serious that the Council on Scientific Affairs (1990: 3320) of the American Medical Association has stated that "environmental monitoring and disease incidence data... point out that public and environmental health... is rapidly deteriorating and seriously affecting the health and future economic vitality on both sides of the border."

Incidents from the export-processing zones of East and Southeast Asia also illustrate the health risks posed by hazardous industry. In November 1993, 81 workers died in a fire in the Zhili doll factory in the Free Trade Zone of Shenzen, China. Thirty-one workers were hospitalized. According to reports at the time, people were trapped in the factory because company officials kept doors and windows locked to ensure that people remained inside during working hours (Johnston and Button, 1994: 207).

Economic Costs

The costs associated with the future cleanup of contaminated sites and improperly disposed wastes are potentially high for both core and periphery countries, but even more so for the latter. The treatment and compensation of victims of hazardous exposures in the periphery are also potentially very costly, though accidents such as the one at Bhopal have proven to be far more so for Indians than for Union Carbide. Destruction of natural resources (including marine life, biodiversity, and soil, water, and air quality) is also likely to be costly. And reductions in human health are costly, for they can impede economic growth (Behrman, 1993). The tangible and intangible economic costs associated with the transfer of hazardous industries to the periphery appear to be substantial.

Social Costs

The benefits and costs associated with the transfer of hazardous production facilities to the periphery are distributed in an uneven fashion. Most benefits go to the core-based TNCs, while the importing countries bear most of the costs. Losses within the peripheral countries are distributed in an unequal fashion: some groups are able to capture benefits and other social groups (because of their class, race/ethnicity, gender, or geographic location) bear the costs. Consider the Bhopal incident: most of those killed were poor and most of those who continue to suffer are poor (Bogard, 1989: 45). Young women in the export zones of Mexico and the newly industrializing countries of Asia have borne many of the health and safety risks of industrial production, but they have enjoyed few of the economic benefits generated in these zones (e.g., LaBotz, 1994; Park, 1993).

Surrounding countries may also bear costs as hazardous residues move across national boundaries through the air, water, and food. In northern Mexico, for instance, wastes created by the maquilas are dispersed into the air and water and often end up in the United States (Barry, 1994). Furthermore, future human generations will bear costs without enjoying any of the benefits generated by the hazardous production operations.[4]

An Approximate Cost-Benefit Assessment

The short-term economic benefits associated with the location of hazardous industries in the periphery must be considered in light of the long-term economic costs. Despite suggestions and efforts to the contrary, there is no sound factual or methodological basis for adequately identifying, estimating, and valuating the costs and benefits associated with the transfer of hazardous industries to the periphery (see Asford and Ayers, 1985). Comments of former World Bank chief economist Lawrence Summers (Economist, 1992) are worth quoting at length because they illustrate some of the difficulties and contradictory outcomes of traditional economic reasoning in such matters:

> Just between you and me, shouldn't the World Bank be encouraging *more* migration of the dirty industries to the LDCs? I can think of three reasons:
>
> (1) The measurement of the costs of health-impairing pollution depends on the foregone earnings from increased morbidity and mortality. From this point of view a given amount of health-impairing pollution should be done in the country with the lowest cost, which will be the country with the lowest wages.
>
> (2) The costs of pollution are likely to be non-linear as the initial increments of pollution probably have been very low cost. I've always thought that under-polluted countries in Africa are vastly under-polluted; their air quality is probably... low compared to Los Angeles or Mexico City...
>
> (3) The demand for a clean environment for aesthetic and health reasons is likely to have very high income-elasticity. The concern over an agent that causes a one-in-a-million chance in the

odds of prostate cancer is obviously going to be much higher in a country where people survive
to get prostate cancer than in a country where under-5 mortality is 200 per thousand.

Such reasoning undervalues nature and is based on the belief that human life in
the periphery is worth much less than it is in the core because of wage differences.
Although most costs are borne by the periphery (and most benefits are captured by
the core), the costs to the periphery are deemed minimal and acceptable because
human life is defined as worth so little.

Even if the economic costs and benefits associated with the transfer of hazardous
industries to the periphery could be meaningfully estimated and valued, it is doubtful
that the benefits accruing to the periphery would cover the costs. Again, consider
Bhopal, the maquiladoras of northern Mexico, and the export-manufacturing zones
of East and Southeast Asia. Little systematic attention has been directed to an examination of the costs and benefits surrounding the Bhopal case, but there is little reason
to believe that the benefits generated by the plant over its six-year life span cover
the full costs associated with the accident (Bogard, 1989; Bowonder, 1987). Sklair's
(1993: 240-266) qualitative assessment of the maquiladora program in terms of six
development criteria (backward and forward linkage creation, foreign currency earn-
ings, personnel upgrading, technology transfer, work conditions, and environmental
conditions) concludes that the mix of costs and benefits of the maquiladora program
is uncertain. Bello and Rosenfeld (1992) paint a far darker picture in their assessment of the costs and benefits of the export zones of Korea, Taiwan, and Singapore.
They conclude that the "strategy of development needs drastic, if not fundamental
revision to avoid the scenario of... (Korea, Taiwan, and Singapore) falling back to
the third world" (Bello and Rosenfeld, 1992: 337; also see Bello, 1996).

Concluding Thoughts

The transfer of hazardous industries to the periphery has been discussed in terms
of its nature and scope, causes, and adverse consequences, but it can also be framed
in terms of responsibility: those who profit from production should bear the costs associated with it. Various strategies have been proposed (by the UN, the World Bank,
numerous NGOs, and many grass-roots environmental groups throughout the periphery) to deal with the problem and several international regimes have emerged to curb
the transnational movement of hazardous production processes (see, e.g., Ashford
and Ayers, 1989; Kitt, 1995; Neff, 1990; Renn et al., 1991). But many obstacles
stand in the way of the effective control of the dispersion of hazardous industry to
the periphery.[5] Until the global political authority exists to effectively monitor and
control the export practices of TNCs or the control of capital is "renationalized" (returned to nation states, cf. Daly, 1996: 145-162), TNCs will continue to externalize
their production costs on the periphery and contribute to the globalization of health,
safety, and environmental risks.

NOTES

1   There is also increased concern with the movement of pollutants from the core to the periphery
     through the air, soil, and water, as well as the pollution of the global commons by the core countries
     (see, e.g., Huq, 1994; Moomaw and Tullis, 1994).
2   Early efforts in the U.S. included the National Environmental Policy Act of 1969, the Occupational,
     Health and Safety Act of 1970, the Federal Water Pollution Control Act of 1972, the 1976 Toxic
     Substances Control Act, and the Resource Conservation and Recovery Act (RCRA) of 1976.
     Subsequent legislation such as the 1980 Comprehensive Environmental Response, Compensation,
     and Liability Act (CERCLA and commonly known as Superfund), the 1984 amendment to RCRA,
     and the 1986 Superfund Amendments and Reauthorization Act (SARA) curtailed the haphazard
     disposal of hazardous wastes into the air and water and increased the amount of wastes earmarked
     for specialized disposal (Fiorino, 1995: 22-99).
3   Wastes include the carcinogen trichlorethylene used as a degreasor in the electronics industry; the
     poison copper cyanide generated in electroplating; and a host of other toxic chemicals such as paint
     strippers and thinners, PCP-contaminated wastes, and methylene chloride (Barry, 1994; Sanchez,
     1990).
4   Ashford and Ayers (1985: 880) state the problem in an unusually precise fashion by noting that
     establishing "a pesticide plant in a developing country may result in economic benefits to the
     corporate owner, corporate shareholders, employees, local farmers, and consumers. The decision
     may also result in adverse health effects to plant employees, people living near the plant, farmers
     who handle the pesticide, and consumers who eat contaminated food. In addition, future generations
     may suffer the depletion or pollution of natural resources and adverse health effects."
5   There are a number of obstacles. International regimes can be easily undermined by uncooperative
     nations. International efforts to control and regulate the movement of hazardous industries to the
     periphery have been dismissed as nothing but attempts to legalize TNC practices. Provision of
     risk information to peripheral countries about hazardous industries is likely to have little impact
     on reducing risks because many peripheral countries are unable to use such information. Codes of
     conduct for TNCs are unlikely to be enforced. Peripheral state efforts to regulate hazardous indus-
     tries are unlikely to be fully effective, because of limited economic resources, limited regulatory
     capacity, and a lack of political will. (See Kitt [1995], Krutilla [1991], and Susskind [1994] for
     further discussion of these and related issues.)

REFERENCES

ASFORD, Nicholas and Christine AYERS
     1985 Policy issues for consideration in transferring technology in developing countries. *Ecology
           Law Quarterly* 12, 871-905.
BARNETT, Richard J. and John CAVANGH
     1995 *Global Dreams*. New York: Touchstone.
BARRY, Tom
     1994 *The Challenge of Cross-Border Environmentalism*. Albuquerque, NM: Resource Center
           Press.
BECK, Ulrich
     1992 *Risk Society*. London: Sage.

BEHRMAN, J.R.
  1993 Health and economic growth. Pp. 21-61 in *Macroeconomic Environment and Health with Case Studies for Countries of Greatest Need*. Geneva: World Health Organization.
BELLO, Walden
  1996 Neither market nor state. *The Ecologist* 26 (July/August), 167-175.
BELLO, Walden and Stephanie ROSENFELD
  1992 *Dragons in Distress*. San Francisco, CA: Food First.
BOGARD, W.
  1989 *The Bhopal Tragedy*. Boulder, CO: Westview Press.
BOWONDER, B.
  1987 The bhopal accident. *Technological Forecasting and Social Change* 32, 169-182.
BOWONDER, B., Jeanne X. KASPERSON, and Roger E. KASPERSON
  1985 Avoiding future bhopals. *Environment* 27 (September), 6-13, 31-37.
BRICKMAN, R., S. JASANOFF, and T. ILGEN
  1985 *Controlling Chemicals*. Ithaca, NY: Cornell University Press.
BROHMAN, John
  1996 *Popular Development*. Cambridge, MA: Blackwell.
BROWN, H.S., P. DERR, O. RENN, and A.L. WHITE
  1993 *Corporate Environmentalism in a Global Economy*. Westport, CT: Quorum Books.
CASTLEMAN, Barry I.
  1985a The double standard in industrial hazards. Pp. 60-89 in *The Export of Hazard*, Jane H. Ives (Ed.). Boston: Routledge and Kegan Paul.
CASTLEMAN, Barry I.
  1985b Response to Levenstein-Eller critique. Pp. 90-93 in *The Export of Hazard*, Jane H. Ives (Ed.). Boston: Routledge and Kegan Paul.
CASTLEMAN, Barry I. and Vincent NAVARRO
  1987 International mobility of hazardous products, industries and wastes. *Annual Review of Public Health* 8, 1-19.
COUNCIL ON SCIENTIFIC AFFAIRS
  1990 A permanent U.S.-Mexico border environmental health commission. *Journal of the American Medical Association* 253, 3319-3321.
COVELLO, Vincent T. and R. Scott FREY
  1990 Technology-based environmental health risks in developing nations. *Technological Forecasting and Social Change* 37, 159-179.
DALY, Herman E.
  1996 *Beyond Growth*. Boston: Beacon Press.
The Economist
  1992 Let them eat pollution. *The Economist* (February 8), 66.
FIORINO, Daniel J.
  1995 *Making Environmental Policy*. Berkeley: University of California Press.
FRENCH, H.
  1992 Strengthening global environmental goverance. Pp. 155-173 in *State of the World, 1992*. New York: W.W. Norton.
FRENCH, H.
  1993 *Costly Tradeoffs*. Washington, D.C.: Worldwatch.
FREY, R. Scott
  1995 The international traffic in pesticides. *Technological Forecasting and Social Change* 50, 151-169.

FREY, R. Scott
1997 The international traffic in Tobacco. *Third World Quarterly* 18, 303-319.
FROEBEL, F., J. HENRICHS, and O. KREYE
1980 *The New International Division of Labor.* London: Cambridge University Press.
HAYS, S.P.
1987 *Beauty, Health, and Permanence.* Cambridge: Cambridge University Press.
HUQ, Saleemui
1994 Global industrialization. Pp. 107-113 in *Industrial Ecology and Global Change*, R. Socolow, C. Andrews, F. Berkhout, and V. Thomas (Eds.). Cambridge: Cambridge University Press.
JAFFE, Adam B., Steven R. PETERSON, Paul R. PORTNEY, and Robert N. STAVINS
1995 Environmental regulation and the competitiveness of U.S. manufacturing. *Journal of Economic Literature* 33, 132-163.
JENKINS, Rhys
1987 *Transnational Corporations and Uneven Development.* London: Methuen.
JOHNSTON, B. and G. BUTTON
1994 Human environmental rights issues and the multinational corporation. Pp. 206-215 in *Who Pays the Price?*, B. Johnston (Ed.). Washington, DC: Island Press.
KITT, Jennifer R.
1995 Waste exports to the developing world. *Georgetown International Environmental Law Review* 7, 485-514.
KOCHAN, Leslie
1989 *The Maquiladoras and Toxics.* Washington, DC: AFL-CIO.
KRUTILLA, Kerr
1991 Unilateral environmental policy in the global commons. *Policy Studies Journal* 19, 126-139.
LABOTZ, D.
1994 Manufacturing poverty. *International Journal of Health Services* 24, 403-408.
LADOU, Joseph
1992 The export of hazardous industries to newly industrialized countries. *Polish Journal of Medicine and Environmental Health* 5, 223-226.
LEONARD, H. Jeffrey
1988 *Pollution and the Struggle for the World Product.* New York: Cambridge University Press.
LERNER, Stephen
1993 The Maquiladora and Hazardous waste. *Transnational Lawyer* 6, 255-270.
LEVENSTEIN, Charles and Stanley W. ELLER
1985 Exporting hazardous industries. Pp. 51-59 in *The Export of Hazard*, Jane H. Ives (Ed.). Boston: Routledge and Kegan Paul.
LOGAN, Bernard I.
1991 An assessment of the environmental and economic implications of toxic-waste disposal in sub-Saharan Africa. *Journal of World Trade* 25, 61-76.
LOW, Patrick and Alexander YEATS
1992 Do 'dirty' industries migrate? Pp. 89-103 in *International Trade and Environment*, Patrick Low (Ed.). Washington, DC: World Bank.
LUCAS, R., D. WHEELER, and H. HETTIGE
1992 Economic development, environmental regulation and the international migration of toxic industrial pollution. Pp. 67-85 in *International Trade and the Environment*, Patrick Low (Ed.). Washington, DC: World Bank.

MELIUS, J.M.
: 1992 The bhopal disaster. Pp. 921-926 in *Environmental and Occupational Medicine*, W.N. Rom (Ed.). Boston: Little, Brown.

MICHAELS, D., C. BARRERA, and M.G. GACHARNA
: 1985 Occupational health and the economic development of Latin America. Pp. 94-114 in *The Export of Hazard*, Jane H. Ives (Ed.). Boston, MA: Routledge and Kegan Paul.

MOOMAW, William and Mark TULLIS
: 1994 Charting development paths. Pp. 157-172 in *Industrial Ecology and Global Change*, R. Socolow, C. Andrews, F. Berkhout, and V. Thomas (Eds.). Cambridge: Cambridge University Press.

Multinational Monitor
: 1995 Border health hazards. *Multinational Monitor* (April), 22-23.

NEFF, Alan
: 1990 Not in their backyards, either. *Ecology Law Quarterly* 17, 477-537.

PARK, K.
: 1993 Women and development. *Comparative Politics* 25, 127-145.

PEARCE, N., E. MATOS, H. VAINIO, P. BOFFETTA, and M. KOGEVINAS (Eds.)
: 1994 *Occupational Cancer in Developing Countries*. Lyon, France: International Agency for Research on Cancer.

PEARSON, Charles S. (Ed.)
: 1987 *Multinational Corporations, Environment, and Third World Business Matters*. Durham, NC: Duke University Press.

REICH, Michael and Toshiteu OKUBO (Eds.)
: 1992 *Protecting Workers' Health in the Third World*. New York: Auburn House.

RENN, O., H.S. BROWN, and A.L. WHITE
: 1991 Doing the right thing in exporting hazardous technologies. *Environment, Science and Technology* 25, 1965-1970.

ROSS, R. and K. TRACHETE
: 1990 *Global Capitalism*. Albany: State University of New York Press.

SANCHEZ, Roberto A.
: 1990 Health and environmental risks of the Maquiladora in Mexicali. *Natural Resources Journal* 30, 163-186.

SANCHEZ, Roberto A.
: 1991 Environment: Mexican perspective. Pp. 303-335 in *U.S.-Mexican Industrial Integration*, Sidney Weintraub (Ed.). Boulder, CO: Westview Press.

SCRAMSTADT, B.
: 1991 Transboundary movement of hazardous waste from the United States to Mexico. *Transnational Lawyer* 4, 253-290.

SKLAIR, Leslie
: 1993 *Assembly for Development*. San Diego: Center for U.S.-Mexican Studies, University of California.

SURO, R.
: 1994 *The New York Times* (May 31), 18.

SUSSKIND, Lawrence E.
: 1994 *Environmental Diplomacy*. New York: Oxford University Press.

TOBEY, James A.
: 1990 The effects of domestic environmental policies on patterns of world trade. *Kyklos* 43, 191-209.

UNITED NATIONS CENTRE ON TRANSNATIONAL CORPORATIONS
  1988 *Trasnational Corporations in World Development*. New York: United Nations.
UNITED NATIONS ENVIRONMENT PROGRAM
  1984 *Industry and Environment*. Nairobi, Kenya: United Nations.
WORLD RESOURCES INSTITUTE
  1996 *World Resources, 1996-1997*. New York: Oxford University Press.

Concepts and Indicators of Development
An Empirical Analysis[1]

BAM DEV SHARDA*, GEORGE A. MILLER*
and ARCHIBALD O. HALLER**

ABSTRACT

A number of concepts and measurement procedures have been proposed to describe the development-level differences among nations. This paper reviews them and examines their interrelationships. Fifteen variables and their intercorrelations are discussed. Of these, 10 were deemed acceptable on theoretical and empirical grounds for factor analysis. Two strong, orthogonal factors were found to meet the conventional criteria. They were labeled *domestic development* (*DD*) and *authority* (*A*). *DD* loads most on life expectancy, infant mortality (negative), $\log_n$ GNP/c, and population growth rate (negative). *A* loads most on $\log_n$ population, Wallerstein's "core-periphery," and Rossem's "prominence." Thus the two factors reflect two very different phenomena. *DD* expresses the meaning of development commonly held by economic planners. *A* expresses the relative power of one nation to exert influence on another, with total population and core status serving as resources by which the outcomes of negotiations among nations may be influenced.

THE CONTEMPORARY INTEREST in development research goes back at least to the 1940's when the Latin American structural school of development economics was founded. Raol Prebish, an Argentinean economist, and Celso Furtado, a Brazilian economist, played central roles in the formation of this school. In 1948, the Economic Commission for Latin America (ECLA) was formed under Prebish's direction. ECLA attacked the theory of comparative advantage, which was dominant in economics at the time. The theory was originally propounded by David Ricardo (1817), who suggested that nations produce what they can produce more efficiently and exchange those products with what other countries produce more efficiently. In this exchange, both counties benefit. The great depression of 1930's devastated the economies of many primary producing countries. For example, the world prices of coffee—a major export of Brazil and other Latin American countries plummeted but

* Department of Sociology, University of Utah, Salt Lake City, Utah 84112, U.S.A.
** Department of Sociology, University of Wisconsin-Madison, Madison, Wisconsin 59706, U.S.A.

the price of industrial goods increased—devastating countries dependent on primary exports.

ECLA proposed the new theory, emphasizing the economic structure of underdevelopment. Contrary to the tenets of the neo-classical economic theory, ECLA recommended industrialization and state intervention as essential to Latin American national development. Further impetus to the popularity of this school occurred with the work of Andre Gunder Frank who first made explicit the dependency theory of South American underdevelopment. Frank's work was influenced by a neo-Marxist paradigm of underdevelopment, especially of Paul Baran in the United States. Dependency theory has since been incorporated in the World System approach of Wallerstein, which we will discuss later.

Development also was a new theme of the 1950's and 1960's in the United States and Europe, after the successful outcome of the Marshall Plan in Europe, and, in a sense, even before, in Truman's Point 4 Program. The European reconstruction after the devastation of World War II showed that aid could be used as a new strategy of development. Development was needed in the newly decolonized nations of Asia and Africa and the poor countries of the Western Hemisphere. It was also seen as a response to the Cold War, as two great power blocs with competing visions of development vied for hegemony over the poorer regions of the world. Industrialization was considered an essential feature of development by most social scientists. However, the term remained ill-defined. Per capita energy consumption, percent labor force not in agriculture, or even telephones per 1,000 households were used as indicators of industrialization, and hence development. However, for researchers, the handiest indicator came to be the Gross National Product per capita (GNP/c), based on Kuznet's concept of the GNP (1963). Economic development was thus mainly equated with per capita income, assuming that benefits of growth would "trickle down" (Streeten, 1981: 108).

Economic theory tends to set the form of scholarly thinking about development, and in the West at least, economists almost wholly dominate development planning. Nonetheless, theory and research on national development incorporate contributions from various disciplines: economics, anthropology, political science, and sociology in particular. The debates about development concepts, therefore, are truly interdisciplinary. The different disciplines have tended to emphasize different variables as most central to the conception and measurement of development. This may have contributed to confusion over the very concept of development that the debate is supposed to resolve. This paper is an effort to resolve this confusion by an empirical demonstration of the relationships among key indicators of competing conceptions.

In the economics literature it is, of course, recognized that nations of the modern world are linked to each other with trade, considering each as an autonomous unit as regards economic activity. The development of populations occurs within the confines of the boundaries of the nation states. In essence, even though the political units of the world—the nations—are linked by trade, they pursue their own policies of economic growth and development. Sociologists have criticized this position as politically naive.

In the world system perspective held by many sociologists, nation states are not seen as completely autonomous. Some are seen as more autonomous than others. The world system perspective puts heavy emphasis on the international division of labor, in which different sets of nations play different roles in the world economy. The international division of labor is considered to be enforced by political power, implicitly backed by military power—though in a much different way than during the colonial era. The appropriate units of the world system are not seen as nation states but politico-economic units consisting of sets of them. Originally, Wallerstein (1974) conceived the world in three tiers: the *core*—a rich and politically powerful bloc of nations, at one extreme; the *periphery*—the poor and politically powerless countries, often also called "underdeveloped" or "third world" nations, at the other; and the *semi-periphery* set in between. Thus Chirot (1986: 97) has noted: "Internal class structures, or the distribution of power and wealth within particular societies, are related to the international distribution of power and wealth between societies." With the end of colonialism after World War II, third-world nations, impoverished and politically weak, embarked on finding strategies of development.

Chirot (1986: 98-99, passim) then outlined three analytically distinct, though "correlated dimensions" that allocated societies to different blocs in the world system: (i) sheer political and military power, the ability of a state to impose its will on others, (ii) the degree of economic development—international strength as a function of a state's level of economic development, sheer size and degree of internal cohesion, and (iii) a lower-end derivative of the level of economic development, the degree to which an economy is dependent on primary exports. Economic development, therefore, played a key role in the development of international stratification—the order of power and privilege among nations.

Bornchier and Chase Dunn (1987: 1) have held that the:

> problem of development and modernization has been recast by a new awareness of the hierarchical structure of the world-economy. What were formerly understood to be relatively independent national societies, some advanced and some backward or traditional, are now seen as differentiated parts of a larger world-economy... The basic contention of such a sociological paradigm is that national development cannot be explained by looking at isolated countries, but rather a country's position in the larger world division of labor and power structure must be taken into account in order to explain the nature and rate of national development.

In order to understand the relationship empirically, we need to define the concept of international stratification system and national development and identify indicators of measurement. Sociologists such as Wallerstein (1974) and Bornschieir and Chase-Dunn (1987) were hardly the first to comment on this process.

International linkages and their role in development were noted by Lenin (1917: 91) who argued that "capitalism is growing with the greatest rapidity in the colonies and in the overseas countries," as Marx had claimed earlier. But Lenin also saw that this rapidly developing capitalism was imperialist and not indigenous. Since capitalists are interested only in profit and interest, the colonies could never come out of this trap and would become even more impoverished. He pointed out that colonies were used for cheap raw materials and were a dumping ground for cheap goods by the imperialist powers, thus destroying local production systems. This was the reason why the imperialist powers developed and the colonies remained underdeveloped.

Economic growth and development: Classical growth theory in economics was propounded by Adam Smith and his colleagues. Smith argued that the benefits of economic growth will "trickle down" to the lowest rungs of society. Growth, therefore, would bring "universal opulence." The factors responsible for economic growth are capital accumulation, institutional factors, trade, and technology. It is the invisible hand of the market that brings growth. He did not want governments to interfere in that process: the so-called "hands off" policy. It was Ricardo (1817) who propounded the theory of "comparative advantage" in international trade. Ricardo was writing against state intervention and in favor of the free market. The modernization theories of the 1960's were derived from this classical perspective. W.W. Rostow's (1960) theory of the stages of economic growth was one of them. Industrialization, at the appropriate stage, would bring growth and development. However, the evidence showed that nations that were developing were also increasing in income inequalities. *Neo-classical theories* propounded the curvilinear hypothesis (the inverted U-shape curve) of income inequality with development: in the initial stages of development, income inequality increases, but as development proceeded income inequality would decline (Kuznets, 1955, for explanation see Williamson, 1991).

By early the 1970's, a quarter century after the push for development began, the evidence showed that rather than 'universal opulence', *absolute* poverty, no matter how measured, was still the lot of much of the world's population (McNamara, 1973). This is the level of an endless day-to-day struggle for mere survival. It should not be confused with the *relative* unequal distribution of income, which is a question of equity rather than survival. The *basic needs* approach was articulated as a response to the problem of continued high levels of absolute poverty. In 1976, the International Labor Office (ILO) increased its emphasis on poverty alleviation through meeting the basic needs of people by year 2000, a proposal which was endorsed by all the member states. The basic needs were identified as health, education, food, water supply, sanitation, and housing. Following this, Morris and

Liser (1977) proposed a Physical Quality of Life Index (PQLI), to be used to measure the average life conditions of the people of each of the world's nations. The three indicators included in the scale: life expectancy at birth, literacy (primary school enrolment as percent of population age 5-14), and the inverse of infant mortality per thousand live births, defined basic needs. It was argued that infant mortality is also an indirect indicator of both sanitation and access to potable water (FAO, 1985; Hicks and Streeten, 1979: 578). The World Bank promoted the ILO's program, arguing these indicators are essentially linked to the development of "human capital:" health and education. There was a more radical proposal called *basic needs first* that demanded redistribution of land and which did not have much success with planners.

The 1960's were called the "decade of development," and there was interest in the development process in political science as well. Also, political scientists were interested in the newly independent nations. Their focus was on the study of nation building, political efficacy, commitment to democracy and nationalism as indicators of development: for example, Michigan State University's reported attempts to build a national government in South Vietnam in those years.

As this review shows, various indicators of development have surfaced over the decades. They are usually tied both to specific disciplines and to specific theoretical paradigms. This paper reviews indices that are frequently used in the literature of the 1990's and provides an empirical examination of the underlying themes they represent.

Indicators of National Development

In this section, we present the indicators of national development that appear to be in common use today, along with several related variables. In succeeding pages, empirical data describing the interrelations among them will be examined.

As we have seen, the notion of development is not new. It became a major concern right after World War II. The end of the War marked the end of an era of European colonialism. At this juncture, the centers of world power also shifted away from Europe to the United States and to the former Soviet Union. Many former colonies of European empires, and other countries with low incomes and living standards, were labeled as "underdeveloped." However, it was soon realized that some of these countries were experiencing reasonable rates of economic growth. Hence the static label of underdeveloped changed to that of "developing" nations. These developing nations were collectively known as the "Third World," to distinguish them from the First World "free market" nations and the Second World "command economy" nations. There are no universally accepted definitions of either of the terms "Third World" or a "developing country."

GNP/c: Economists, the World Bank, and other development banks usually categorized countries by per capita income and total national income. In that respect, an increase in national income/per capita income is widely considered to be a measure or indicator of economic development. Many economists argue that although there are a number of problems for the measurement of both per capita income and its rate of growth, both are the best available indicators to provide estimates of the level of economic well being within a nation and its growth.

There are, of course, conceptual and measurement difficulties in using this "conventional" measure of national development/underdevelopment: the GNP or the GNP/c (GNP per capita). There are the awkward borderline cases. Even if the analysis is confined to developing countries, a handful of countries (e.g., oil producing) rank far above others in terms of per capita incomes even though it is obvious that the development levels of their people are often low. Secondly, there are technical difficulties in comparing national incomes across countries because of differences in official exchange rates at which national incomes are converted into the common denominator of the American dollar, and of the problems of estimating the value of noncash components of real incomes in developing countries.

Real GDP/c: In order to deal with the difficulty of comparison, efforts were made to adjust the GDP and GDP/c of various countries to the Purchasing Power Parity (PPP). It is argued that the goods and services produced and bought and sold in a country should be reflected in the calculations of products and services, and that the indicator of income thus arrived at is a true reflection of the country's development compared with other countries. The data for this indicator come from the calculations of Summers and Heston (1988).

The Human Development Index: In 1990, the United Nations Development Program (UNDP) produced a "Human Development Index" that the UNDP argues is a better measure of development. The UNDP argued that: "People are the real wealth of a nation. The basic objective of development is to create an enabling environment for people to enjoy long, healthy, and creative lives" (Human Development Report, 1990: 9). The report, as with later annual reports, then went in great detail to define and develop the Index (HDI).

Brazil in particular came under severe criticism in the Human Development Report (1990: 56) and was described under the title: "Missed Opportunities for Human Development." The report stated that: "Brazil failed to achieve satisfactory human development" because of (i) extreme inequality of income and (ii) insufficient targeting of public resources—much of the housing and social security subsidy went to urban rather than rural residents. (This criticism seems a bit odd when applied to a nation in which only 20-25% of the population is rural and in which the incidence of absolute poverty plummeted over the 1970's (Pastore et al., 1983).) Similarly, China was treated under the title: "Disrupted human development." It was claimed that China's health care and basic needs gains of the 1960's had stagnated or had even reversed. This further indicates that the index is sensitive to short-term variations of components on which the index is based.

If the intent indicated here is to measure some form of human welfare, then that purpose is just about the same as that of prior measures of development such as the PQLI—the Physical Quality of Life Index (Morris and Liser, 1977). Our purpose in this paper is to compare various indicators of development and report what each of them measures.

The World System: rank and prominence: The World System concept was first proposed by Wallerstein (1974). The system emerged over a long period of time, starting with the emergence of capitalism and the industrial revolution. The system, however, became much more elaborate, with an international division of labor in which various nations occupy unequal positions. The World System theory argues that a system of dependency becomes institutionalized in the network of unequal exchange relations. Hence the theory incorporates earlier theories of imperialism and dependency as well. Quantitative analyses classified countries into a hierarchy of core, semiperiphery, and periphery (divided today into advanced periphery and true periphery). This measure is called the World System Ranks (WSR).

A recent operationalization of the World System concept, resulting in an empirical assignment of each nation to a WSR category, was performed by Rossem (1996). It classifies countries by prominence (PROM) in the World System. PROM was created by mapping five network dependence relations, imports, exports, trade in major conventional weapon systems, the presence (really: absence) of foreign troops, and the presence of diplomatic representation (see Rossem, 1996 for details). Contrary to criticisms stemming from the Human Development Index (1990) and even to Wallerstein's assignment of them to the semiperiphery, both Brazil and China have high prominence scores and are classified by Rossem's technique as members of the *Core*.

Basic Indicators: In addition to the indices that we have discussed above, other basic indicators include population, population growth rate (1980-1988), daily caloric supply, infant mortality, life expectancy at birth, percent of age 5-14 enrolled in primary schools, gross domestic savings as percent of GDP, official disbursement of aid, and average rate of growth of GNP (1965-1988). Some of these have been discussed for their relevance and others are well understood by scholars. The data (circa 1988) for the "basic indicators" are provided in Stern (1991).

Dimensions of Development

It is clear from the above description that commonly used indicators of development measure aspects of national populations which are at least nominally different. However, as yet the empirical relations among them have not been shown despite the efforts that have been made to specify indices composed of a few of them. (The recent creation of the UNDP's Index of Human Development is an example.) Are these indices valid measures of development? The answer depends largely upon how well they relate to other dimensions of development. We proceed with a two-stage analysis. In the first, we report correlations among 15 presumably important indicators/indices of development. In the second, we factor analyze a smaller set of these indicators for the purpose of extracting their common themes.

Coefficients of correlation for the 15 indicators are reported in Appendix A. The list of nations for which complete data are available is presented in Appendix B. For the purpose of computing correlations reported in Appendix A, we used pairwise deletion method in order to maximize available information. The correlations are practically all in the predicted directions, with a few exceptions that we will discuss below.

Preliminary comments: Variables that either do not work or that overlap with others: Several preliminary comments are in order. First, we have included two measures of per capita national income: GNP/c and RGDP/c—Gross National Product per capita and Real GDP per capita. The correlation of the two is very high: $r = 0.92$, and the correlations of both measures with other development indicators are almost identical. Therefore, in the factor analysis we simply used GNP/c rather than RGDP/c as a measure of per capital national income.

The second (taken on data from 1987 and 1991) concerns the HDI scores published in 1990 and 1994. It is one of the most widely used measures of national development. The *Human Development Report* (1990: 9) stated: "The basic objective of development is to create an enabling environment for people to enjoy long, healthy, and creative lives." Much emphasis has been given to the supposed reliability of the HDI (for a critique, see Srinivasan, 1994). Face validity is also claimed for it. A more informative way to assess its validity would be through construct validity—correlating the indices with other available indicators of socio-economic development for which data are available. Fortunately, these can be had. They were published by Stern (1991) who took them from the *Human Development Report* (1990) itself.

Let us examine the available HDI indices—called HDI 1990 and HDI 1994—carefully. If they are valid measures of development, they should meet four criteria. First, they should be highly correlated with each other. Second, their correlations with other proposed development measures should not change much over the four years between the measurements (1987 and 1991). This is because societal-led phenomena do not change much over short periods except in violent revolutions or other calamities. Third, they should be highly correlated with other variables thought to measure development. Fourth, the correlations with other development indicators should not change much over brief periods of time.

                     BAM DEV SHARDA ET AL.

The two HDI indices meet the first criterion rather well: $r = 0.97$ (see Appendix A). Second, their correlations (see Table 1) with nine of the 13 other indicators are reasonably consistent, varying from $r = 0.650$ and $r = 0.532$ (GNP/c) to $r = -0.022$ and $r = -0.021$ (population). However, their correlations with the other four variables differ sharply: from $r = -0.635$ and $r = -0.283$ (population growth) to $r = 0.637$ and $r = 0.453$ (caloric intake per capita). Third, their correlations with other presumptive development variables vary markedly. They are highest with Life Expectancy and Infant Mortality: $r = 0.900$ and 0.847, and $r = -0.939$ and -0.896. They are also rather high with GNP/c, RGDP/c, Education, the disbursement of official Development Assistance as a percent of GDP, and (ambivalently) with caloric intake. Their relations with the remainder are either uniformly or ambivalently low. Fourth, their correlations with most other indicators, including two of their three components (Late Expectancy and RGDP/c), declined over the four years.[2]

So what is to be concluded? It is not at all clear that the HDI index is a good measure of national development level, although the evidence is not totally negative. It does relate well to itself over four years, and it is highly correlated with some of the other indicators. But two findings argue against it. For one, its correlations with two of the hypothetically most important indices (National Prominence and World System Rank) changed markedly over the four years. The other is the fact that its correlations with at least 10 of the 13 others declined over the period. This suggests

Table 1

Coefficients of Correlation of Human Development Index (1990 and 1994) with Indicators of National Development

	Human development index, 1990	Human development index, 1994
GNP/c	0.650	0.532
RGDP/c	0.749	0.653
EDU	0.733	0.733
LIFE	0.900	0.847
IMOR	−0.939	−0.896
CAL	0.637	0.453
POP	−0.022	−0.021
POP GRO	−0.635	−0.283
GROWTH	0.379	0.402
SAVE/GDP	0.546	0.535
DEV ASSIS	−0.604	−0.625
PROM	0.504	0.197
WSR	0.559	0.226

Note: See Appendix B for description of indicators and sources.

that its efficacy may be declining rather rapidly. It must be concluded that the HDI is of dubious value as a measure of national development.

Obviously, better measures are needed. Since we have the indicators that HDI is composed of, we decided not to include the Index itself for further analysis. More important, we believe it is not very useful for policy purposes.

Therefore, along with the decision to drop RGDP/c, we excluded both of the HDIs (1990 and 1994) from the remaining analyses. In addition, we also excluded two more indicators that were in the original correlation matrix: official development assistance disbursed as a percentage of GDP (DEV ASSIS) and savings as percentage of GDP (SAVE/GDP). Limited data were available for these variables and most

Table 2

Coefficients of Correlation, Means, and Standard Deviations for Selected Indicators of National Development (N = 88)

	1	2	3	4	5	6	7	8	9	10
CAL	1.00									
LIFE	0.76	1.00								
IMOR	− 0.74	− 0.92	1.00							
EDU	0.44	0.72	− 0.71	1.00						
LGNP/c	0.80	0.85	− 0.84	0.51	1.00					
WSR	0.56	0.55	− 0.46	0.38	0.54	1.00				
PROM	0.55	0.48	− 0.44	0.26	0.57	0.80	1.00			
LPOP	0.13	0.09	0.00	0.12	− 0.01	0.69	0.60	1.00		
POP GRO	− 0.66	− 0.68	0.68	− 0.38	− 0.68	− 0.44	− 0.47	− 0.11	1.00	
GROWTH	0.35	0.42	− 0.38	0.44	0.29	0.28	0.15	0.20	− 0.32	1.00
Mean	2,658.15	63.77	56.38	91.89	7.30	2.25	0.21	2.61	2.10	1.81
Standard deviation	538.50	10.81	43.93	25.36	1.49	0.96	0.17	1.40	1.17	2.11

CAL = Daily caloric supply per capita, 1986.

LIFE = Life expectancy at birth, 1988.

IMOR = Infant mortality rate.

EDU = Percent 5-14 age group enrolled in primary education, 1987.

LGNP/c = Natural log of GNP/c, 1988.

WSR = World system rank (see Rossem, 1996).

PROM = Prominance scores (see Rossem, 1996).

LPOP = Natural log of opulation (millions) in mid-1988.

POP GRO = Average annual population growth (1980-1988).

GROWTH = Average annual growth rate of GNP/c (1965-1988).

Sources:

(1) Nicholas Stern, 1991. "Public Policy and the Economics of Development." *European Economic Review* 35, 243-250. (Reproduced in Gerald M. Meier, 1995. *Leading Issues in Economic Development*, Sixth edition. New York: Oxford University Press.)

(2) R.V. Rossem, 1996. "The World System Paradigm as a General Theory of Development: A Cross-National Test." *American Sociological Review* 61, 508-527.

pertain to the less developed nations, so they would have biased the results. Besides this, their correlations with other variables ranged from modest to low. Furthermore, we logged population and GNP/c and recomputed the correlations (Table 2) for the 88 countries for which complete data are available (see Appendix B). We factor analyzed the remaining 10 indicators. The results are reported below.

Factor analysis: Factor analysis is commonly used to identify the more fundamental conceptual variables, if any, which underlie their empirical manifestation in specific indicators. A factor loading of .30, is often considered to be a cutting point. Those items with a .30 loading are considered as significant whereas those below .30 are dropped as insignificant. This is an arbitrary criterion justified on pragmatic grounds but is consistent with previous research (Sharda, 1989). Results of this analysis are reported in Table 3.

Factor I—Domestic development: Following varimax rotation, nine of the 10 items had a factor loading of 0.30 and above (in fact the minimum loading was 0.46) on the first factor. It accounted for nearly 56% of the matrix variance. The factor was significant with an eigenvalue of 5.56. Its theme is composed of national income and economic growth (GNP/c and GROWTH), international standing (WSR and PROM), basic needs/human development (CAL, LIFE, IMOR), human capital development (EDU), and concern with population growth (POP GRO), all of which hang together. This factor truly represents the theme of national domestic development; we named it "domestic development." The several components this dimension encompasses are

Table 3

Factor analysis of basic development Indicators (circa 1988)

	Rotated score	
	Factor I: Domestic development	Factor II: Authority
LIFE	0.94	–
IMOR	− 0.95	–
LGNP/c	0.89	–
CAL	0.81	–
POP GRO	− 0.75	–
WSR	0.42	0.84
PROM	0.39	0.81
EDU	0.72	–
GNP G	0.46	–
LPOP	–	0.92
Eigenvalue	5.56	1.74
Percent variance	55.6	17.4

Notes: (1) See Table 2 for description of indicators and sources.
(2) − = score less than 0.30.

repeated time and again as goals of development by different traditions, academic disciplines, and development agencies. They all are significant and it would appear that they deserve to be included in any assessment of development levels of nations. In fact, either life expectancy or the inverse of infant mortality might alone serve as an indicator of development. Indeed, scholars and agencies often select a few items and exclude others in the formation of indices of development, the most recent example being the HDI.

It is also significant that the factor loading of population—more accurately the log of population (LPOP)—did not significantly load on the first factor. This may simply mean that development occurs in both the large and small nations alike and hence population size is not as significant a factor as is sometimes alleged. Population size, however, is highly significant for the second factor.

Factor II—Authority: The second factor, which we call Authority, expresses a country's position and power in international relations. It is led by the log of population size (LPOP). Recall that population size has almost no relationship with any of the variables (see Appendix A) and LPOP had nonsignificant loadings on Factor I. However, LPOP has the highest loading of 0.92 on Factor II, along with PROM with a factor loading of 0.81, and WSR with a factor loading of 0.84. This factor is also significant with an eigenvalue of 1.74. It explains another 17.4% of the variance. This indicates that the dimension expressed by these three items is uniquely different from the theme of domestic development. These items are often neglected in economic literature but are emphasized by sociologists who study the effects of international dominance and status of nations through the operation of the world system. It is, therefore, clear that both factors (domestic development and authority) should be employed in studies of development.

It is our contention, then, that larger countries pursue development goals which may or may not be consistent with the "welfare" dynamics of their citizens but are related to their position in the international authority structure. These countries may have to spend portions of their resources, both financial and human, on military pre- paredness, and they develop influential trade and political blocs, etc. We suppose that all nations pursue policies to increase their power and prestige, expending resources which might otherwise be used for the welfare of their citizens. Perhaps this works in the long run. With increased status and power in the international arena, nations might gain better access to international markets and/or generate more resources for the welfare of their citizens. If so, the second factor might turn out someday to be significant for national development.

In any case, it is clear that the main factor, domestic development, focuses on differences among nations regarding the degree to which they meet the needs of their populations. It looks inwardly, so to speak. The second factor, could be said to look outwardly in that it is mostly concerned with the potential for directly affecting the decisions of other nations. Of course, one nation's position on either factor might influence other nations. But there is a difference: the first factor would exert its influence mostly by the *policy example* one nation sets for another, the second by the *pressure* one nation might or might not exert upon another.

Discussion and Conclusions

We set out to review the development literature and to identify some key indicators of development from various traditions. We examined the set of coefficients of correlations among such indicators (Appendix A) and argued that some indices of development (e.g., HDI, 1990 and 1994) constructed with few items may not have captured the greater themes of development that nations pursue. We dropped those indices but kept the items on which they are based. We dropped two others as well. We then subjected the remaining indicators to factor analysis. Two factors appeared. We called them domestic development and authority.

Factor I is the most comprehensive of the two. It clearly expresses major components of domestic development: elimination of absolute poverty, the provision of basic needs, human development, human capital development, and concern with population growth. Factor II loads heavily on the position of nations regarding total population, international dominance, and prestige. It could be argued, therefore, that development goals of nations have tended to be more comprehensive than has been recognized in the literature so far. This neglect, we believe, is due to the lack of integration of development literature among the various disciplines, notably economics. For example, the field of development economics incorporates many variables that are important to sociologists: demographic variables (life expectancy, infant mortality), education (school enrollments) but hardly ever are references made to the work of sociologists. There is almost a complete neglect of international dominance and prestige (WSR, PROM) of nations in the economic development literature, although our evidence shows that they are powerful aspects of development—aspects that are quite different from domestic development. We argue, therefore, that since the two themes of national development and authority are each justifiable on theoretical grounds and supported by hard evidence, they should both be taken into account in future research, free from disciplinary constraints.

It is, therefore, our conclusion that differential weight be put on variables in the definition of development. The domestic development variable has many correlates, as is clear from the factor analysis we have presented. For policy purposes, it must be tempting to construct a scale of domestic development, using the Factor I (national development) scores as weights in its construction. However, we realize there are limitations that need to be addressed before such a scale should be constructed.

These limitations also apply to the whole of the present analysis. But this should not vitiate our findings: among the 88 nations covered and among the variables examined, it is safe to say that we have presented strong evidence for the existence of two different fundamental dimensions of national development, domestic development, and authority. Yet we have been able to examine only 15 of the variables that might measure development, and of course, only 88 countries. It is possible—though unlikely—that the inclusion of all other nations, and whatever other variables might be relevant, might change the factor pattern. This should be tested. Or it might simply reinforce the present findings. This seems likely. For example, the authority factor might turn out to be loaded on the absolute size of the national GNP.[3] In the future, we hope to check this and other possibilities.

NOTES

1 The authors express their thanks to the Department of Sociology at the University of Utah and the Department of Rural Sociology at the University of Wisconsin-Madison for their support for research reported in this paper. The senior author was an Honorary Fellow in Wisconsin when the manuscript was written and has received considerable encouragement from the Department of Rural Sociology for which he is also grateful. Address all correspondence to: Bam Dev Sharda, Department of Sociology, University of Utah, Salt Lake City, Utah 84112 (E-mail: Sharda@Freud.sbs.utah.edu).

2 HDI 1994 was *more* highly correlated than HDI 1990 with only two other variables: economic growth and development assistance.

3 This brings up another issue as yet not directly treated in the literature. There exists a formal authority structure among peoples. It consists of nationhood as defined by the United Nations and international law. Future research should examine the relationship between the formal, or *de jure*, international authority structure, and the informal, or *de facto*, structure of authority among nations.

REFERENCES

BORNSCHIER, V. and C. CHASE-DUNN
1987 *Transnational Corporations and Underdevelopment*. New York: Praeger.
CHIROT, D.
1986 *Social Change in Modern Era*. New York: Harcourt, Brace, Jovanovich.
FOOD AND AGRICULTURAL ORGANIZATION
1985 *Fifth Food Survey*. Rome: F.A.O.
HICKS, N. and P. STREETEN
1979 "Indicators of Development: The Search for a Basic Needs Yardstick." *World Development* 7 (6).
KUZNETS, S.
1955 "Economic Growth and Inequality." *American Economic Review*, March.
KUZNETS, S.
1963 "Quantitative Aspects of Economic Growth of Nations: VIII—Distribution of Income by Size." *Economic Development and Culture Change* (January), Part II.
LENIN, V.I.
1917/1939 *Imperialism: The Highest State of Capitalism*. New York: International Publishers.

McNAMARA, R.
1973 "Address to the Board of Directors." (World Bank Reprint) Narobi, Kenya: September 4.
MORRIS, M and F. LISER
1977 "The PQLI: Measuring Progress in Human Needs." *Communique on Development Issues* 32. Washington, D.C.: Overseas Development Council.
PASTORE, J., H. ZYLBERSTAJN, C. PAGOTTO, and A.O. HALLER
1983 *The Decline in the Incidence of Extreme Poverty in Brazil, 1970-1980.* Madison: University of Wisconsin, Department of Rural Sociology: A Report to the Inter-American Foundation.
RICARDO, D.
1817 *"The Principles of Political Economy and Taxation,"* Vol. 1. In *Works and Correspondence,* Piero Sraffa and M.H. Dobbs (Eds.). Cambridge University Press, 1951-1955.
ROSSEM, R.V.
1996 "The World System Paradigm as a General Theory of Development: A Cross-National Test." *American Sociological Review* 61.
ROSTOW, W.W.
1960 *The Stages of Economic Growth: A Non-Communist Manifesto.* Cambridge: Cambridge University Press.
SHARDA, B.D.
1989 "Schooling and Modernity: Theory and Evidence." In *Social Development: Processes and Consequences,* P.N. Pimpley, K.P. Singh, and A. Mahajan (Eds.). Jaipur, India: Rawat.
STERN, N.
1991/1995   "Public Policy and the Economics of Development." *European Economic Review* 35 (Reprinted in G.M. Mier, *Leading Issues in Economic Development.* New York: Oxford University Press, 1995).
SRINIVASAN, T.N.
1994 "Human Development. A New Paradigm or Reinvention of the Wheel?" *American Economic Review, Papers and Proceedings* (May), 238-243.
STREETEN, P.
1981 "Development Ideas in Historical Perspective." In *Development Perspectives.* New York: MacMillan.
SUMMERS, R. and A. HESTON
1990 "The Penn World Table (Mark 5): An Extended Set of International Comparisions, 1950-1987." National Bureau of Economic Research and University of Pennsylvania.
UNITED NATIONS DEVELOPMENT PROGRAM (UNDP)
1990 *Human Development Index.* New York: Oxford University Press.
WALLERSTEIN, I.
1977 *The Modern World System: Capitalist Agriculture and the Origins of the European World Economy in the Sixteenth Century.* New York: Academic Press.
WILLIAMSON, J.G.
1991 *Inequality, Poverty, and History: The Kuznets Memorial Lectures of the Economic Growth Center.* Yale University. Cambridge, MA: Blackwell.

Appendix A. Coefficients of correlation among national indicators of development, circa 1988

	1	2	3	4	5	6	7	8	9	10	11	12	13	14	15
LIFE		0.40	−0.89	0.90	0.85	0.75	0.66	0.71	−0.59	0.52	0.51	0.47	0.02	−0.56	0.42
CAL			−0.57	0.64	0.45	0.27	0.63	0.64	−0.42	0.43	0.46	0.41	−0.01	−0.45	0.24
IMOR				−0.94	−0.90	−0.71	−0.64	−0.74	−0.60	−0.56	−0.48	−0.45	−0.00	−0.61	−0.40
HDI90					0.97	0.73	0.65	0.75	−0.60	0.55	0.56	0.50	−0.02	−0.64	0.38
HDI94						0.73	0.53	0.65	−0.62	0.54	0.23	0.20	−0.02	0.28	0.40
EDU							0.28	0.39	−0.53	0.42	0.36	0.27	0.10	−0.31	0.41
GNP/c								0.92	−0.34	0.35	0.48	0.60	−0.05	−0.58	0.18
RGDP/c									−0.41	0.45	0.48	0.56	−0.05	−0.54	0.26
DEV ASSIS										−0.62	−0.37	−0.41	−0.14	0.19	−0.33
SAVE/GDP											0.37	0.27	0.16	−0.34	0.34
WSR												0.85	0.27	−0.40	0.21
PROM													0.22	−0.44	0.14
POP														−0.01	0.11
POP GRO															−0.32
GROWTH															
$\bar{x}$	62.0	2,644.8	62.7	0.64	0.53	89.8	4,257.8	3,527.4	8.1	16.5	1.9	0.16	48.9	2.3	1.7
Std. dev.	12.1	639.5	45.7	0.27	0.22	27.1	6,289.6	3,676.9	10.9	14.4	1.0	0.16	155.4	1.2	2.3
(N)	(118)	(114)	(118)	(130)	(125)	(107)	(109)	(113)	(84)	(104)	(162)	(163)	(118)	(118)	(100)

LIFE = Life expectancy at birth, 1988.

CAL = Daily caloric supply per capita, 1986.

IMOR = Infant mortality rate (per 1,000 live births), 1988.

HDI90 = HDI 1990 (*Human Development Report*, 1990).

HDI94 = HDI 1994 (*Human Development Report*, 1994).

EDU = Percent of 5-14 age group enrolled in primary education, 1987.

GNP/c = GNP per capita, 1988.

RGDP/c = Real GDP per capita (Summers and Heston, 1990).

DEV ASSIS = Disbursement of official assistance (percent GDP), 1988.

SAVE/GDP = Gross domestic savings (percent GDP), 1986.

WSR = World system rank (see Rossem, 1996).

PROM = Prominance scores (see Rossem, 1996).

POP = Population (millions) in mid-1988.

POP GRO = Average annual population growth (1980-1988).

GROWTH = Average annual growth rate of GNP/c (1965-1988).

Appendix B. Countries with complete data for 10 indicators ($N = 88$)

Low-income economies ($N = 28$)	
Ethiopia	China
Chad	India
Tanzania	Pakistan
Bangladesh	Kenya
Malawi	Togo
Somalia	Central African Republic
Zaire	Haiti
Burkina Faso	Benin
Mali	Ghana
Burundi	Lesotho
Uganada	Sri Lanka
Nigeria	Indonesia
Niger	Mauritania
Rwanda	Sudan

Lower-middle-income economies ($N = 29$)	
Bolivia	Jamaica
Philippines	Ecuador
Senegal	Colombia
Zimbabwe	Paraguay
Egypt Arab Republic	Tunisia
Dominican Republic	Turkey
Côte d'Ivoire	Peru
Papua New Guinea	Chile
Morocco	Syrian Arab Republic
Honduras	Costa Rica
Guatemala	Mexico
El Salvador	Mauritius
Thailand	Malaysia
Botswana	Brazil
Cameroon	

Upper-middle-income economies ($N = 10$)	
Algeria	Venezuela
Hungary	Trinidad and Tobago
Uruguay	Korea
Argentina	Portugal
Yugoslavia	Greece

High-income economies (21)	
Saudi Arabia	Austria
Spain	France
Ireland	Canada
Israel	Denmark
Hong Kong	Germany Federal Republic
New Zealand	Finland
Australia	Sweden
United Kingdom	United States
Italy	Norway
Kuwait	Japan
Netherlands	Switzerland

Global Agri-Food Sector and the Case of the Tuna Industry

Global Regulation and Perspectives for Development

ALESSANDRO BONANNO and DOUGLAS CONSTANCE*

ABSTRACT

Employing the case of the global tuna fish industry the paper investigates the effect of globalization on political institutions and social agents. Three interrelated points are argued. First, it is maintained that while the process of globalization is pervasive, it is also flexible, i.e., the outcomes of globalization are contested and no particular agent has total control. Second, in the domestic arena the regulatory ability of the nation-state has to be redefined. Third, despite possibilities for some subordinate groups to advance, weak segments of the labor force, particularly in developing countries such as Latin American countries, continue to be marginalized. A possible alternative strategy calls for attempts to establish international solidarity. The latter, however, should be based on awareness of the limits of protectionist and/or domestic center strategies in the global era.

Introduction

THROUGH THE USE of the case of the tuna-dolphin dispute this study investigates the relationships among capital (tuna processors, tuna fleets, and related trade associations), labor (tuna boatworkers and processing plant workers), the State (represented by the Mexican State, the Venezuelan State, and the U.S. State), and U.S. environmentalists. For the last thirty years these actors have interacted to define the regulation of tuna fishing. Environmentalists have fought and won legislation that mandated the elimination of dolphin kills associated with current techniques of tuna fishing. The tuna industry has disputed the implementation of the law from the beginning with injunctions and restraining orders. The U.S. executive branch and associated departments worked to weaken pro-environmental legislation and stalled its implementation.

* Department of Sociology, Sam Houston State University, Huntsville, Texas 77341, U.S.A.

The first part of the paper provides our theoretical framework and illustrates relevent literature on globalization, the transition to Post-Fordism, and the role of the State. In this context, three hypothesis are formulated. First, the process of globalization is contested terrain. The concept of contested terrain refers to the fact that while the process of globalization is pervasive, it is still flexible. Globalization opens opportunities to some classes or groups and closes some to others. This is not to say that the competing agents have equal power, but to imply that domination is not absolute. Second, within the process of globalization, the nation-States' regulatory abilities to manage its affairs are weakened as internationalized capital makes domestic accumulation and legitimation more problematic. Third, while some social movements, such as environmental movements, do have some opportunities to gain, weak social groups (e.g., labor, particularly in the third world) are increasingly marginalized as transnational capital sources the world for lowest costs of production, docile labor, favorable regulation climate, and better access to important markets.

The second part of the study presents the tuna-dolphin case through which the above mentioned hypotheses are analyzed. The conclusions illustrate some developmental alternatives for Latin America and present some observations on the global patterns of regulation of actors in the agro-food sector.

Economic Growth and the Creation of Free Spaces

From its outset, capitalism has generated both intense fragmentation and extensive interdependence. Marx, for instance, made this point compellingly by stressing, on the one hand, that capitalism instituted highly complex modes of social cooperation in the firm, interfirm cooperation, the much enlarged regulatory State, and world market (Marx, 1977: 439-454). Yet, on the other hand, Marx also argued that constant revolutionizing of the means of production generates an unrelenting destruction and regeneration of social organization, association, culture, and identity (Marx, 1981). Durkheim (1984) attacked reductionist, market-centered ideas of society even more directly, arguing that expansive and unregulated individual interest and utility maximization results in social disintegration rather than spontaneous order. He held that the capitalist market, itself, depends on social interdependence in noneconomic facets of culture, association, and social organization. In different ways, Simmel, Weber, Gramsci, and many other classical social theorists recognized that completely unrestricted markets would destroy their own socio-cultural foundations.

Following the classical sociological tradition, it can be argued that capitalism depends on a combination of flexibility and control. Capitalism requires a structure of accumulation that provides opportunities for economic dynamism without socially unbearable consequences. The State has been the primary mechanism for mediating the relationship of market and society (O'Connor, 1986; Offe, 1985).

The historical existence of control of the flexibility of accumulation of capital through the action of the State opens the possibility for the creation of "free spaces" in the political sphere. Corporations have historically counted on the support of the State to enhance accumulation of capital and legitimize this action to the rest of the population (Block, 1980; Offe, 1985). For instance, the State has been instrumental in the control of labor, in generating the legal and social instruments for the availability of labor and in constraining the actions of subordinate classes seeking the satisfaction of their needs. In the historical implementation of these actions, however, the State has been forced to extend concessions to subordinate classes. In this respect, the action of the State in favor of subordinate classes has partially limited its ability to assist corporations in their pursuit of capital accumulation (Offe, 1985). More importantly, the State has allowed, in various degrees and according historical and geographical contexts, the societal incorporation of norms which represent gains for members of subordinate classes. The establishment of social programs, consumer oriented programs and programs in defense of the environment are all cases in point. In essence, the State has maintained "free spaces" accessible to subordinate classes which allow the participation of the public in decision making processes and the establishment of democratic contexts which have been used historically by subordinated classes to exercise their participatory rights in public life.

The Post-Fordist Globalization of the Economy and Society and the Crisis of the State

A significant number of studies (e.g., Harvey, 1990; Lipietz, 1987; Friedmann and McMichael, 1989) have underscored the fundamental changes in the organization of production which took place in the early portion of the 1970s. In essence it is argued that the crisis of accumulation of the 1970s was addressed by replacing Fordist "rigidity" with "Post-Fordist" global flexibility (Harvey, 1990; Bonanno et al., 1994). Although the attempt to diminish rigidity and increase flexibility involves many multisided processes, operating in a relatively autonomous fashion in different spheres (i.e., spatial, cultural, ideological, organizational etc.), the most decisive dimension is the effort to eliminate all constraints to the free mobility of capital and to maximize its speed of movement. Above all, this is the central meaning of flexibility. This process is manifested in the enhanced capacity of capital to weaken or even eliminate local, regional, and national controls and blockages.

Post-Fordist flexibility also significantly reduced the State's capacity to mediate and organize the relations between capital and society and establish social limits to the mechanisms of accumulation. During the later 1970s and 1980s, the State was not able to maintain growth and, at the same time, contain capitalist dynamism within social acceptable limits. In particular, post-Fordism substantially reduced the (local, regional, and national) State's control over its economic and noneconomic environments. This does *not* mean that all dimensions of the State have been necessarily weakened (e.g., police and military power and assistance to financial segments of society have often been increased (Pitelis, 1991)). However, post-Fordism destroys the spatial-temporal unity of the polity and economy, characterizing the earlier phases of capitalist development. The conception of democratic capitalism presumed this unity; the State's capacity to establish socio-cultural limits to capitalist development provided community and national institutions a relative autonomy and safety from the forces of economic rationalization.

Capitalism operates increasingly without spatial boundaries, while the State remains confined to finite jurisdictions. This gap restricts the State's regulatory role. The fact that it can not effectively mediate economic growth and social stability gives rise to important contradictions. Most notably, its ability to provide infrastructure and coordination for stable or longer-term profit seeking and corporate planning is limited in decisive ways. The State's capacity to defend social "rights" (e.g., of workers, minorities, alternative social movements) is also attenuated. Such public protections and provisions for needs are devalued by economic actors by-passing State regulations and legislation (e.g., Bonanno et al., 1994; Friedmann and McMichael, 1989; Constance and Heffernan, 1991; Harvey, 1990). For instance, corporations' tendency to seek less expensive labor abroad jeopardizes the State's effort to maintain adequate wage levels within the national territory. The implications for labor interests are manifold. For domestic labor, the result is a net loss of employment and/or the existence of lower paying jobs; for foreign labor, one implication is the creation of low-wage employment. For the entire international labor community there is the constant threat of job elimination through relocation and the decreased possibility of labor mobilization for economic claims. In terms of regional development, there is a decreased possibility of long and sustained economic growth, as local demand and the emergence of external economies are hampered by a system of low wages.

Post-Fordist globalization involves limitations to the State in other areas, as well. Among these are State action in favor of the protection of the health and safety of workers, the protection of consumers and the preservation of the environment. State implemented measures in these areas can be significantly diminished and/or eliminated by the simple relocating of production to regions where they do not exist or are less stringent than in the original country of operation. The well documented relocation of agricultural-related production processes to Mexico is a case in point (Barkin, 1990; Wright, 1986). In Mexico the pressure to attract foreign investments has given a very low priority to environmental protection, as well as to practices which enhance the quality and safety of agricultural products and the safety and health of workers. As reported by numerous studies (e.g., Restrepo and Franco, 1988; Wright, 1986), industrially polluted soil and water are used for the manufacture of agricultural products which are then exported world wide, through transnational corporations (TNCs), including to the United States. Similarly, agricultural inputs banned in many advanced countries, such as DDT, are still permitted in agricultural production in Mexico. The international commercialization of products treated with these substances nullifies other countries' existing laws against their use. The case of tuna fish also illustrates capital's strategy to move around State regulations.

In essence it can be said that post-Fordist globalization has activated processes which jeopardize the availability of "free spaces" for public participation in decision-making processes. Capital's strategy of flexible accumulation or restructuring has forced the nation-States with protectionists policies to deregulate or risk capital flight. Deregulation implies the closing of "free spaces." In the event that these spaces are closed the possibility of participation on the part of subordinate classes is severely compromised. Consumer protection, product quality, and the protection of labor and the environment pertain to this issue as well. Indeed, they all represent instances in which the political forum, where the interests of subordinate classes have customarily been articulated, is greatly devalued of its function. The inability of public institutions to enforce measures which directly affect these sectors of socio-economic life represents, then, a shift of decision making processes from the public domain to the private sphere. In the public domain the possibility of participation in the decision making process is available, at least in principle, to all segments of society. In the private domain, however, this possibility does not exist. It follows that such a change jeopardizes the continuous existence of effective spaces in which the subordinate classes can exercise their right to participation in the management of society.

The Case of the Global Tuna—Dolphin Controversy

The diminishing of free spaces associated with the consolidation of post-Fordist globalization can be viewed as a progression toward the permanent de-democratization of society. Indeed a number of scholars (e.g., Borrego, 1981; Ross and Trachte, 1990) have argued the totalizing dimension of global capitalism and the inability of subordinate classes to respond to the establishment of restrictive forms of democratic social arrangements. Neoliberal views of globalization, conversely, have stressed the beneficial effects of a minimal State and market-dominated "opportunity society" (e.g., Kindleberger, 1986; Friedman, 1982). In their analysis, the unrestricted mobility of capital generates greater and renewed opportunities for accumulation which are then transferred, albeit in differing rates, to various segments of society.

These two opposing views stand in contrast with a third interpretation which underscores both the limits to democracy as well as the possibilities of resistance associated with the contradictions of post-Fordist global capitalism. In this third view, the domination of TNCs at the global level is limited by their inability to surrogate the action of the State apparatus, to legitimize international competition and to satisfy the demands for homogenization of production and international relations. Furthermore, this position stresses the power that subordinate classes have at the global level to counter the action of TNCs. For instance, subordinated classes have established a presence in some of the emerging transnational political institutions such as the European Community. Simultaneously, new movements have emerged worldwide with regard to issues such as the protection of the environment, food security and safety, and consumer rights along with the development of international labor solidarity (McNally, 1991: 244-245). Albeit limited, this power constitutes a significant obstacle to TNCs total domination.

The case of the global restructuring of the tuna-fish industry is illustrated as an example of this latter posture and of the contradictions embedded in the evolution of Post-Fordist global capitalism. Over a thirty year period segments of the tuna industry, environmental groups, and fractions of the U.S. State and other nation-states have struggled to advance their agendas regarding tuna fishing and dolphin safety.

The Case

Since the 1960s environmental groups, segments of the tuna industry, and fractions of the U.S. State have interacted to define the regulations of tuna fishing. Environmentalists fought and won legislation that mandated the elimination of dolphin kills associated with current techniques of tuna fishing resulting in the Marine Mammal Protection Act of 1972 (MMPA). The tuna industry disputed the implementation of the law from the beginning with injunctions and restraining orders. The U.S. executive branch and associated departments worked to weaken MMPA and stalled its implementation. Environmentalists obtained court orders to force implementation of the MMPA. The tuna fleets reflagged under foreign ownership to avoid U.S. regulations. The environmentalists organized a consumer boycott and found congressional support to force foreign fleets to honor MMPA. The tuna processors responded to the consumer boycott and vowed to buy only dolphin-safe tuna, effectively abandoning the U.S. and Latin American fleets. The tuna industry also scaled back U.S. and Latin American processing plants and moved to Asia. Environmentalists won lawsuits forcing embargoes on Mexico, Venezuela, and Vanuatu who still caught non-dolphin safe tuna. Mexico filed under GATT (General Agreement on Tariffs and Trade) accusing the U.S. of protectionism. GATT found in favor of Mexico. Mexico didn't press the GATT charges to keep the NAFTA (North American Free Trade Agreement) talks going. Environmentalist lawsuits extended the boycott to "transhipping to third party countries"—this action affected over 20 countries. Several countries, including the EEC (European Economic Community), filed under GATT. U.S., Mexico, Venezuela and GATT all called for an international forum to resolve the tuna-dolphin dispute. A tuna accord was finally agreed upon in late 1992 by Mexico, Venezuela, and U.S. establishing a five-year moratorium on purse-seine fishing, thereby avoiding a GATT showdown.

The three hypotheses identified in the introduction will be analyzed in regard to the events of the case. Their presentation will follow an analytical scheme rather than a chronological one. First, the contested terrain hypothesis is examined, to be followed by the those of the limits of the State and labor and global restructuring respectively.

The Contested Terrain

New Technologies, Increased Accumulation, and a Legitimation Crisis

Prior to the 1960s tuna fishing technology consisted of a pole and bait method that was relatively labor intensive. In the Easter Tropical Pacific (ETP), a triangle which stretches from San Francisco, to Hawaii, to Peru, large yellowfin tuna swim under dolphin. Fisherman use the dolphin to find the tuna. During the 1950s San Diego fishermen developed purse-seine fishing which involves the use of a large net that encircles the tuna (and dolphins) and allows the capture of a large number of tuna in one setting of the net. The purse-seine method was developed in response to high numbers of U.S. tuna boat seizures by foreign nations over territorial fishing rights and to counter the low-cost dumping of tuna in the U.S. by Japanese tuna fisherman (Tennesen, 1989; Kraul, 1990).

Territorial fishing rights and tuna markets were contested by competing nations and their tuna fleets resulting in new technologies utilizing large nets and dolphins. The new technologies based on "setting on dolphins" facilitated huge tuna catches (Tennesen, 1989; Brower, 1989). By 1976, the U.S. tuna fleet had grown to 130 huge purse-seiners (Kraul, 1990). The new technology provided very high levels of accumulation—the problem was that it systematically killed hundreds of thousands of dolphins a year (Brower, 1989: 37).

In 1972, public indignation over dolphin killing associated with tuna fishing brought passage of the MMPA. This act mandated that over a period of time "commercial operators' marine mammal kills be 'reduced to insignificant levels approaching zero'" (Godges, 1988: 24). MMPA banned the killing of marine mammals but contained an exception for commercial tuna fishing. The American Tunaboat Association, a trade association of U.S. fishermen, was accorded a general permit to kill dolphins in the course of its commercial fishing operations (Trachtman, 1991). As part of MMPA the National Marine Fisheries Service (NMFS) under the U.S. Department of Commerce organized an observer program which placed observers on one-third of U.S. tuna boats to document the number of dolphin kills associated with tuna fishing (Holland, 1991). At the time of the 1972 MMPA, the U.S. tuna fleet was responsible for 85% of dolphin kills in the ETP (368,600 of 423,678) (Godges, 1988). The intent of the law was to reduce dolphin kills to insignificant levels approaching zero which became the basis for the conflict among various collective actors, both domestically and internationally. Even though environmental groups had won a legislative battle, the war over who would get to define the regulations of tuna fishing was far from over. The tuna industry and fractions of the U.S. executive branch contested the implementation of the law from its inception.

Environmental Lawsuits and Amendments to MMPA

Responses to the perceived inadequacy of the implementation of the law prompted lawsuits from the environmental community during the late 1970s. Congress responded by adopting a quota system for reducing dolphin kills. To implement the law, the NMFS set yearly dolphin-mortality quotas that dropped rapidly from 78,000 in 1976 to 20,500 in 1981 (Godges, 1988). Under President Reagan, industry pressure ended the managed decline in dolphin quotas (Brower, 1989: 38). In 1980, the NMFS issued a five-year permit which set an annual quota take of 20,500. In 1984, the MMPA was amended to extend this quota indefinitely (Holland, 1991). Instead of abolishing the intentional netting of dolphins, the MMPA's quota system institutionalized the practice (Davis, 1988: 486). Under the Reagan Administration, the U.S. tuna industry was able to more effectively contest the 1972 MMPA and thereby significantly weaken, and even alter the intent and language of, MMPA—insignificant dolphin kill levels approaching zero were redefined by industry and fractions of the U.S. State to be equal to 20,500 per year.

In an attempt to control the foreign tuna fleet, in 1984 the U.S. Congress added two amendments to the 1972 MMPA. The amendments stated that tuna caught using purse-seine nets in the ETP may only be imported if the government of the foreign country of origin demonstrates that it (1) has implemented a dolphin protection program "comparable" to that of the U.S. fleet, and (2) has an average incidental dolphin kill rate "comparable" to that of the U.S. fleet (Trachtman, 1991). Under environmental group pressure, Congress ordered the NMFS to close the U.S. tuna market to nations failing to require dolphin protection measures comparable to those in the U.S. (Levin, 1989). Early in 1988, at the request of the conservation groups, a federal judge ordered the fisheries service to place observers on all U.S. tuna boats, instead of on only a certain percentage to better monitor the dolphin kill (Levin, 1988: 35; New York Times, 1989a; 1989b).

Earth Island Institute (EII) and the Marine Mammal Fund filed a lawsuit that sought to force the U.S. Department of Commerce to impose a ban on imports from foreign violators and to properly enforce the dolphin quota on U.S. boats and also urged Heinz and Ralston Purina to voluntarily end tuna purchases from nations that violate the quota. The National Audobon Society joined the EII to amend MMPA to reduce the quota to "zero" (Audobon, 1988). The Cetacean Society, Earth Island Institute, Greenpeace, Sierra Club, and the Whale Center and other groups pooled their resources as the Marine Mammal Protection Act Reauthorization Coalition to push needed improvements in the law and at the same time ask for boycotts (Godges, 1988).

In 1988 EII sponsored Sam LaBudde's investigative work on a Panamanian tuna boat. An 11-minute edited version of the video "where dolphins squealed in pain as they succumbed—in some cases being ground up alive in the gears of the nets—was first aired in March of 1988, to horrified audiences" in the U.S. (Kraul, 1990: d6). This video made the issue of dolphin killing terribly real to millions of Americans (Kraul, 1990).

Environmentalists used the courts and sympathetic legislators to force compliance from the NMFS and Department of Commerce. They also continued their battle in the judicial and legislative branches to reduce dolphin kills to "0" while the U.S. tuna industry used its influence in the NMFS and Commerce Department to block implementation of the MMPA.

The Consumer Boycott of the BIG 3 Tuna Processors

The limited effect that U.S. legislation had on reducing dolphin mortality generated further responses from the environmental groups which supported the MMPA. Having failed to win legislation mandating a phase-out of purse-seine netting, environmental and animal-rights groups attacked the problem at the consumer level. In January of 1988, they launched a boycott of the three major tuna producers in the U.S. (i.e., Chicken of the Sea owned by Ralston Purina, Star Kist owned by Heinz, and Bumble Bee, then owned by Pillsbury) which processed about 70% of the tuna consumed in the U.S. (Newsweek, 1990; Sharecoff, 1990).

First Embargo and Calls for an International Forum

In early 1990 Federal Judge Thelton Henderson of San Francisco ordered the Bush Administration to impose an immediate embargo on imports of tuna caught by foreign fleets until they proved that they were reducing the number of dolphins killed. This affected mostly Mexico, Venezuela, Panama, Ecuador, and Vanuatu (Morain, 1990). Judge Henderson said that the Bush Administration was taking too long in determining whether foreign fleets were complying with U.S. law (New York Times, 1990). Again, environmentalists had to use the justice department to get the Commerce Department to obey the law.

The Commerce Department appealed the judge's decision in district court. In August of 1990, the district court found in favor of the environmentalists and ordered the U.S. Secretary of Treasury to impose embargoes on imports from Mexico, Venezuela, Vanuatu, and other countries which still relied on purse-seine nets fishing techniques. The next day the NMFS made positive findings for Mexico, Venezuela, and Vanuatu allowing the embargo to be lifted on them (Trachtman, 1992). EII then sought a restraining order on Mexico because the NMFS had not counted their dolphin kill rates correctly. In October of 1990 the district court granted the temporary restraining order, and converted it into a preliminary injunction reinstating the embargo on Mexico. The U.S. Government appealed the injunction, arguing that it was the Government's discretion (Commerce Department) to interpret MMPA. The U.S. Court of Appeals found in favor of the Commerce Department and removed the embargo on November 14, 1990. In February of 1991, the appellate court vacated the "stay" of the appeals court, and reinstated the embargo. In March the embargo was extended to include Venezuela and the tiny island nation of Vanuatu (formerly New Hebrides). The appellate court held on April 11, 1991 that the NMFS's interpretation conflicted with the statutory language and congressional purpose (Trachtman, 1992). The U.S. Department of Commerce lost its appeal. This is another example of the fractional nature of the State which is the forum for the contest to define the interpretation and implementation of the law.

The embargo on Mexico prompted accusations of U.S. protectionism. According to Mexico's Secretary of Foreign Relations, "In accordance with international law, no country has the right to impose their own criteria on others, much less apply sanctions" (Scott, 1991: 6). Several prominent Mexican politicians and business leaders saw the embargo as a ploy to protect U.S. market share by forcing a poor, developing nation to meet unreasonably high ecological standards. "This is a particularly severe warning for the free-trade agreement negotiators of the loop-holes to watch out for," said Hermenegildo Anguianos, a congressman belonging to the Institutional Revolutionary Party or PRI (Scott, 1991: 6).

A spokesman for President Salinas de Gortari stated the official Mexican position was that the disagreement on the tuna issue should be handled outside the free-trade talks. Both Salinas and Bush administration officials agreed that standards for protecting dolphins should be set in international forums, as has been done with the whales (Scott, 1991). Both countries called for an international mediator to settle the dispute, a form of an international State.

Environmentalists Call For An International Tuna Policy

In late 1990 EII reported that Bumble Bee had lied about accepting only dolphin-safe tuna and had accepted a shipment of non-dolphin safe tuna in Thailand. Bumble Bee first said that the buyers were not actually Unicord companies (Parrish, 1990a: d2), then later admitted that it did buy the tuna without checking papers (observers document) but that it was a mistake (Meier, 1990b). In a move to monitor the global tuna fishing industry and verify the dolphin-safety of tuna products such as the Bumble Bee incident, Greenpeace and the Dolphin Coalition drafted a five-point corporate policy that they wanted the international tuna-packing industry to adopt—an international code of ethics. A canner's claim to be selling only dolphin-safe

tuna, "must be binding worldwide, including all subsidiaries, controlled bodies...
enterprises which purchase, process or sell canned tuna or tuna products for export"
(Parrish, 1990b: d4). The environmentalists' call for an international body to regulate
the industry globally is an embryonic attempt to surrogate failing nation-State actions
at the world level.

Mexico, GATT, and NAFTA

Faced with further losses or potential sanctions for its $450 million export fishing
sector, Mexico began proceedings against the U.S. at GATT (Uhlig, 1991). In March
of 1991, Mexico was granted a panel before GATT (Trachtman, 1992). The GATT
hearings occurred when Mexico and the U.S. were trying to negotiate the NAFTA
accord. The tuna issue threatened the Bush Administration with a volatile trade
battle with Mexico at the very moment they were trying to defend Mexico as a major
trading partner. Mexican critics of the free-trade accord seized upon the conflict as
an example of American domination under any such pact. Latin American tunaboat
competition with U.S. tunaboats is highest in the ETP. But out in the Western Pacific
where U.S. fleets can go, Latin American boats do not have the same access to ports
or fishing rights. In Mexico there was suspicion that the law was to protect U.S.
fishermen and not dolphins and raised the issue according to GATT of whether the
U.S. had the right to unilaterally enforce a limit on third countries.

American conservation groups cited the behavior of the Mexican tuna fleet to
emphasize what they said was the need for tough environmental scrutiny of all
aspects of a free-trade accord (Uhlig, 1991). According to environmentalists, even
with sanctions and embargoes, foreign fleets in Mexico, Venezuela, and Vanuatu
continue to use the "dolphin set on" method. "In terms of sheer numbers, Mexico
kills the most dolphins of any country by far," said David Phillips of EII (Uhlig,
1991: D2).

The Secondary Embargo

In January of 1992 Federal Judge Theldon E. Henderson ordered the U.S. Commerce Department to ban $266 million worth of imports (about 1/2 of U.S. tuna
imports) from about 20 countries who buy tuna from Mexico, Venezuela, and Vanuatu and then import it to the U.S. (Bradsher, 1992). The new countries embargoed
could remove themselves from the embargo by providing "certification and proof"
that they had prohibited the import of tuna from the three target countries (Bradsher,
1992: d16). While U.S. environmentalists applauded the secondary embargo, U.S.
fishermen opposed it because it would raise the cost of tuna (Facts on File, 1992).
David G. Burney, executive director of the U.S. Tuna Foundation, said the tuna industry would lobby for new legislation in Congress that would effectively overturn

Judge Henderson's ruling. The Bush Administration tried to overturn the embargo, claiming the action went well beyond the intent of the environmental law it was based on (Wastler, 1992: 3a).

In February of 1992 the NMFS began to enforce the secondary embargo. The embargo was targeted at Mexican and Venezuelan tuna processed in other countries and included Britain, Canada, Colombia, Costa Rica, Ecuador, France, Indonesia, Italy, Japan, Malaysia, Panama, the Marshall Islands, the Netherlands Antilles, Singapore, South Korea, Spain, Taiwan, Thailand, Trinidad, Tobago, and Venezuela (New York Times, 1992a).

EEC officials protested the U.S. embargo of yellowfin tuna before GATT in February of 1992. The U.S. ruling affected $4 to $5 million in tuna exported to the U.S. from France, Italy, and Britain (Maggs, 1992). EEC officials maintained that the EEC had regularly protested the trade penalties under MMPA and would renew this effort before GATT. The EEC stated that they would press for the adoption of Mexican GATT ruling even though the Mexicans seem reluctant to push to ruling while negotiating NAFTA (Maggs, 1992).

To recapitulate, the events illustrated above support the hypothesis that TNCs don't have absolute power in domestic and international arenas. First, pro-environmental legislation was created and partially implemented countering the interests of TNCs. Second, TNCs' attempts, supported by the U.S. executive branch, to combat pro-environmental legislation fell short of their proposed objectives. More importantly TNCs were not able to create an international system in which they could continue to profit from fishing in the ETP using conventional technology. Simultaneously, however, subordinate groups have also encountered strong opposition regarding the implementation of pro-environmental legislation. These situations matured in a context in which fractions of the U.S. State opposed each other and the State apparatus as a whole was increasingly unable to fulfill its role as mediator between various social groups. Indeed, GATT calls into question the durability of MMPA and the ability of the U.S. State to enforce MMPA. The limits that the State encounters in controlling and regulating TNCs' actions and in satisfying demands stemming from others social groups (i.e., environmentalists) are analyzed in the following section.

The Limits of the State

In the attempt to by-pass U.S. State legislation TNCs shifted their operations to foreign fleets while still using conventional technology based on purse-seine nets in the ETP. This action can be viewed as an example of the limited ability of individual States to control activities of economic actors which are increasingly global in scope. Simultaneously, as indicated above, the State embodies conflicting demands stemming from both TNCs and environmentalists which require some forms of organization and control of economic activities. TNCs are interested in maintaining a business climate conducive to further capital accumulation. Environmentalists, in this case, are interested in the enforcement of anti-dolphin killing legislation. The control and regulation of global economic activities, therefore, are pursued through efforts to establish new forms of transnational regulatory agencies.

Industry Moves and Tuna Boats Reflagg

Between 1981 and 1987 at least 21 U.S. tuna boats reflagged under other nations to avoid limits imposed by MMPA (Brower, 1989; Davis, 1988; Levine, 1989). These limits included among other things a low number of dolphin kills allowed and the presence of observers on one-third of U.S. tuna boats which translated into higher production costs. The NMFS reported that U.S. dolphin kills went down from 368,600 in 1972 to less than 20,000 in 1987—mostly due to the fact that the U.S. fleet had shrank dramatically from 93 boats in 1981 to 35 boats in 1988. Although the kill rate decreased on U.S. tuna boats, dolphin kill rates were still very high in the ETP because of increased use of the purse-seine method in the ETP by foreign fleets and the transfer of U.S. fleet tuna boats over to foreign flags (Levin, 1989). According to Joshua Floum, lawyer for EII, the foreign flagged vessels are responsible for most of the current dolphin kills (New York Times, 1989: a17).[1] "Many of the departed seiners have reflagged to avoid high U.S. operating costs and to escape the MMPA and other U.S. regulations" (Brower, 1989: 57).

In addition to reflagging the tuna boats, the by-passing of U.S. laws was carried out through a process of relocation of the tuna industry. In November of 1988 Ralston Purina sold its Van Kamp Chicken of the Sea division to Mantrust of Indonesia. In August of 1989 Pillsbury sold its Bumble Bee subsidiary to Unicord of Thailand. Pillsbury's decision to sell Bumble Bee was motivated by the increasing costs of operating facilities in the United States. Simultaneously, Unicord's purchase of Bumble Bee was made "to counter stiff U.S. tariffs and quotas on imports of canned tuna and to protect Unicord's stake in the U.S. market" (Handley, 1989: 108). The tuna industry restructuring is a classic example of capital avoiding dependence on high-cost labor, by-passing State regulations that restrict accumulation, and sourcing low-cost production sites. In this case the tuna industry found it beneficial to have some production within the U.S. for tariff and market access purposes, but also have other lower-cost production sites elsewhere.

Industry analysts stated the relocations reflect the food industry's increasing concerns about costs. According to Nomi Chez, an analyst with Goldman, Sachs & Co. in New York, "The food business is consolidating on a worldwide basis and there is a lot of production in the Far East. It's a labor intensive business and labor costs are low there" (Kraul, 1989: 2). Tuna caught by Asian fleets in the western

Pacific Ocean and Indian Ocean do not associate with dolphin. Transnational tuna firms are by-passing the increased costs of fishing in the ETP by moving to the western Pacific where regulations are minimal and labor costs are low. One such firm is Unicord.

Unicord was established in 1978 and was Thailand's largest canned-tuna exporter by the mid 1980s. "Bumble Bee was acquired at auction in the first step by Unicord to form a global tuna organization" (Handley, 1991a: 48). Unicord's global strategy foresees a network of factories in five continents that will give the company easy access both to fish and to its main markets. At the core of the strategy is a new tuna-handling process which cuts transport costs and enables Unicord to avoid high import duties in the U.S. and Europe. Unicord sells tuna to the U.S. under its own brand labels and also sells under Bumble Bee. Bumble Bee has canneries in San Diego and Santa Fe Springs, CA, Puerto Rico, and Ecuador. Despite their higher wage rates, the U.S. canneries are an advantage because they allow Unicord to avoid import duties on canned tuna and are also relatively close to fishing grounds in Atlantic and ETP. The new technology removed the loins which were then cooked, frozen and shipped for canning within the U.S. and saved large amounts of money on shipping costs. Unicord was also setting up a loin operation in Ghana to serve the European market (Handley, 1991b).

U.S. State Action, Counteractions and Compromises

U.S. State action to counteract TNCs by-passing of State powers consisted primarily of attempts to enforce MMPA beyond national boundaries, i.e., the first and second embargoes. This action was resisted by foreign nations, which as indicated above, viewed it as limiting their sovereignty. GATT rulings support their positions.

In September of 1991 U.S. officials (State, Commerce, and Trade Departments) reached an understanding with Mexico over the embargo on Mexican tuna. To avoid undercutting NAFTA talks, Mexican President Salinas de Gortari backed off of the complaint lodged with GATT over the tuna dispute. In late September, Salinas announced as "a show of good faith" that Mexico would "postpone" the final GATT decision and pursue a bilateral solution (Scott, 1991). In exchange for the Bush Administration's pledge to try to change the MMPA, Mexico issued a 10-point plan to reduce dolphin kills. The promise to try to amend the law was "brokered" in Mexico by Secretary of State James Baker, Secretary of Commerce Robert Mosbacher and U.S. Trade Representative Carla Hills (Maggs, 1991: 3a).

Environmentalists argued the GATT ruling in favor of Mexico could set a precedent that could undermine their efforts on a range of fronts. "If the GATT ruling goes through, international trade sanctions designed to halt trade of endangered species, trade in rare hardwoods, and shipments of toxic wastes could be declared illegal. It would be a very serious blow," said a spokesman with EII (Scott, 1991: 8).

"The administration is working behind the scenes to achieve some of the deregulation that it was not able to get in the open," charges Lori Wallach, a lawyer at Congress Watch, a group founded by Ralph Nader (Magnusson, Hong, and Oster, 1992: 130). U.S. Congress, especially Representatives Waxman and Gephardt, are strongly opposed to amending MMPA to suit the U.S. Government and the U.S. tuna industry or to any Mexican deal that imperils U.S. health, safety, labor or environmental laws (Magnusson, Hong, and Oster, 1992). According to Chief William K. Reilly of the U.S. Environmental Protection Agency, "If this becomes the basis of GATT policy, it would unravel all the strings" of U.S. environmental policy (Magnusson, Hong, and Oster, 1992: 130). If the GATT decisions prevailed, U.S. trade officials said it might also weaken enforcement of international environmental accords, e.g., sea turtles, ozone, rain forests, endangered species, whaling, ivory and elephants. According to GATT, such problems concerning the "global commons" should be solved through "international environmental agreements" (Brooke, 1992a: 7). Even GATT called for an international forum to resolve "global commons" issues such as MMPA.

GATT's call for an international forum to resolve "global commons" issues highlights the contradictory position nation-States confront. On one hand, GATT's statements acknowledge the inability of domestic bodies to face the demands stemming from this case. On the other hand, GATT becomes the forum where transnational regulatory functions are proposed. It is interesting to note that the political agenda established by GATT during the 1980s has been aimed at deregulation. Accordingly, GATT becomes a political terrain where regulating and deregulating forces and demands confront each other.

The Second Compromise and the IATTC Accord

In March of 1992 the U.S., Mexico and Venezuela reached a preliminary agreement to protect dolphins. GATT officials reported that the three countries had agreed to a five-year moratorium, beginning in 1994, on purse-seine nets (Davis, 1992: B10). According to Representative Seade of Mexico, "The main message that should sink in (for environmentalists) is international cooperation" and he hoped other nations would adopt the accord (Davis, 1992: B10). EII attacked the pact and congressional aides said the agreements would face a tough time winning approval. Phillips of EII, said the agreements represented a "bad approach" because it would lift trade pressures that had led to sharp declines in dolphin kills. "The current regulatory mechanism is resulting in significant conservation of dolphins" said Phillips (Davis, 1992: B10). The agreement failed to obtain U.S. congressional backing and failed. In April of 1992 an agreement negotiated by the Inter-American Tropical Tuna Commission (IATTC), the first major international accord to save dolphins, the ten nations that fish for tuna in the ETP agreed to cut killing dolphins by 80%

during the 1990s. "The resolution sets into motion a program to reduce dolphin mortality to insignificant levels, to levels approaching zero," according to Dr. James Joseph, director of the IATTC (Brooke, 1992b: C4).

EII argued that the accord was too little, too late. "The reduction is way too little, and the killing of dolphins will continue way too long. In the U.S., consumers, companies, and Congress are saying: eliminate the setting of nets on dolphins," says Phillips of EII. "We do not believe that you can chase down and encircle 1000 dolphins in a mile-long net and avoid killing them" (Brooke, 1992b: C4). According to Richard C. Atchison, Executive Director of the American Tunaboat Association, the accord is "reasonable, practical, and achievable" (Brooke, 1992: C4).

The Third Compromise

In June of 1992 the U.S., Mexico, and Venezuela agreed to stop the setting of nets around dolphins and tuna. The Stubbs Bill was introduced to U.S. Congress on the 16 of June 1992 and was supported by EII (New York Times, 1992b). The unlikely alliance of the Bush Administration, Congress, environmentalists, and the governments of Mexico and Venezuela forged a tentative agreement to stop the killing of thousands of dolphins. After months of negotiations, the Bill had bipartisan support and had already been agreed to by the Mexican and Venezuelan governments. The agreement would end the embargo on Mexico and Venezuela and place a five-year moratorium on purse-seine fishing in the ETP and possibly end purse-seine fishing is the ETP forever (Parrish, 1992a).

According to EII, it was only these "incredible constraints on the market" which brought Mexico and Venezuela, the last countries with big fishing fleets in the ETP, to the bargaining table. "The market for dolphin-unsafe tuna is collapsing. They can't find places to sell the tuna... the U.S. won't buy it. England, France and Germany won't buy it. Thailand won't process it, and now very recently some of their last remaining markets in Spain and Italy are collapsing" (Parrish, 1992a: A20).

Mexico and Venezuela have agreed to halt the killing of dolphins by their tuna fishers by March of 1994. The formal agreement with Mexico and Venezuela is expected to be signed after the bill—The International Dolphin Conservation Act—is ratified. In a key concession to environmentalists, Mexico and Venezuela agreed to face stiff penalties if they resume killing dolphins—a U.S. embargo of all seafood products, except for shrimp (Maggs, 1992). In the final hours of the congressional session, the U.S. Senate passed the International Dolphin Conservation Act of 1992 (IDCA), which President Bush signed in late October (Parrish, 1992b). Though President Bush signed the IDCA, "the IDCA will only go into effect if Mexico agrees to comply with its terms, a step which Mexico has so far refused to take" (Public Citizen, 1993: 9).

From the illustration of the events mentioned above, it can be concluded that the action of the U.S. State in response to demands from social groups is problematic when lodged in a transnational arena. The by-passing of State action through tuna boat re-flagging and industry relocation demonstrated that the ability of the State to perform its historical roles has been weakened. The State is increasingly unable to regulate TNCs' actions (i.e., enforce compliance of MMPA), to enhance TNCs interests (defeat pro-environment groups) and to respond to demands stemming from other social groups such as the environmentalists (implementation of MMPA). Also problematic are attempts to extend State regulation of economic activities at the international level. The various compromises reached by the U.S., Venezuelan, and Mexican States have been designed to respond to the global hyper-mobility of TNCs (i.e., the move to Asia which will be further discussed in the next section) and to foster legitimative and accumulative actions at the domestic level (respond to environmentalists' demands in the U.S. and loss of employment and economic opportunities in the U.S., Venezuela and Mexico).

These territorially-limited accords do not match the spatial sphere of action of economic actors. More specifically, TNCs did escape the pro-environmental regulations associated with them by moving to Asia where they continue to use the existing purse-seine method and therefore can avoid the costly adoption of new environmentally sound technology. The present situation indicates that TNCs' activities can be regulated when in the ETP. Yet they are, at least temporarily, out of reach when operating outside that area. Moreover, despite the existence of multinational accords, TNCs have no immediate interests in re-shifting their operations back to the American continent.

Labor and Global Restructuring

Effects of Restructuring on U.S. Tuna Industry

The transnational move of the tuna fish industry had important repercussions in terms of employment and the overall economic well-being of fishing communities. First, the introduction of the purse-seine net technology in the ETP expanded employment and economic opportunities in the U.S. Later, the passage and contested implementation of MMPA fostered the shift of tuna industry operations to Latin America with the consequential growth of employment in those regions and economic decline among tuna fishing communities in the U.S. Finally, the secondary embargoes on Latin American producers stimulated a shift of the industry to Asia curtailing employment and economic growth in Latin American fishing areas.

In response to the Big 3 tuna processors' decision to not accept dolphin unsafe tuna, boatowners in San Diego maintained that this decision was tragic and that they had been fighting it for twenty years along with boat seizures, the closing of

U.S. tuna canneries, and foreign fleets slashing prices to capture the U.S. market. According to Peter Schmidt, President of Marco Seattle, whose Campbell Industries subsidiary in San Diego is on of the world's leading builders of the purse-seine boats, "This could be the last nail for the American tuna boats" (Kraul, 1990: d1). The last six canneries in San Diego closed in 1984 and local tunaboat owners "must now unload their fish at cannery plants in American Samoa and Puerto Rico" (Kraul, 1990: d6).

As a result of the dolphin unsafe consumer boycott, the Big 3 U.S. tuna canners turned to Asian suppliers such as the Philippines and Thailand to assure that the tuna they buy has not been caught with purse-seine nets that can kill dolphins. These actions decreased the volume of tuna caught by the U.S. fleet (Thurston, 1990). In the year following the Big 3 boycott of ETP tuna, the number of U.S. fishing boats in the ETP dropped from 30 to 9 (Wallace, 1991). By 1993, forty percent of the U.S.—owned canneries in Puerto Rico had shut down (Kroman, 1993). Since the environmentalists' victories of the 1990s, several boats in the U.S. tuna fleet, once the world's largest, had also gone broke and others were sold to foreign interests. Tuna boat captains had to relocate to the Western Pacific and have shouldered $1 to $2 mil. retrofits for larger nets, bigger hydraulics, and new engines (Kroman, 1993).

Prices paid to tuna fishermen dropped 22%, to the lowest in 10 years. Within days of the U.S. boycott, the bottom fell out of the tuna market. Yellowfin from the ETP, the best tuna in world, fell from $1,075 a ton to $835 a ton (Kroman, 1993). The shift of 16 U.S. boats to the Western Pacific and abundant supplies of skipjack tuna and yellowfin increased yields and depressed prices. Dolphin-safe policies benefitted newcomers on the tuna scene, notably Korea and Taiwan, who built boats and canneries as fast as they could. These nations were already blessed with being close to waters that provide dolphin-safe tuna, not to mention low overhead and regulatory costs that U.S. fishermen bear (Kroman, 1993). Economic opportunities and employment opened for Asian processors and closed for U.S. and Latin American processors as MMPA was increasingly enforced. The industry moved to Asia to source dolphin-safe tuna and low-cost labor which marginalized labor, both tuna fishermen and tuna processing workers, in the U.S. (especially Puerto Rico), and Latin America.

Although Heinz's Star Kist operates the world's largest tuna cannery in Mayaguez, Puerto Rico, U.S. tuna marketers are increasingly importing canned tuna to take advantage of lower labor costs in developing countries. U.S. and foreign tuna firms are increasingly using non-U.S. labor for processing (Thurston, 1990). Except for Star Kist's Puerto Rican plant which employs 4,300, the local tuna industry is virtually controlled by Asians. Unicord of Thailand—Bumble Bee, Mantrust of Indonesian—Chicken of the Sea (Mantrust's National Packing Plant with 600 workers), and Japanese (Caribe Tuna of Mitsubishi Corp. of Japan and Neptune Packing of Mitsui and Co.) dominate the Puerto Rican tuna canning industry. For all of these firms, tax benefits under Section 936 of the U.S. Internal Revenue Code are crucial to their remaining in Puerto Rico (Luxner, 1990).

Bumble Bee in Puerto Rico employs 2,200 workers and processes between 200 and 300 tons of tuna a day and accounts for more than 50% of Bumble Bee sold in U.S. mainland. "Bumble Bee started out in Astoria, Ore. We had plants in Hawaii, Maryland and San Diego, but currently operate tuna canneries only in Puerto Rico," according to Mr. Dan Sullivan, president of Bumble Bee (Luxner, 1990: 4A).

When the ETP was profitable and legitimate, the TNCs set up operation in Puerto Rico and Latin America to process for the U.S. market. When MMPA made the ETP illegitimate, Puerto Rican and Latin American processing facilities became less convenient and the industry moved operations to the western Pacific.

The Move to Asia

The move to Asia is a strategy designed to decrease the costs of production. However, the shift to Asia jeopardizes the access to affluent markets such as the U.S. and Europe. Accordingly, this strategy is complemented by another one which attempts to secure footholds in these markets. Unicord for example is Southeast Asia's largest investor in the U.S. Before Unicord bought Bumble Bee, it was the world's largest supplier of tuna, but was at the mercy of industry middlemen who bought the fish for resale to major brands. "Now Unicord can be assured of a distribution network in the United States, while Bumble Bee is sure of its supply," said Unicord Chairman Kamchorn Sathirakul. "Now we've become a truly integrated, global business" (Wallace, 1992: H3).

Unicord's strong point has been low wages at its Thailand factory, where it employs 7,000 people to process raw tuna. "Thai companies, especially in the food-processing business, are aggressively seeking out U.S. companies which control their markets in order to lock up a foothold in fortress Europe and fortress U.S.A.," said Graham Catterwell, an analyst at Crosby Securities in Bangkok (Wallace, 1992: H3). These are good examples of globally sourcing markets before protectionist policies may arise.

Impact on Latin America: Mexico and Venezuela

Mexican and Venezuelan tuna-related economic activities were damaged by negative publicity and declining exports. Under MMPA, Venezuelan and Mexican industries couldn't export tuna products to the U.S. because in 1991 their boats had a dolphin kill rate higher than 125% of the U.S. fleet average. Venezuela contends that the U.S. set standards that are impossibly high for third world fleets in order to protect the American fleet at a time when tuna demand is flat (Brooke, 1992a: 7). In response to the embargoes, both countries joined the IATTC and opened their tuna fleets to inspection by IATTC observers. Mexico pledged $1 million and Venezula $500,000 for research on dolphin safe fishing (Brooke, 1992b).

Years of highly publicized campaigns and boycotts by environmental groups forced most of the U.S. fleet out of the ETP, westward to near New Guinea where tuna and dolphin stay apart and where the U.S. has fishing treaties with surrounding islands. Mexico and Venezuela lack such treaties to gain access to other fishing waters and the Latin American boat owners are not eager to pay the $1 million deemed necessary to equip each boat for such long voyages. Mexico's tuna industry was extremely vulnerable due to the Tuna Wars and a tuna glut on foreign markets. The price per ton fell more than 30% in the first half of 1991 (Ellison, 1991). Claiming to be prisoners of geography, Venezuela says it is too far for them to fish in the western Pacific where they do not have fishing rights (Brooke, 1992).

As a result of the U.S. tuna embargo, in Cumana, Venezuela, more and more tuna boats are at dock and more sailors and canners are out of work. Sealed off from the world's largest market since August of 1990, Venezuela's tuna fleet has shrunk from 118 boats in 1988 to 34 boats in 1992. As a result of the depressed economy, a crime wave is sweeping Cumana due to high unemployment from the embargo (Brooke, 1992a). According to Laura Rojas, Director General of Venezuela's Institute of Foreign Trade, "The U.S. has passed domestic legislation that has jurisdiction outside the U.S. Environmental protection can't be had at the cost of another country" (Brooke, 1992a: 7).

In February of 1992, Venezuela joined members of the EC and 23 other nations in urging the U.S. to abide by a GATT ruling that the unilateral American ban on tuna imports from Mexico and Venezuela is illegal. According to David Phillips of EII, "They are kidding themselves if they think GATT can force the U.S. to abandon laws to protect the global environment. In the 1990s, free trade and efforts to protect the environment are on a collision course" (Brooke, 1992a: 7). According to Oliver Belisario, a Caracas-based consultant for Venezuela's tuna industry, "Tuna is the debut for a great debate between environmentalists and traders" (Brooke, 1992a: 7).

With Venezuelan and Mexican tuna shut out from U.S., Australia and most of Europe, tuna landed in Venezuela sells at a steep discount from world prices, e.g., $600/ton versus $1000/ton if "dolphin-safe." Cans labeled "dolphin-safe" account for 95% of U.S. sales and the U.S. has half of the world's consumer tuna market. According to John M. Werner, president of the local subsidiary of the H.J. Heinz company in Venezuela, "We don't even can tuna in Venezuela for Venezuelan consumption any more. Heinz has a worldwide "dolphin-safe" tuna policy" (Brooke, 1992a: 7).

U.S. and foreign tuna boat owners say the ban on purse-seine nets in the ETP would cripple their livelihood. "Our vessels and, I believe, the international fleet, would not be able to fish" in the ETP without purse-seine nets, says Richard Atchison, Exec. Dir. of the San Diego-based American Tunaboat Assn... "It's not technically feasible or economically feasible" (Parrish, 1992a: A20).

Conclusion

The tuna-dolphin case demonstrates the contested nature of the transnational arena as neither the TNCs nor the environmentalists and the various States' officialdoms were able to fully assert their agendas. It also shows the limits of the regulatory capacity of the nation-State along with the difficulties which exist in the development of larger-than-national forms of regulation. The accords among the U.S., Venezuelan, and Mexican governments, the various appeals to GATT, and domestic attempts to implement policy are all cases in point.

In this respect, it can be concluded that the regulatory situation at the transnational level is extremely unsettled and characterized by a combination of old forms of regulation paralleled by emerging new ones. The former refers to the various nation-States' attempts to continue their mediative and organizational roles both domestically and internationally. New forms of regulation are embodied in the increasingly important role performed by transnational organizations which in this particular case refer to GATT and the IATTC. The unsettled character of this situation is supported by the inability of these institutions to maintain levels of control which encompass the sphere of action of TNCs and which address the demands from other social actors.

The case further demonstrates that issues concerning the protection of the environment and labor cannot be addressed unless some forms of regulation are carried out. More specifically, this case points out the validity of the assumption held by some of the most prominent classic social thinkers, such as Marx, Durkheim, Weber, Spencer, Smith, and Gramsci, indicating that unrestricted development of capitalism creates unbearable consequences for society. Accordingly, this case study speaks directly against the neo-liberal assumption maintaining that unregulated capitalism can successfully address economic growth, employment, and protection of the environment. TNCs' constant attempts to avoid pro-environmental legislation, the waves of negative consequences for labor in the U.S. and Latin America, and the use of global sourcing by TNCs to avoid the task of developing environmentally-sound fishing technologies point out the limits of the neo-liberal proposal.

Unrestricted capitalist development and its current reliance on flexible accumulation also speaks against the maintenance of "free spaces." The Fordist accord provided "free spaces" for labor which characterized the expansion of the living standards of the working and middle classes in the U.S. and in many other advanced and developing nations in the world. During the post-Fordist restructuring, "free spaces" for labor contracted, while some new "free spaces" concerning the protection of the environment were established. The tuna industry abandoned U.S. and

Latin American processing plants which serviced their ETP operations. The case study illustrates, however, that even in the case of the environment, the availability for democratic control appear increasingly problematic, especially in light of possible GATT rulings. It is evident that the enforcement of pro-environmental legislation pushed TNCs to reconsider their plans of action. At the same time, TNCs were not forced to alter their methods of production, although the TNCs were compelled to move their operations out of the ETP.

If the scenario is correct, then the task of regulating global capitalism assumes central importance. There are two general categories of alternatives which have been recently discussed. The first is protectionism. Protectionism has been advocated to limit the transnational mobility of capital and labor and to enhance the ability to control undesirable consequences of economic activities. In recent years, protectionist strategies have called for items such as the adoption of increased import tariffs, tougher controls for commodities and labor at the border, and various incentives to enhance domestic production and consumption of domestic products (i.e., buy American).

The limits of the protectionist strategy can be synthesized into two objections. The first is that protectionism counters global capital's post-Fordist strategy of flexible patterns of accumulation. Flexible patterns of accumulation are key in overcoming the crisis of Fordism and expanding the avenues for capital growth. Accordingly, protectionist strategies would involve hampering the functioning of a system that is increasingly interrelated globally and which finds in the global character its ultimate strength.

The second objection refers to the nation-State's decreasing capacity to enforce local legislation. In this case, as documented above, there is no reason to justify the conclusion that protectionism would enhance the State's capacity to enforce effectively its regulations in the international arena.

The other general alternative is to be found in international accords aimed at regulation. This alternative is based on the principal that the unity of the polity and the economy must be reconstructed. This reconstruction implies that the global sphere of economic action must be matched by an equally global sphere of action by political regulatory forces. This alternative would involve the creation of transnational polity forms which surrogate the functioning of the nation-State at the transnational level such as IATTC. In essence, this alternative would involve the creation of international alliances and/or organizations which would control capital flexibility. The modalities and forms with which these alternatives can be constructed are to be found in the historical conditions of the present era.

In order to do so, one of the major aspects that needs to be overcome is the fragmentation emerging in production and cultural spheres. As indicated in the case study, progressive movements such as the environmentalists and pro-labor organizations, as well as local communities, are pitted one against the other. Accordingly, the communalities shared by these movements and communities, both at the economic and solidarity levels,[2] are weakened by the emphasis on locality and particularity of interest. This situation matures in a context in which the interests of transnational capital are not fully criticized.

The case of the tuna industry shows that while the U.S. national controversy centered on the banning of established fishing techniques, it ignored domestic labor issues. Alternatively, the international controversy barely touched the issue of the industry restructuring around new technologies but instead focused on the localized impacts of labor dislocation. The international discourse centers on local advantages and gains of local groups without questioning the tuna industry's insistence on purse-seine technologies. Gains are framed in a taken-for-granted discourse which addresses immediate concerns but never embrace the more probing issue of long-term social arrangements. In other words, the objective of profit generation is ultimately maintained along with the "alternative" goals of constructing a sound environment and developing the world's poor regions.

In conclusion, these contradictory elements point to the historical difficulties of bridging environmental, labor, local and global interests around common goals. Therefore, the alternative of creating international attempts (i.e., organizations and/or accords) to control economic activities, while perhaps more desirable than protectionism, is certainly no less problematic. The 30-year struggle between the tuna industry and environmentalists richly captures the problematic character of national regulation within an international arena. Although the environmentalists appear to have won the latest battle, the onus of GATT casts significant doubts over the eventual outcome of the war.

NOTES

1 It also important to note that according to the environmental group Earth Island Institute (EII) Federal agencies are not enforcing the law to require foreign fleets to comparable kills as the U.S. fleet. Furthermore, the EII maintains that fines and penalties for violations of MMPA are so low that skippers of tuna boats accept the low fines in order to maintain higher levels of returns.

2 This should not be interpreted as a stand against diversity. On the contrary, it speaks to the shattering of common experience which constituted in the past the backbone of collective movements such as unions and other political organizations of the working class.

REFERENCES

Audobon
    1988 "Porpoise Mortality Numbers Skewed." *Audobon* (Sept.) 90 (5), 16.
BARKIN, David
    1990 *Distorted Development.* Boulder: Westview Press.

BLOCK, Fred
> 1980 "Beyond Relative Autonomy: State Managers as Historical Subjects." Pp. 227-240 in R. Miliband and J. Seville (Eds.). *Socialist Register* London: Merlin Press.

BONANNO, Alessandro, Lawrence BUSCH, W.H. FRIEDLAND, Lourdes GOUVEIA and Enzo MINGIONE (Eds.)
> 1994 *From Columbus to ConAgra: The Globalization and Agriculture and Food.* Lawrence: University Press of Kansas.

BORREGO, John
> 1981 "Metanational Capitalist Accumulation and the Emerging Paradigm of Revolutionist Accumulation." *Review* IV (4), 713-777.

BRADSHER, Keith
> 1992 "U.S. Told to Bar Tuna Over Dolphin Killings." *The New York Times* (Jan. 15) 141, D16.

BROOKE, James
> 1992a "America—Environmental Dictator?" *The New York Times* (Jan. 17) 141, F7.

BROOKE, James
> 1992b "10 Nations Reach Accord on Saving Dolphins." *New York Times* (Feb. 7) 141, C4.

BROWER, Kenneth
> 1989 "The Destruction of Dolphins: in Spite of Laws Intended to Protect them, Federal Indifference and Cruel Fishing Methods once Again Endanger Dolphins." *The Atlantic* (July) 263 (1), 35.

CONSTANCE, Douglas and William D. HEFFERNAN
> 1991 "The Global Poultry Agro/Food Complex." *International Journal of Sociology of Agriculture and Food* 1, 126-142.

DAVIS, Bob
> 1992 "U.S., Mexico, Venezuela Set Accord on Tuna." *The Wall Street Journal* (March 20) B10(E).

DAVIS, Andrew
> 1988 "Caught in the Tuna Nets: the Slaughter of Dolphins." *The Nation* (Nov. 14) 247 (14), 486.

DURKHEIM, Emile
> 1984 *The Division of Labor in Society.* New York: The Free Press.

ELLISON, Katherine
> 1991 "U.S. Quest for Dolphin-Safe Tuna Hurts Mexican Fisherman." *Journal of Commerce and Commercial* (Oct. 28) 390 (27 592), 5A.

Facts on File
> 1992 "Yellowfin Tuna Ban Enforced." *Facts on File* (Feb. 6) 52 (2672), 78.

FRIEDLAND, William H.
> 1991 "The Transnationalization of Agricultural Production: Palimpsest of the Transnational State." *International Journal of Sociology of Agriculture and Food* 1, 48-58.

FRIEDMAN, Milton
> 1982 *Capitalism and Freedom.* Chicago: The University of Chicago Press.

FRIEDMANN, Harriet and Philip MCMICHAEL
> 1989 "Agriculture and the State System." *Sociologia Ruralis* 29 (2), 93-117.

GODGES, John
> 1988 "Dolphins Hit Rough Seas Again." *Sierra* (May-June) 73 (3), 24.

HABERMAS, Jürgen
> 1975 *Legitimation Crisis.* Boston: Beacon Press.

HANDLEY, Paul
> 1989 "Unicord's Big Catch." *Far East Economic Review* (Sept. 7) 145 (36), 108-109.

HANDLEY, Paul
   1991a "Off the Hook." *Far East Economic Review* (May 23) 151 (21), 48-49.
HANDLEY, Paul
   1991b "Row of Canneries." *Far East Economic Review* (May 23) 151 (21), 50.
HARVEY, David
   1990 *The Condition of Postmodernity.* Oxford: Basil Blackwell.
HOLLAND, Kerry L.
   1991 "Expolitation on Porpoise: The Use of Purse Seine Nets by Commercial Tuna Fisherman in
        the Eastern Tropical Pacific Ocean." *Syracuse Journal of International Law and Commerce*
        17, 241.
KINDLEBERGER, Charles P.
   1986 "International Public Goods Without International Government." *American Economic Review*
        76 (1), 1-13.
KRAUL, Chris
   1989 "Pillsbury to Sell Bumble Bee Unit to Thai Firm." *Los Angeles Times* (Aug. 17) 108, 2.
KRAUL, Chris
   1990 "U.S. Fishermen fear Decision May be Final Blow." *Los Angeles Times* (April 14) 109, D1.
KROMAN, Mick
   1991 "Fishing Morally Correct Tuna." *Journal of Commerce and Commercial* 390 (27 613), 8A.
LEVINE, Myron
   1989 "Dolphin Demise; Foreign Tuna Fishing Fleets Blamed for Most of the Sharp Increase in
        Killings." *Los Angeles Times* (March 5) 108, 3.
LIPIETZ, Alain
   1991 "A Regulationist Approach to the Future of Urban Ecology." *Capitalism, Nature, Socialism*
        3 (3), 101-110.
LIPIETZ, Alain
   1987 *Mirages and Miracles.* London: Verso.
LUXNER, Larry
   1990a "Puerto Rico Lures Asians to Tuna Business." *Journal of Commerce and Commercial* 384
        (27 202), 4A.
MAGGS, John
   1991 "Bush Team Feels Heat over GATT Tuna Ruling." *Journal of Commerce and Commercial*
        30 389 (27 573), 3A.
MAGGS, John
   1992 "EC Will Protest U.S. Tuna Embargo against 20 Nations." *Journal of Commerce and Com-
        mercial* 391 (27 684), 5A.
MAGNUSSON, Paul, Peter HONG, and Patrick OSTER
   1992 "Save the Dolphins—or Free Trade?" *Business Week* (Feb. 17) 3252, 130-131.
MARCUSE, Herbert
   1964 *One Dimensional Man.* Boston: Beacon Press.
MARX, Karl
   1977 *Capital,* Vol. 1. New York: Vintage Books.
MARX, Karl
   1981 *Capital,* Vol. 3. New York: Vintage Books.
MCNALLY, David
   1991 "Beyond Nationalism, Beyond Protectionism: Labour and the Canada-U.S. Free Trade
        Agreement." *Capital & Class* 43 (2), 233-252.

MEIER, Barry
 1990 "Tuna Company Protests Accusations about Dolphins." *The New York Times* (Dec. 6) 140, D4(L).
MORAIN, Dan
 1990 "U.S. Told to Ban Tuna Imports." *Los Angeles Times* (Dec. 9) 109, A3.
Newsweek
 1990 "Swim with the Dolphins; Tuna Fishing will Change." *Newsweek* 115 (17), 76.
O'CONNOR, James
 1986 *Accumulation Crisis*. New York: Basil Blackwell.
OFFE, Claus
 1985 *Disorganized Capitalism*. Cambridge: MIT Press.
PARRISH, Michael
 1990a "Film Turns Tide for Dolphins at StarKist Tuna." *Los Angeles Times* (April 14) 109, D1.
PARRISH, Michael
 1990b "Fight for 'Dolphin-Safe' Tuna Flares up Again." *Los Angeles Times* (Nov. 29) 109, D2.
PARRISH, Michael
 1992a "U.S. Approves Pact to Protect Pacific's Dolphins." *Los Angeles Times* (October 9) 111, D2.
PARRISH, Michael
 1992b "Pact May Stop Dolphin Deaths in Tuna Fishing." *Los Angeles Times* (June 17) 111, A1.
PITELIS, Christos
 1991 "Beyond the Nation-State?: The Transnational Firm and the Nation-State." *Capital & Class* (43), 131-152.
Public Citizen
 1993 "Why Voters Are Concerned: Environmental and Consumer Problems in GATT and NAFTA." *Public Citizen, Inc.* (Jan.) 7-12.
RESTREPO, Ivan and Susana FRANCO
 1988 *Naturaleza Muerta*. Mexico City: Centro de Ecodesarrollo.
ROSS, Robert J.S. and Kent C. TRACHTE
 1990 *Global Capitalism: The New Leviathan*. Albany: Suny Press.
SCOTT, David Clark
 1991a "Mexico Wins Battle over U.S. Tuna Ban, but Backs off to Save Image, Trade Talks." *Christian Science Monitor* (Sept. 27) 83 (213), 8.
SCOTT, David Clark
 1991b "Mexico Chafes as U.S. Revisits Ban on Tuna Imports Involving Dolphin Kills." *The Christian Science Monitor* (Feb. 27) 83 (64), 6.
SHARECOFF, Philip
 1990 "Big Tuna Canners Act to Slow Down Dolphin Killings; 70% of Market Affected; 3 Concerns Will Stop Buying Fish Caught in Nets that are Trapping Mammals." *The New York Times* (April 13) 139, A1.
TENNESEN, Michael
 1989 "No Chicken of the Sea." *National Wildlife* 27 (3), 10-13.
The New York Times
 1989a "Judge Extends Order that U.S. Protect Dolphin." *The New York Times* (Jan. 19) 138, A17.
The New York Times
 1989b "U.S. Defends Law on Monitoring Dolphin Killings." *The New York Times* (Aug. 23) 138, A14.

The New York Times
    1990 "Judge Orders Tuna Import Ban over Dolphin Kill." *The New York Times* (Aug. 30) 139, A21.
The New York Times
    1992a "U.S. Enforces Tuna Embargo." *The New York Times* (Feb. 3) 141, D3.
The New York Times
    1992b "Pro-Dolphin Accord Made." *The New York Times* (June 16) 141, D9.
THURSTON, Charles
    1990 "Save-the-Dolphin Drive to Spur Asia Tuna Imports: Some Suppliers out of Stock." *Journal of Commerce and Commercial* 384 (27 209), 1A.
TRACHTMAN, Joel P.
    1992 "International Trade—Quantitative Restrictions—National Treatment—Environmental Protection—Application of GATT to U.S. Restrictions on Import of Tuna from Mexico and other Countries." *American Journal of International Law* 1, 142-151.
UHLIG, Mark A.
    1991 "U.S.-Mexico Pact Faces Hurdle on Tuna Fishing." *The New York Times* (April 4) 140, D14.
WALLACE, Amy
    1991 "Dolphin-Safe Tuna Fishing is Aim of Bumble Bee Study." *Los Angeles Times* (May 2) 110, D1.
WALLACE, Charles
    1992 "Southeast Asia Nations Scrambling to Gobble up U.S. Firms." *Los Angeles Times* (August 4) 111, H3.
WASTLER, Allen R.
    1992 "Tuna Importers Struggle to Escape Embargo's Snag." *Journal of Commerce and Commercial* 391 (27 661), 1A.
WRIGHT, Angus
    1986 "Rethinking the Circle of Poison: the Politics of Pesticide Poisoning among Mexican Farm Workers." *Latin American Perspectives* 13 (4), 341-361.

Geopolitics, Global Production, and the Three Paths of Development in East Asia

ALVIN Y. SO* and STEPHEN W.K. CHIU**

ABSTRACT

Why did the East Asian region experience, not one, but three different paths of development (Japan's rise from a core to a global economic power, China's shift from revolutionary Maoism to market socialism, and the upgrading of Hong Kong, South Korea, and Taiwan to the status of the NIEs)? And why did the entire East Asian region become an epicenter of capitalist accumulation for the global economy in the 1990s? Adopting a regional framework, this paper argues that an examination into the geopolitics of American polarization project in the 1950s and the 1960s, the Japanese economic integration project in the 1970s and the 1980s, and mainland China's national reunification project in the 1980s and the 1990s will help in understanding some of the puzzles of the profound transformation of East Asia during the second half of the twentieth century.

THE EAST ASIAN REGION has undergone dramatic transformation during the second half of the twentieth century. At the mid-twentieth century, mainland China, Korea, Taiwan, and Hong Kong were facing enormous economic and political problems, and Japan was badly damaged by its defeat in World War II. However, by the late 1960s, Japan quickly emerged as a capitalist core state; mainland China tried to achieve semiperipheral ascent through revolutionary socialism; and Hong Kong, South Korea, and Taiwan began to participate in export-led industrialization. Finally, by the 1990s, Japan further grew to a global economic powerhouse; mainland China shifted to market socialism and sought foreign investment; and Hong Kong, South Korea, and Taiwan were upgraded to the NIEs (Newly Industrializing Economies).

What explains the drastic transformation of the East Asian states at the end of the twentieth century? Why did the East Asian region experience, not one, but three different paths of development (Japan's rise from a core to a global economic power, China's shift from revolutionary Maoism to market socialism, and the upgrading of

---

* Department of Sociology, University of Hawaii, Honolulu, HI 96822, U.S.A.
** The Chinese University of Hong Kong, Hong Kong.

Hong Kong, South Korea, and Taiwan to the status of the NIEs)? And why did the entire East Asian region experience upward mobility in the postwar era?

There are three general explanations for East Asian development. First of all, there is the *cultural* explanation. The culturalists argue that what the successful East Asian economies have in common is their Confucian traditions. Confucianism placed the family as the paramount institution within society, which led to the emergence of family entrepreneurship in East Asia. Furthermore, Confucianism shaped a new pattern of personalistic corporate management different from the West's rational, bureaucratic management. Finally, Confucianism glorified the established authority of the better-educated and rationalized their claims of superiority on the basis of possessing specialized wisdom (e.g., Rozman, 1992).

Secondly, the *neoclassical economists* argue that the growth of exports in the East Asian NIES accounted for their GDP growth rates, which were among the highest for developing countries. Exports contributed to resource allocation according to comparative advantage, helped these nations overcome the limitations of their small domestic markets, and provided the "carrot and stick" of competition. The East Asian NIEs adopted such export policies because of their stable incentive system, limited government intervention, and reliance on private capital (Balassa, 1988).

Thirdly, the *statist* perspective contends that East Asian states play a strategic role in taming domestic and international market forces and harnessing them to national ends (Amsden, 1989). Onis (1991) points out that East Asian industrializing states benefitted from the unusual combination of both bureaucratic autonomy and public-private cooperation. As a result, strong autonomous states emerged in East Asia, capable of not only formulating strategic developmental goals, but of also translating them into effective policies to promote rapid industrialization in Japan, South Korea, and Taiwan.

The above theoretical frameworks, however, have failed to analyze why the East Asian states adopted different paths of development and to account for their changing status in the global economy, or to investigate why the entire East Asian region could achieve upward mobility by the end of the twentieth century.

The aim of this paper, therefore, is to offer an alternative regional explanation of East Asian development. After criticizing the "country-by-country approach" in East Asian literature, Cumings (1987: 47) asserted that "an understanding of the Northeast Asian political economy can only emerge from an approach that posits the systemic interaction of each country with the others, and of the region with the world at large." In addition, Arrighi (1994) proposes a "three-stage rocket" theory to examine the pattern of regional development in East Asia. In the first stage, the main agency of expansion was the U.S. government, whose strategies of geopolitics propelled the upgrading of the Japanese economy. In the second stage, Japanese business itself became the main agency of expansion, and the catchment area of its subcontracting networks came to encompass the entire East Asian region. In the incipient third stage, it was the Chinese capitalist diaspora that emerged as the leading agency of expansion.

Following Cumings (1987) and Arrighi's (1994) framework, this paper will examine how the three regional projects of the U.S., Japan, and China have shaped the contour of the East Asian states in the second half of the twentieth century. It will focus upon geopolitics and the global production orientation of these three regional projects in East Asia. *Geopolitics* is the study of the strategic value of space in the context of the competing territorial, economic, and political ambitions of states. In this paper, geopolitics refers to a state's strategic location and its role in warfare, inter-state alliance, and national integration in the region. *Global production* refers to the global manufacturing system and commodity chains (Gereffi, 1994; McMichael, 1995). As there is a shift from company-based to global production, export, and marketing networks across different states (Bernard and Ravenhill, 1995), it is no longer a question of whether national firms or nation states have attained industrialization or not. They certainly have. Instead, the critical question is how national firms and nation states could capture a larger share of the value-added production process in global production networks. Unlike the "flying geese" literature (Ozawa, 1993) which points to the technical and harmonious aspects of the value-added process of production networks, this paper emphasizes the politics and struggles over technology, market, labor, and sourcing in the value-added hierarchy.

To begin the discussion, this paper will examine the American regional polarization project in the post-World War II era.

The American Regional Polarization Project: The Primacy of Geopolitics

After World War II, the U.S. replaced Great Britain as the new hegemonic world power, leading to an unprecedented expansion (the upward phase) of capitalist world-economy. In response to the threat of communism, the U.S. developed a regional polarization project in the late 1940s. East Asia was divided into two opposing spheres: (1) A communist bloc composed of mainland China, North Korea, and the Soviet Union. The U.S. attempted to contain the spread of communism in East Asia by sending warships to protect the defeated Nationalist Party in Taiwan, soldiers to fight against the communists in Korea, imposing an economic embargo on mainland China products, and preventing mainland China from gaining a seat in the United Nations. (2) The U.S. designated Japan as a critical element in a U.S.-led East Asian order. Later in the Korean War, South Korea and Taiwan were included in this U.S.-led anti-communist front as well.

In this respect, geopolitical concerns—not profitability in global production—were at the heart of the U.S. regional polarization project. In order to build up a strong anti-communist bloc in the Pacific rim, the U.S. provided economic aid, loans, industrial contracts, and opened its domestic markets to its East Asian allies, while tolerating their continued discrimination against dollar imports. From 1946 to 1977, military and economic aid to South Korea and Taiwan (US$ 18.5 billion) accounted for 10.5% of all American foreign aid, exceeding the totals for all of Africa or Latin America (Bello and Rosenfeld, 1990: 438; Cumings, 1987: 67; Eckert, 1992: 295). The U.S. patronage of capitalist allies and its assault on communist foes in East Asia had a profound impact on the contour of development in this region.

China: Revolutionary Maoism

Intense hostility from the U.S. served to preclude certain developmental options for socialist China. Cut off from contacts with capitalist core states, the Chinese socialist state could not possibly pursue either export-oriented industrialization (due to the closure of Western markets) or import-substitution (due to the economic embargo). Thus socialist China was forced to miss a golden opportunity for achieving ascent during this upward phase of the world-economy.

On the other hand, the Korean War, U.S. economic blockage, and forced withdrawal from the world-economy in the 1950s influenced socialist China to adopt a Leninist model for state building to confront the "imperialist enemies" from without and the "counterrevolutionaries" from within. In addition, the Cold War climate influenced the nascent socialist state to accelerate the processes of militarization in addition to collectivization, nationalization, and heavy industry-led growth strategies (Selden, 1995). Moreover, the Chinese Communist Party (CCP) developed a socialist policy in order to secure mass support. Thus entitlement programs for job security, housing, child care, and pensions were granted to the urban working class, while social programs in education, health care, and welfare became increasingly available to the peasantry. Finally, the CCP put forward an inward looking, "self-reliance" model of development, stressing national autonomy, pride in being a poor country, mass mobilization, and labor-intensive industries. During the Cultural Revolution, the new emphases were on developing rural areas rather than urban areas, and heartland provinces rather than coastal provinces. Some key industries were even relocated from coastal provinces to heartland provinces. By dispersing rural communes and relocating key industries to the heartland provinces, the CCP hoped that it could avoid economic ruin due to external invasions from either capitalist core states or rival socialist states (Naughton, 1991).

If the American regional polarization project placed geopolitical concerns at a higher priority than capitalist profitability, revolutionary Maoism also put "politics in command" in order to mobilize support from the masses. Subsequently, moderate socialist programs, such as market reforms in the early 1960s, were unable to gain a foothold during the Cold War era.

Japan: The Ascent to the Core

When mainland China actively promoted revolutionary socialism in the late 1960s, Japan was quickly transforming into a core state. Between 1945 and 1951,

Japan was under the control of the United States. The overriding political objectives of the American Occupation were demilitarization and democratization. The U.S. asked Japan to pay for wartime damages the latter had inflicted upon other countries, attempted to dissolve the *zaibatsu* (prewar corporate conglomerates), encouraged the formation of labor unions, and carried out land reform in the countryside (Halliday, 1975; Nakamura, 1981).

However, by late 1947, the Americans' reformist zeal began to ebb as the Cold War heated up. In that year, Mao's Liberation Army was gaining ground in China. In 1948, in response to the Soviet blockade of West Berlin, the U.S. carried out a massive airlift. Correspondingly, the objectives of the American Occupation then shifted from punishment to rehabilitation in order to build a strong Japan which could contain the spread of communism in East Asia. Anti-trust reforms of the *zaibatsu* were halted; reparation programs were terminated; and labor militancy and strikes were quickly suppressed. It was this sudden reverse course of U.S. Occupation policies in the late 1940s that laid the foundation for the ascent to the core in Japan (Halliday, 1975).

First, a strong Japan required a strong Japanese state committed to development. The previous empire-building project already laid the foundation of the developmental state in Japan. The reforms imposed by the U.S. during its occupation of Japan further increased the power of the bureaucrats vis-à-vis other political groups, as U.S. reforms helped remove influential politicians, smashed the military, dispossessed the landlords, and crushed the labor movement. Thereafter, the Japanese state was empowered to formulate independent industrial and financial policies to promote development.

In addition, a strong Japan required a robust economy. In order to rebuild the Japanese economy after the damage of WWII, the U.S. opened its huge domestic market for Japanese products and provided aids, loans, and procurement to promote Japanese development. As well, the U.S. government tolerated a closure of the Japanese economy to foreign enterprise, thus providing a crucial breathing space to Japanese corporations to recuperate their World War II wounds. In the 1960s, the U.S. government encouraged South Korea and Taiwan to overcome their nationalist resentment of Japan's colonial past and to open up their doors to Japanese trade and investment. Without U.S.'s pressure, it was doubtful whether South Korea would sign the 1965 Normalization Treaty with Japan against a series of nationalist demonstrations (Kim, 1971).

Furthermore, under such favorable developmental conditions given by the U.S., the Japanese state and corporations were able to develop lifetime employment and the seniority-based wage system in the early postwar period as weapons to divide and rule (Fukui, 1992). The American occupation unleashed the mobilization of militant unions which necessitated such a strategy. In addition, the experience of state intervention and close state-business cooperation during wartime mobilization helped the Ministry of International Trade and Industry (MITI) formulate effective policies in the postwar era. Furthermore, wartime mobilization also left a legacy of a dense network of subcontracting relations between large and small firms in Japan. These Japanese subcontracting networks were far more stable and effective instruments of vertical and horizontal inter-enterprise cooperation than U.S. subcontracting networks.

In sum, blessed by U.S. patronage and drawing upon wartime historical legacies, the Japanese state and corporations seized the opportunities created by the favorable postwar global economy. Similar to Japan, Hong Kong, South Korea, and Taiwan were also blessed by the U.S.'s project of regional polarization.

Hong Kong, South Korea, and Taiwan: Export-Led Industrialization

In Hong Kong, the Chinese Communist Revolution prompted a massive inflow of refugees from China. This particular conjuncture of refugee capital and refugee labor provided the impetus for Hong Kong's export-oriented industrialization in the early 1950s. Intense conflict between socialist China and the capitalist power bloc also explained the lack of political unrest in Hong Kong in the 1950s. As immigrants fleeing from Communist rule, the new Chinese capitalists and working class in Hong Kong tolerated the British monopoly of the colonial state machinery in order to prevent any political instability that would threaten the business environment. Moreover, unions tended to be small and ideologically divided between pro-Communist China and pro-Taiwan factions. The favorable world market situation and lack of domestic class struggle help to explain the liberal, non-interventionist policy of the Hong Kong state. It did not need to militarize itself or promote an anti-communism ideology to justify its colonial rule, nor did it need to involve itself in export industrialization because the Chinese capitalists already gained a head start in exports in the 1950s.

Taiwan and South Korea, too, benefitted from the Cold War geopolitical environment. The U.S. polarization project helped build up a strong authoritarian state in Taiwan and Korea. Military tensions in the East Asian region justified the actions of the Taiwanese and Korean states in building up the military, banning labor unions and strikes, and suspending democratic elections. Moreover, U.S. aid not only helped solve their economic problems in the 1950s, but also presented the states with powerful tools with which to intervene in the economy, enforce compliance in the private sector, and build up a strong military for defense. Furthermore, the Chinese Communist Revolution and the Korean War helped establish anti-communism as a hegemonic ideology to control civilians.

In addition, foreign economic assistance carried great weight in alleviating huge government budget deficits, financing investment, and paying for imports. U.S. Foreign aid to South Korea averaged 9.4% of the GNP, 39.7% of the government budget, 65% of total investment, 70% of imports, and nearly 80% of total fixed capital formation during the period from 1953 to 1961. In Taiwan, U.S. aid financed 95% of its trade deficit in the 1950s; and, through foreign savings, it almost totaled 40% of gross domestic capital formation (Cumings, 1987; Kurian, 1979). Nearly all U.S. aid before 1964 was provided on a grant basis, thus making it possible for South Korea and Taiwan to begin their export-led growth without a backlog of debt. The U.S. was also willing to open its own market to them while tolerating their continued discrimination against dollar exports. Finally, their fledgling electronic industry greatly benefitted from US's orders for military radios and radars during the Vietnam War. In the late 1960s, Vietnam War-related revenues accounted for about 4% of South Korea's GNP and up to 58% of total exports in 1967 (Lie, 1992).

Nevertheless, their industries in the 1960s were the type of "export-platform," consisting of low value-added and labor-intensive assembly of manufactured goods in export-processing zones. Thus researchers in the dependency tradition stressed the constraints of this type of low-valued production on their development possibilities.

The Demise of the U.S. Project in the Early 1970s

The American polarization project radicalized the CCP to pursue the Maoist revolutionary policy of self-reliance and mass mobilization as a development strategy. It contributed to the rise of Japan as a model of development and the growth of export-led industrial strategies in Hong Kong, Taiwan, and South Korea. These three paths of development in East Asia in the 1960s, therefore, owed much to the geopolitics of the U.S. regional polarization project.

However, by the early 1970s, the U.S. project had run its course. There was the end of the radical phase of China's Cultural Revolution; the beginning of U.S. withdrawal from Indochina; and the U.S.-China diplomatic breakthrough which transformed the lines of regional power, paving the way for China's full re-entry to the capitalist world-economy. As the U.S. shifted its strategy from regional polarization to peaceful coexistence, geopolitics also began to play a much lesser role in the U.S.'s policy toward East Asia.

At the same time, the golden era of postwar economic expansion came to an end in the early 1970s. Burdened by a huge military, humiliated by defeat in the Vietnam War, unable to carry out its welfare promises to its citizens, and plagued by growing budget deficits and the decline of its dollars, the U.S. gradually turned into a declining hegemon. As its industrial, commercial, and financial supremacy were increasingly challenged by rival core powers, protectionism was on the rise in the U.S. Many Latin American NIEs slipped into recession by the end of the 1970s due to the downward turn of the world-economy and the closing of the U.S. market. What, then, explains the continual economic growth of the East Asian states?

The Japanese Economic Integration Project: The Primacy of Global Production

Japan adopted a new regional project of *global localization* in the 1970s, which implies that core manufacturing began to be governed by a global outlook with local preference (Hill and Lee, 1994). To maintain global competitiveness, Japanese corporations retained high-value added production processes at home, and developed technology that dramatically increased productivity in their domestic plants. Unlike the American corporations, Japanese corporations transferred not only routine, low value-added production but also some medium value-added production to host countries. Japanese corporations have been found to be more willing than U.S. firms to accept minority equity restrictions, engage in technological cooperation, make loans, and invest in ways compatible with the industrial strategies of the East Asian states.

This is because as Japan's market strength grew during the 1970s, so did its trade surplus with the rest of the world. Japan's trading partners reacted with protective measures, including quotas and tariffs therefore forcing Japan to raise its yen value. Developing countries raised local content requirements. To circumvent trade restrictions, Japanese corporations upgraded their subsidiaries, expanded their production facilities and encouraged more of their suppliers to go offshore.

In addition, as a result of rapid economic growth, intense inter-enterprise competition and rising wages, Japan's wages were no longer cheap by the standard of advanced industrial countries. The oil shock and the sharp rise of the yen in the 1970s and 1980s further led to a rapid increase in the costs of production in Japan. These economic pressures prompted Japanese corporations to engage in a transborder expansion into developing countries.

Subsequently, a new "flying geese" ideology emerged (Hill and Fujita, 1995). In this model, Japan played the lead position in the East Asian region because it had the most advanced level of technological sophistication. Ranked behind Japan in a spreading "V" of decreasing levels of technical sophistication were first the NIEs (Hong Kong, Singapore, South Korea, and Taiwan) and then the Southeast Asian states (Malaysia, Thailand, Indonesia, and the Philippines). The "geese" behind Japan would learn from the progress of those up ahead and eventually close the technological gap. This model predicted that the NIEs would follow the Japanese pattern, while the Southeast Asian states would follow the NIEs. As a result, every player could supposedly improve its position in following the Japanese leadership in East Asia. The impact of this Japanese regional integration project on the further development of Taiwan, South Korea, Hong Kong, and mainland China has been outstanding.

Hong Kong, South Korea, and Taiwan: Upgrading to the NIEs
What Japanese capital was seeking were locations close at hand with efficient, cheap, flexible labor supplies, and with maximally privileged an access to the United

States and other core markets. From this viewpoint, Japan's former colonies of South Korea and Taiwan, which had as privileged an access to the U.S. domestic market as did Japan, and the city-states of Singapore and Hong Kong, were good locations.

The first wave of the Japanese transborder expansion in the 1970s consisted of mostly traditional, labor-intensive industries (such as textile, apparel, and footwear) that relied on low wages and an unskilled workforce in the export processing zones. However, Gereffi (1992) observes that there was a very pronounced shift in the 1980s toward an upgraded, skill-intensive version of export-led industrialization in the East Asian NIEs. These new export industries included higher value-added items that employed sophisticated technology and required a more extensively developed, tightly integrated local industrial base. Products ranged from computers and semiconductors to numerically controlled machine tools, automobiles, televisions, videocassette recorders, and sporting goods. This export dynamism in East Asia did not derive solely from introducing new products, but also from continuously upgrading traditional ones. The upgrading of the East Asian NIEs can be seen in the case of Hyundai, the South Korea automaker. Hyundai, after forming an alliance with Japan's Mitsubishi Motors, was able to manufacture the Pony Excel and the Sonata automobiles and export both cars to the U.S. (Hill and Lee, 1994).

The transfer of some medium value-added production processes from Japan to the NIEs is explained by Japan's lack of a strong military, and the lingering suspicions that remain from WWII that other Asian states view the prospects of Japanese regional political dominance with alarm. As a Japanese transnational executive explains, "We don't have military power. There is no way for Japanese businessmen to influence policy decisions of other countries" (Friedland, 1994: 42). Subsequently, Japanese corporations had to engage in hard bargaining with the strong states and corporations in the East Asian NIEs. For example, Taiwan and South Korea's states set ceilings on foreign ownership, demanded local production for domestic markets, technology transfer, and research and development sharing through joint-ventures. Competition among Japanese and U.S. corporations, saturated demand in the U.S., growing trade barriers in the core states, and the rising incomes of East Asian states made East Asian markets highly attractive to Japanese corporations.

What resulted was the formation of a East Asian regional production network based not just on product cycles but also on a value-added hierarchy. Technology tie-ups between Japan, South Korea, and Taiwan are becoming more common; local sourcing of components are more frequent due to the high value of the yen; and Japanese auto assemblers and suppliers have been yielding market-entry niches to South Korea and Taiwan.

China: Shift to Market Socialism

While the East Asian NIEs experienced robust economic development in the 1970s, socialist China experienced economic stagnation. Its economic productivity reached a plateau and could not be raised anymore through mass mobilization; its industrial technology was outdated, its industrial bureaucracy ossified, and its state workers were not motivated to work hard. China also faced very serious unemployment problems, as its population doubled from around 500 million in 1953 to 1,000 million in 1980.

Consequently, when the U.S. terminated its polarization project and welcomed China back to the capitalist world-economy, and when the old revolutionary generation passed away in the mid-1970s, the leaders in the CCP replaced revolutionary Maoism with market socialism. First of all, the CCP tried to bring market forces back in. In the countryside, communes were gradually dismantled. Peasant families were given plots of land to cultivate, and they were responsible for their own gains and losses. They were also encouraged to sell their products to rural markets and seek work in nearby township enterprises. In the cities, urban youth were encouraged to engage in petty trading and industrial activities, while state and collective enterprises were asked to contract out their unprofitable operations to small private enterprises.

Then the CCP developed an open-door policy toward foreign investment through the establishment of special economic zones (SEZs) and the opening of coastal cities and delta areas. The CCP wanted to attract large-scale, high-tech, capital investment from the U.S. and Japanese corporations. The preferred form of operation was a "joint-venture" between the mainland Chinese government and the transnationals, so that Chinese managers could acquire advanced technology, Western management know-how, and information on world-market conditions from their foreign partners. It was hoped that these joint-venture projects would invigorate aging state enterprises, raise industrial production to levels comparable to those of core states, help Chinese industries to break into the world-market, and earn the needed foreign currency through export-industrialization.

In order to attract foreign investment, special privileges such as cheap factory sites, low rates of taxation, low wages, and tariff exemptions were granted to the transnationals. However, this open-door policy failed to achieve its goals of attracting high-tech capital investments from transnationals. This was due to frequent complaints about unnecessary regulations and bureaucratic red tape, operational problems, including rigid labor laws, difficulties in getting reliable supplies of high quality raw materials, lack of enterprise autonomy, and an inability to remit foreign currency profits out of China and the closed Chinese market.

Extending the Japanese Project in the Late 1980s

In the early 1970s a Japanese regional integration project in East Asia followed the U.S.'s hegemonic decline. Japanese corporations transferred some medium value-added production processes to Japan's East Asian neighbors, leading to the latter's industrial upgrading and advancement in value-added hierarchy. Gaining an East

Asian hinterland, in turn, strengthened Japan's export and financial power, enabling it to become a global economic power. Japan is now the center of international trade in East Asia, overshadowing the U.S. Japan's huge trade surpluses and its yen appreciation in the 1980s made it the largest source of new foreign direct investment there. The "demonstration effect" of Japan and the East Asian NIEs, in turn, lured mainland China to open its door to foreign investment and to pursue market socialism in order to promote economic development. In East Asia, the transformations to global economic power, the NIEs, and market socialism in the 1980s were therefore highly related to the Japanese regional integration project.

However, by the late 1980s, the Japanese East Asian project had run its course. As Hong Kong, South Korea, and Taiwan were upgraded to the status of NIEs, they gradually lost their geopolitical privileges with the U.S. They, too, had to face the trade restrictions (tariffs, quotas, rising foreign currency value) that the U.S. had imposed upon Japan earlier. Furthermore, as a result of their economic success, there were labor shortages, increasing labor disputes, escalating land prices, and the emergence of environmental protests—all of which served to raise the cost of production in the East Asian NIEs.

In the late 1980s, in order to secure a stable supply of a cheap, docile labor force, Japan extended its regional project from East Asia to the ASEAN states (Thailand, the Philippines, Indonesia, and Malaysia). The NIEs quickly followed suit in the late 1980s. What resulted was a complicated division of labor management, marketing, and production across different states in East and Southeast Asia.

This complicated multi-regional production network can be seen in the case of Jinbao, a calculator-producing factory in Thailand (Bernard and Ravenhill, 1995). In Jinbao, the innovation, product's brand name, and marketing are Japanese. All key components are imported from Japan. All procurement and administration are controlled from Taipei, and plant management is Taiwanese. The labor is Thai. Plant output is exclusively for export. In international trade data, Jinbao's production is recorded as Thai exports of electronic goods. To purchasers at the other end the products appear to be Japanese. The direct foreign investment statistics indicate a Taiwanese investment. The ASEAN's experience did prompt mainland China to initiate a new national reunification project to promote development.

The Chinese Reunification Project: Balancing Geopolitics and Global Production

Unlike the geopolitical-oriented American project and the global production-oriented Japanese project, the Chinese project is oriented toward both geopolitics and global production.

Since the open-door policy could not achieve its goal, mainland China in 1988 proposed a national reunification project to encourage Hong Kong and Taiwanese investment in Guangdong, Fujian, and other coastal provinces. This coastal-development strategy had the following characteristics. First, instead of appealing to U.S. and Japanese investors, the coastal-development strategy was targeted at investors from Taiwan and Hong Kong. Second, instead of aiming to attract large-scale investments from the transnationals, the strategy was targeted at small investment projects from the small and medium size firms in Taiwan and Hong Kong. Third, instead of demanding high-tech, capital-intensive investment and the utilization of local materials, the strategy allowed investment in labor-intensive industries which relied solely on raw material imports. Assembly-line industries would help solve the serious unemployment problem, and foreign raw-material imports would help ease the shortage of raw materials in mainland markets. Fourth, instead of encouraging joint-venture contracts, the present strategy preferred wholly-owned foreign investment because of capital shortages. In short, through the coastal-development strategy, mainland China declared that it was willing to enter global production network at the low value-added level, just like the ASEAN states.

Nevertheless, the national reunification project also had a geopolitical orientation. For the old generation of CCP leaders, national reunification was perceived as a historical mission which they were duty-bound to accomplish in their lifetime. In the 1980s, the CCP formulated a "One Country, Two Systems" model for reunification. In this model, the capitalist economies and lifestyles of Hong Kong and Taiwan would remain unchanged after national reunification with the socialist mainland. As special administrative regions (SARs) of the mainland, the Hong Kong and Taiwan governments would have a high degree of autonomy and self-governance. For Taiwan, the KMT would even be allowed to retain its military forces and conduct an independent foreign policy.

The national reunification project, therefore, had both global production and geopolitics orientations. On the one hand, the CCP was willing to act like a periphery in order to attract Taiwan and Hong Kong investment in low value-added, labor-intensive industries. The CCP officials showed flexibility in enforcing labor practices, foreign currency policies, and tariffs towards their Hong Kongese and Taiwanese compatriots because these favors can be legitimized through appeals for national unification. If the same favors were granted to Western businessmen, the officials would be condemned for betraying national interests! On the other hand, the CCP acted as a core power in pushing for political unification with Hong Kong and Taiwan. The CCP hoped that increasing economic integration with Hong Kong and Taiwan would strengthen their dependence on the mainland's labor, natural resources, and markets, by which a vested interest group within their civil societies could be developed that would push their states towards political unification.

Hong Kong, South Korea, and Taiwan: Consolidating NIE Status

Hong Kong corporations were the first to respond to the Chinese project. By 1990, over 60% of all DFI in mainland China were from Hong Kong, which amounted to US$ 10 billion out of a total of US$ 16 billion in actual investment. Hong Kong investment was concentrated in the nearby Guangdong province in the Pearl River Delta and took the form of "outward processing" through which the Hong Kong investor supplies the machinery, material, technology, product design, and marketing services, while the Chinese partner provides the plant, labor, water, electricity and other basic facilities, and assembles the product according to Hong Kong design. The Hong Kong investor pays the Chinese partner a "processing fee" which covers workers' wages and the above-mentioned expenses incurred on the Chinese side. By the early 1990s, Hong Kong firms employed more than 3 million workers in Guangdong, about six times more than these firms employed in the colony itself.

What is more, Hong Kong has been turned into a service center for mainland China. Hong Kong was developed as a facilitator or intermediary for mainland trades and investment, providing China with valuable information channels and, serving as a contact point for its trade. Also it finances China's modernization, and acts as a conduit for technology transfer, providing a training ground where China can learn and practice capitalist skills in a market environment.

In the late 1980s, Taiwan's mainland investment also increased rapidly from US$ 100 million in 1987 to US$ 4 billion by mid-1992. Similar to Hong Kong's investment, Taiwan's mainland investment exhibited the following characteristics. First, with respect to locale, most Taiwanese investment has been in Guangdong and Fujian—the two mainland provinces closest to Taiwan. Second, investors came mostly from small and medium enterprises. Third, it is estimated that 70% of Taiwanese investment was sole ownership enterprises rather than joint ventures with mainland companies. Finally, most investment is in such labor-intensive industries as shoemaking, plastic products, and textiles. Mainland investment enhanced the economic competitiveness of Taiwanese corporations in the global market because it provided them with cheap labor, resources, and investment opportunities.

However, mainland economic integration also complicated the geopolitics of Hong Kong and Taiwan. In Hong Kong, the deepening of borderland integration finally led to the national reunification with mainland China in 1997. Since the mid-1980s, Beijing's intrusion into Hong Kong politics complicated the colony's democratic transition, and political alienation and emigration grew to be prevalent among Hong Kong's new middle-class professionals. In Taiwan, the prospect of political reunification deepened the division between the Guomindang and the Democratic Progressive Party. Both parties watch each other closely to ensure that the other does not to go too far in its campaigns for unification or independence. Aware of their less than equal bargaining position with Beijing, the Taiwan government has been unwilling to enter into any political negotiations.

Japan and South Korea: Following the Bandwagon

Since the late 1980s, South Korean corporations started to invest in mainland China. Like their Hong Kong and Taiwan counterparts, their investments tended to be in labor-intensive projects such as toys, sporting goods, and daily consumer items. Nevertheless, due to geographical proximity, Korean investment is now concentrated in North China's Yellow Sea Economic Zone, especially around Liaoning and Shandong provinces.

Although Japan's investment in China was behind that of Hong Kong and Taiwan, it returned to China much more quickly than other investors in the wake of the Tiananmen Incident in June 1989. By 1990 Japan had invested $2.5 billion in 691 projects. However, Selden (1995) notes that only 17% of this investment was in manufacturing, far below the 38% of Japanese investment in Asia as a whole. As others far surpass Japan's foreign investment in China, it is clear that the Japanese preference is to foster trade relations and provide loans and technology in selected areas (steel and oil technology, for example, but not cutting edge technology in microelectronics and biotechnology).

Without its rationale for national reunification, mainland China is not willing to accommodate the demands of the Japanese and South Korean corporations as it did towards Hong Kongese and Taiwanese corporations. Thus, complaints from Japanese and Korean corporations about a rigid labor market, too many bureaucratic rules and regulations, and poor raw materials supply are common. No matter how fast Japanese investment grew thereafter, it seemed to follow rather than lead the boom of foreign investment in China.

The Prospect for the Chinese Reunification Project

To recapitulate, since the open-door policy of mainland China failed to attract high-tech investment from the Japanese and U.S., mainland China put up a national reunification project to attract labor-intensive investment from small and medium firms in Taiwan and Hong Kong.

On the one hand, the Chinese national reunification project may be endangered by the conflict over global production and geopolitics. Since China's trade surplus with the U.S. has kept increasing, the U.S. will soon likely set up trade regulations for mainland China, as it did with the East Asian NIEs a few years back. Without the patronage of the U.S. market, mainland China would lose its attractiveness to NIE's' investors. In addition, as mainland China presses for political unification, it may create political instability and economic downturns in Taiwan and Hong Kong. Subsequently, geopolitical rivalry may threaten the prospect for stronger economic integration among the three Chinese states.

On the other hand, there seems to be a bright future for the Chinese national reunification project. Chen (1993) points out that overseas Chinese investments contributed to mainland development by providing employment opportunities, market stimuli to local enterprises, and vital information and contacts for reentering the world-market. Furthermore, state managers of mainland China successfully developed close business partnerships with the capitalists of Hong Kong and Taiwan, and this "unholy alliance" will most likely continue into the next century.

In this respect, although the prospect for national unification promoted political rivalry among mainland China, Taiwan, and Hong Kong, their economic integration worked very well in promoting their industrialization and increasing their competitive power in the global market. Subsequently, the entire East Asian region has become an epicenter of capitalist accumulation for the world-economy in the 1990s.

Conclusion

This paper argues that an examination into the geopolitics of the American polarization project in the 1950s and the 1960s, the Japanese economic integration project in the 1970s and the 1980s, and mainland China's national reunification project in the 1980s and the 1990s will help in understanding some of the puzzles of why Japan emerged from a core to a global economic power, why China shifted from revolutionary Maoism to market socialism, why Hong Kong, South Korea, and Taiwan were upgraded to the status of NIEs, and why the entire East Asian region has become an epicenter of capitalist accumulation for the global economy in the 1990s.

The above discussion points to the significance of the interplay between geopolitics and global production in the East Asian region. On the one hand, there is the regionalization of global dynamics, as regions are the condensation of contradictions and opportunities embodied in the world-economy. In the post WWII-era, the upward phase of the world-economy, the Cold War, and global U.S. hegemony appeared in East Asia as the American regional polarization project, assaulting China while patronizing Japan, Hong Kong, South Korea, and Taiwan. In the 1980s, a global commodity chain was embedded in the hierarchial Japanese production network in East Asia, with Japan monopolizing high-tech while transferring medium value-added processes to Hong Kong, Taiwan, and South Korea and low value-added processes to mainland China.

On the other hand, there is the nationalization of regional dynamics, as the latter works through national structure and became internalized in domestic political economy. At the height of the Cold War in the 1960s, intense military tension in East Asia prompted Chinese mass mobilization during the Cultural Revolution, paternalistic industrial relations in Japan's *Zaibatsu*, and authoritarian states and repressive labor laws in South Korea and Taiwan. When global production became the focus of the East Asian region in the 1980s, South Korean and Taiwanese states tried their best to safeguard their own markets, and Hong Kong capitalists actively sought mainland China's support to relocate their labor-intensive production processes across the border.

The above regional analysis, needless to say, is not aimed at refuting entirely the current economic, cultural, and statist literature on East Asian development. Obviously, markets and private enterprises, Confucian cultural practices, and the developmental state are important factors in East Asian development. What this paper hopes to contribute, however, is the often-neglected interplay between geopolitics and global production forces in the shaping of the origins and transformation of the East Asian economic phenomenon in the second half of the twentieth century.

REFERENCES

AMSDEN, Alice
    1989 *Asia's Next Giant.* New York: Oxford.
ARRIGHI, Giovanni
    1994 "The Rise of East Asia: World-system and Regional Aspects." Paper prepared for the conference "L'economia mondiale in transformazione," Rome, Oct. 6-8.
BALASSA, Bela
    1988 "The Lessons of East Asian Development: An Overview." *Economic Development and Cultural Change* 36 (3rd supplement), S273-S290.
BELLO, Walden and Stephanie ROSENFELD
    1990 "Dragons in Distress." *World Policy Journal* 7, 431-468.
BERNARD, Mitchell and John RAVENHILL
    1995 "Beyond Product Cycles and Flying Geese." *World Politics* 47, 171-209.
CHEN, Edward
    1993 "Foreign Direct Investment in East Asia." *Asian Development Review* 11, 24-59.
CUMINGS, Bruce
    1987 "The Origins and Development of the Northeast Asian Political Economy." Pp. 44-83 in *The Political Economy of the New Asian Industrialism*, Frederic Deyo (Ed.). Ithaca: Cornell University Press.
ECKERT, Carter J.
    1992 "Korea's Economic Development in Historical Perspective, 1945-1990." Pp. 289-308 in *Pacific Century*, Mark Borthwick (Ed.). Boulder: Westview.
FRIEDLAND, Jonathan
    1994 "The Regional Challenge." *Far Eastern Economic Review* June 9, 40-42.
FUKUI, Haruhiro
    1992 "The Japanese State and Economic Development." Pp. 199-226 in *States and Development in the Asian Pacific Rim*, Richard P. Appelbaum and Jeffrey Henderson (Eds.). Newbury Park: Sage.
GEREFFI, Gary
    1992 "New Realities of Industrial Development in East Asia and Latin America." Pp. 85-112 in *State and Development in the Asian-Pacific Rim*, Richard Appelbaum and Jeffrey Henderson (Eds.). Newbury Park: Sage.
GEREFFI, Gary
    1994 "Capitalism, Development and Global Commodity Chains." Pp. 211-231 in *Capitalism and Development*, L. Sklair (Ed.). London: Routledge.
HALLIDAY, Jon
    1975 *A Political History of Japanese Capitalism.* New York: Pantheon Books.

HILL, Richard Child and Yong Joo LEE
1994 "Japanese Multinationals and East Asian Development." Pp. 289-315 in *Capitalism and Development*, Leslie Sklair (Ed.). London: Routledge.

HILL, Richard Child and Kuniko FUJITA
1995 "Product Cycles and International Divisions of Labor." Pp. 91-108 in *A New World Order? Global Transformation in the Late Twentieth Century*, David A. Smith and Jozsef Borocz (Eds.). Westport: Praeger.

KIM, Kwang Bong
1971 *The Korea-Japan Treaty Crisis and the Instability of the Korean Political System*. New York: Praeger.

KURIAN, George
1979 *The Book of World Rankings*. New York: Facts on File Inc.

LIE, John
1992 "The Political Economy of South Korean Development." *International Sociology* 7, 285-300.

MCMICHAEL, Philip
1995 *Development and Social Change*. Thousand Oaks: Pine Forge Press.

NAKAMURA, Takafusa
1981 *The Postwar Japanese Economy*. Tokyo: University of Tokyo Press.

NAUGHTON, Barry
1991 "Industrial Policy during the Cultural Revolution." Pp. 153–182 in *New Perspectives on the Cultural Revolution*, William A. Joseph, Christine Wong, and David Zweig (Eds.). Cambridge: The Council on East Asian Studies.

OZAWA, Terutomo
1993 "Foreign Direct Investment and Structural Transformation." *Business and the Contemporary World* 5 (2), 129-150.

SELDEN, Mark
1995 "China, Japan, and the Regional Political Economy of East Asia, 1945-1995." Paper presented to the Japan in Asia Workshop, Cornell University, March 31.

ROZMAN, Gilbert
1992 "The Confucian Faces of Capitalism." Pp. 310-318 in *Pacific Century*, Mark Borthwick (Ed.). Boulder: Westview Press.

Emerging Global Environmental Standards
Prospects and Perils[1]

J. TIMMONS ROBERTS*

ABSTRACT

Increasing economic and political integration has positive and negative environmental implications. On the positive side, globalization is driving some internationalization of environmental regulations and performance, through environmental treaties, side agreements for economic integration treaties, uniform practices within transnational corporations, and in international "green labeling" or standards schemes such as ISO 14000 and BS7750. However it appears unlikely that these will reach far beyond the large-scale and export sectors (about 25-50% of the economy). Further, environmental protection is often threatened by diminished regulatory capacity of states facing austerity programs, and can be undermined by the cutthroat international competition engendered by globalization.

Introduction

DOES THE INCREASING integration of the global economy through trade bode well or poorly for the protection of the environment and for health and safety precautions in workplaces? Are firms fleeing to unregulated "pollution havens" either in poor regions of the U.S. and Europe or to poorer "developing" nations (see, e.g., Covello and Frey, 1990; Kazis and Grossman, 1992)? Do the pressures of these unregulated sites for industry drive down the ability of all locations, whether in rich or poor nations, to regulate their industries? Will trade treaties such as the General Agreement on Tariffs and Trade (GATT) make it impossible for nations to enforce higher environmental and health standards because they are seen as protectionist? Or will new global environmental standards and international treaties emerge which push industry to higher levels of protection?

As corporations "go global," many argue, so must environmental protection laws and enforcement mechanisms. This paper seeks to lay out what's currently

* Department of Sociology/Program in Latin American Studies, Tulane University, New Orleans, LA 70118, U.S.A.

at stake and some of the major forces on the sides of increasing exploitation or protection of workers and the environment in the globalizing economy. I first review briefly the processes by which nations are being more tightly connected to the world economy. I then go on to examine three types of international standards which influence environmental (and worker) protections: trade treaties and their side agreements; environmental treaties; and finally industry-led initiatives to develop international standards. Since I have discussed the first two elements more fully elsewhere (Roberts, 1996a; 1996b), I review those briefly while focusing here on the third: Environmental, Health and Safety (EHS) management guidelines being developed by international industry groups. These new international environmental standards or "green labels" have the potential to revolutionize environmental regulations and compliance by polluters around the world. They include the British Standards Institute's BS7750 series of environmental certifications, the International Standards Organization's ISO 14000 and ISO 20000 standards, and single-industry voluntary programs such as the Chemical Manufacturers of America's "Responsible Care" Initiative. As an illustrative case study of industry initiatives on the environment, in Section Five I examine briefly the case of the rapidly restructuring oil and chemical products industry, focusing on the U.S., Mexico, and Brazil.

At the outset I would first like to acknowledge the complexity of this issue and the difficulty in predicting where efforts to develop global environmental standards are heading. Second, we must recognize that the effects of increasing economic and political global integration on worker safety and the environment will vary sharply in comparatively wealthy and poorer nations. Further, the effects of global restructuring on workers and the environment are being felt in different ways by workers in different sectors of a single country's economy. However, recognizing stratification in wealth and power among and within nations can move us towards developing a dynamic understanding of who will be likely to develop and enforce global environmental and labor standards, and who probably will refute and ignore them. This raises crucial policy implications for planning by national, local and international environmental enforcement agencies and activists.

The questions underlying this research, then, are three. Can the impacts of increasing export production by "developing" nations be mitigated by the growing number of international treaties and business initiatives on the environment? What forces generate pressures to protect the environment, and how durable and significant are they? How serious are firms about environmental protection and worker health and safety in their push for "green labels?" What barriers keep some firms from adopting these measures? I believe that the initial responses by firms to the emerging global environmental standards will have critical implications for their long-term acceptance and effectiveness.

Global Economic Restructuring and the Environment

The rash of factory closings in wealthy nations and the growth of manufacturing in Third World nations since 1970 raised awareness worldwide that a major economic shift is occuring. While I obviously cannot detail those changes here, I would summarize them in three trends (see Roberts, 1996b). First, a "New International Division of Labor" is emerging wherein wealthier nations are now specializing in design, high-tech and services while poorer nations are gaining an increasing share of low-skilled assembly and manufacturing jobs (e.g., Frobel et al., 1980; Dicken, 1992; Korzeniewicz and Martin, 1995). Second, much of this expansion of production in the poorer "peripheral" nations is due to investments by transnational corporations, headquarted mostly in the USA, Japan and Europe (the core nations, in World-Systems Theory parlance). Another segment of new industries in the periphery were firms established by the governments of those nations in an attempt to replace products they once imported or to increase their exports (Gereffi, 1989; etc.). Many of these projects were finance by massive loans from development agencies such as the World Bank and from many private core-headquartered banks who were looking for borrowers who would pay higher interest rates (McMichael, 1996). Locally-owned production units are increasingly linked by relations of subcontracting and marketing "commodity chains," whereby a Third World-owned firm produces something to specifications sent by core-based companies who put their label on it (Gereffi and Korzeniewitz, 1994). As we will see below, this is an important way core consumers might influence environmental practices by firms around the world. The third and final major trend in restructuring is that the 1980s and 1990s have brought waves of "free trade" and privatization ideology across the world. These have intensified the rate at which nations are becoming linked to the world economy. As we approach the end of the century, it appears that the rises and falls in economies of nations in all regions of the planet are woven into one global economy (Chase-Dunn and Grimes, 1995).

Is increased trade likely to worsen environmental conditions and work conditions around the world or improve them? Several experts and activists have argued that increasing integration into world trade networks might increase countries' GNPs but that it will drive down labor and environmental protections. This argument is based on the view that firms can simply move to another nation if they are bothered by the laws, unions or citizen of the one in which they are operating. This "footloose capital" conception sees cities, regions and nations bargaining down regulations and taxes in their eagerness to draw companies and retain them in the face of threatened relocations. If capital is truly mobile and environmental and labor protections (including wages) are important parts of the costs of their doing business, then capital can indeed use this advantage in a time when so many nations are desperate for investors. However, the avoidance of taxes and regulations undermines local conditions and the ability of those very states to enforce laws and provide services which might buffer the effects of a few factories (Barkin, 1995). Further, increasing openness to trade is likely to intensify precisely the *type* of growth which is driven by foreign productive technologies and brings with it unsustainable imported consumption values (e.g., Serbin et al., 1993; Barkin, 1995).

Elsewhere I argue that in most cases, if trade does in fact increase economic growth, that growth will lead to immediate environmental damages of many types (Roberts 1996b). Many pollutants have been seen to increase in concentration in direct proportion with level of development (e.g., CO2, nitrogen oxides, municipal waste).[2] The relation for carbon dioxide emissions has borne out with very few exceptions in world history, and as "development" has proceeded over the last 200 years it appears that each increment in economic growth has brought with it greater accumulation of carbon in the atmosphere (Grimes and Roberts, 1995).

However, the environmental damage which results from the growth in trade and of the world product will depend on the efficiency and cleanliness of the technology applied by companies in production. Of course, it will depend on the extent to which greater income translates into more unsustainable consumption patterns like those those of the core nations. On the side of globalization increasing environmental consciousness of firms, pressure by consumers in search of "green products" has grown tremendously in the last decade, and the effort to establish "green labeling" is especially strong in Europe. Many observers hope that together these movements could pressure firms to choose to install cleaner technologies and only to buy from "environmentally-friendly" suppliers. At the same time, increasing global links of support and communication between environmentalists around the world are forcing companies to realize that they cannot commit atrocities in the Third World without much negative publicity quickly reaching the core wealthy nations (Roberts, 1996b). Internationalization has strengthened the position of Latin American environmental movements, for example, by providing them this new leverage *vis-à-vis* transnational corporations and their states (Roberts, 1996b; Christen et al., 1998). I return to these points later, but for now suffice to say that the patterns of economic restructuring have developed partly in response to social pressures from workers, environmentalists and citizens more broadly. I turn now to the first emerging type of international environmental standards: international treaties.

International Environmental Treaties

Since the 1960s there has been a growing awareness that many environmental problems cannot be solved by unilateral actions within one nation. Pollutants spread across artificial political boundaries, and increasingly we understand that they spread around the globe. A series of environmental treaties have been promulgated over the past three decades, from those on nuclear testing and ocean pollution to CFC emissions, global warming and biodiversity. Do these pacts have the potential to create globally standardized environmental controls which will eliminate the ability of firms to escape regulations?

There are several types of international environmental agreements, each with different implications for their durability and enforcement (see, e.g., Young, 1982; 1989; 1994). First of all, binational agreements attempt to resolve disputes such as transboundary air or water pollutants between neighboring countries. They begin as local matters, but have often provided frameworks for the initial discussion of issues which later are incorporated into wider regional and global pacts. Second, multilateral environmental treaties such as those on ozone protection, endangered species and nuclear testing attempt to create a consensus among the largest possible number of nations on issues considered most critical to our survival. Since so many environmental issues are global in scope (either in systemic or cumulative ways: see Stern et al., 1992), solving them requires a majority of nations to sign. While these treaties are normally proposed and drafted by core nations, Third World nations have certain bargaining power since they can threaten to deny drafters the consensus they see as necessary for their success (Miller, 1995a; 1995b; Young, 1994).

Which nations tend to sign and which to ignore these environmental treaties? Worldwide there is a strong positive relation between a country's wealth and power (in world trading and political systems) and the likelihood that it had signed the nine major environmental treaties put forward during the 1963-1987 period (Roberts, 1996a).[3] Several other factors were seen to also predict environmental treaty-signing by nations: levels of foreign investment had a positive impact while debt service, dependence on one trading partner, regime repressiveness and military spending all had significant negative impacts. These latter findings suggest that the reach of any treaties will vary by country, especially in whether that nation has a repressive government or is highly dependent economically on other nations.

Some commentators rightfully point out that the actual importance of these treaties is unclear since many countries sign and then proceed to flaunt them, and because their enforcement and dispute resolution mechanisms are often weak (see, e.g., Biggs, 1993). We must consider as well that even possessing the political will, many governments may in fact not be *able* to effectively enforce protection of their environments, especially in the face of recent efforts to "shrink the state" (Roberts, 1996b).

Thirdly, the explosion of *free trade* agreements such as the EEC, NAFTA, Mercosul and the Asian trade pacts must be considered. They bring with them both greater environmental perils and some new leverage for enforcing protection. For example, the environmental and labor side agreement to the North American Free Trade Agreement (NAFTA) includes explicit directives towards the "harmonization" of environmental protection in Canada, the U.S. and Mexico. In the years leading

up to its taking effect January 1, 1994 and in the period since, Mexico has substantially increased regulations, spending and enforcement of environmental laws.
A considerable official oversight structure is being formed along the border and in
Washington, Mexico City and Ottowa which combines government officials, aca-
demics and activists.[4] The success and durability of these efforts remains to be seen,
especially as national and international attention shifts elsewhere.

The EEC treaties have paid the most attention to harmonizing environmental
and labor codes between its nations. While weaker, the NAFTA treaty is environmentally the best agreement drafted so far in this hemisphere, and between countries
at such disparate levels of national wealth. Negotiations for other economic integration treaties have often raised environmental issues but have seldom incorporated
protections in formal mechanisms. The General Agreement on Tarriffs and Trade
(GATT) is in many ways the worst of all treaties for environmentalism since it prohibits nations from excluding imports because of environmental considerations on
how they were produced (Biggs, 1993). This approach, however, answers a fear of
some peripheral nations that environmental restrictions on imports will become a
new camouflage for protectionism of core markets (e.g., Alsogaray, 1993; Ominami,
1993).

One addendum to this section is the role of multilateral lending agencies in
changing patterns of development and environmentalism. Since the end of World
War II, the World Bank for Reconstruction and Development (The World Bank) has
providing low-interest loans and key guarantees for other lenders who support states
and other borrowers in the Third World. Many of these loans went for megaprojects
which were responsible for some of the greatest ecological disasters in history,
including enormous dams, mines, railroads and colonization and ranching projects on
indigenous land in unbroken rainforests. Beginning about 1980, indigenous peoples
and local and international environmentalists and human rights activists protested
these projects, targeting the international press, the United States Congress, and
other lenders such as the European Economic Community and the Interamerican
Development Bank (Swartzmann, 1989). Since 1985 the evaluation components
of World Bank loans have pressured some states to more actively enforce *some*
environmental laws and even to expand their areas under preservation.

At the same time, the massive outstanding debts of many Third World nations
have driven them to accept the conditions of "structural adjustment" loans, which
require them to cut government spending and take other drastic steps to control
inflation (e.g., World Bank, 1995; Rosen and McFadden, 1995). Sharp government
cutbacks can undercut environmental protection efforts by weakening already scant
enforcement efforts and by increasing at least short-term desperation of those slipping
through already-torn social safety nets (Barkin, 1995). I return to this issue below,
but the point can be made here that the leverage which foreign debt provides other
nations over Third World states can have both negative and positive influences on

environmental protection. Even in the positive case, however, such protection may be resented by locals as excessively "top-down" or an infringement on national sovereignty, and an unrealistic, even inhumane luxury in times of desperation.

"Green Labeling" and the ISO 14000 Standards

Finally, I will take the balance of this article to explore more thoroughly efforts by businesses to develop their own environmental standards and labeling. In July, 1996, a new set of globally-uniform environmental standards for industries were finalized by the International Organization for Standardization (ISO). The emergence of these standards (called the ISO 14000 series) has been touted by some authors as marking the beginning of a new "proactive" era, wherein firms continuously move towards pollution *prevention* rather than simply reacting to government regulations by installing scrubbers and filters and funding expensive cleanup procedures. What may be surprising is that efforts to create some types of green labels called global environmental standards are being developed largely by the industries themselves.

Why are industries pushing green labeling? Understanding the drive for the ISO 14000 standards by industries requires a bit of background. Facing criticism from environmental groups, concerned citizens, and state and international agencies, in the 1970s corporations' environmental initiatives initially consisted mostly of direct abatement such as installing pollution control equipment and reorganizing production procedures to reduce emissions. These efforts were usually in direct response to government regulations or the threat of such regulation. More recently, however, as firms felt they were getting little credit in the public eye for very substantial expenditures, in the 1980s these efforts were expanded to include a new series of initiatives such as setting up of nature preserves, supporting local environmental groups and institutions, and orchestrating very visible environmental education programs. These programs are sometimes called "greenwashing" by critics, especially environmentalists (Greer and Bruno, 1997).

In the 1990s, corporations around the world are increasingly facing demands by consumers for products which are certified to have been produced in an ecologically sound manner. These pressures have led to a series of some thirty different "green labeling" schemes being instituted in thirty different nations around the world (West, 1995). Meanwhile, trade groups in many nations have created industry-wide standards and codes of practice of their own, such as the chemical industry's "Responsible Care" Initiative, the automobile industry's "Automotive Pollution Prevention Program," and textile manufacturers' "Encouraging Environmental Excellence" (Hoffman, 1995; Roberts and Hunter, 1995). In an era of increasing free trade and global production and marketing, this is becoming many firms' worst nightmare: the need to be certified in dozens of countries under drastically different green labeling systems and industry programs.

As a response, industries have turned to the International Organization for Standardization (ISO), an industry/U.N. agency, to create one set of global environmental certifications. Being finalized as this is being written, the ISO 14000 environmental certifications are just now being instituted by the first firms. ISO standards are different from many other green labeling schemes because they are *process*, not performance standards. That is, they do not tell companies specifically what environmental performance or levels of emissions they must achieve [see below for more details]. "Instead, it offers companies the building blocks for a system that will help them achieve their own goals" (Tibor and Feldman, 1995).

Efforts by businesses to develop their own environmental standards and green labels cannot be as quickly written off as many critics would have it. First of all, there is a surprisingly large and growing market for green products. An OECD study estimated the market for environmental equipment and services at around US$ 200 billion and growing at over five percent per year (Stevens, 1993), and a 1994 survey by German market researchers projected global purchases of $374 billion in "green technology" products in 1995 alone (Rubin, 1994). Firms supplying these products are obviously interested in regulations and treaties which will drive demand for their products (though they've been critiqued for often stressing clean-up rather than prevention; Karliner, 1994).

Beyond those specializing in green-tech, firms of many types want to be able to display a "green label" on their product to get the attention of socially-conscious purchasers. Driven by this demand for certified "green products," especially in Europe, a series of green labels or "ecolabels" were developed. Germany's "Blue Angel" scheme (named after the adopted logo of the U.N. Environment Programme) was the first, established in 1978 (West, 1995). There are now over 30 ecolabeling schemes operating, including the U.S.'s weaker "Green Seal" program initiated in the late 1980s. With the integration of the EEC, however, industries and consumers sought a universal European green seal, which was created in 1993 (West, 1995).

It is important to point out that while driven by consumer and investor demand, the initiatives to internationalize these ecolabels has come from industry itself, to allow both consumers and industrial purchasers to be able to know what they're buying in an increasingly global marketplace, and to head off regulations and more ecolabeling schemes or stricter regulations. Joe Cascio, IBM program director and chair of a key ISO advisory group, stated frankly that "we saw a proliferation of national and regional environmental management, labeling, and audit schemes that could have impacted international trade in a very severe way. That's the main reason the U.S. went ahead with this" (Begley, 1995: 45).

Some of these standards are beginning to include quality control not only for the final product, but also for the *process* by which they are produced. Even so, this increases "the probability that there will be one world environmental standard," says Joel Charm of the chemical industry giant Allied Signal Corp: "it is likely to become law in Europe and provide a transparency for how to conduct business in the Third World" (Heller, 1993: 31). Marash (1994) points out the central optimistic position on increasing free trade, which directly addresses the need for international environmental standards:

> The success of free trade depends on its implementation; consequently, its implementation must result in benefits beyond simply economic improvements... By internationally harmonizing standards, such as the quality management system standards [ISO], product technical-requirements standards, product testing standards, environmental standards, and occupational health and safety standards, countries can benefit from the exceptional socioeconomic advantages that free trade can bring.

Though there are several agencies vying to become the global standard, the ISO (International Standards Organization), which has 111 member nations, is becoming far more broadly utilized than the others. Their currently emerging set of standards are called the ISO 9000, ISO 14000, and ISO 20000 series (Nash and Ehrenfeld, 1996; Begley, 1996). The ISO 9000 series are certifications a company can receive that its products were produced with differing levels of quality control. The ISO certifications show that firms have developed standardized and well-documented *processes* of production. Thousands of plants worldwide have been certified in the last few years for the ISO 9000 series (see Cartwright, 1992 and other *Chemical Week* magazine citations). The certifications allow companies to sell products internationally without running into the barriers of purchasers needing to examine their plant and its procedures. These provided a competitive advantage initially, but now have become routine. Companies can be certified at lower levels, wherein only the product is guaranteed for quality control, or at higher levels (Heller, 1993: 30+). Certifications are just now being debated for worker health and safety, which if approved by the ISO will emerge around the turn of the century under the ISO 20000 series numbers (Sissell, 1995; 1996; M. Roberts, 1996; Sissel and Mullin, 1996).

How widely will the industry standards be adopted and enforced? How big an impact could ISO 14000 have? Many international pacts and governments are incorporating the ISO standards directly into their regulations. Tibor and Feldman (1995) point out that "ISO 14000 may well have an explosive impact on the global marketplace. Although designed as a voluntary standard, it could become a de-facto market-driven requirement for companies." Proponents cite several reasons firms might want to adopt ISO 14000 certification: to satisfy stakeholders such as investors, the public and environmental groups; to lower insurance rates and gain better access to capital; cost savings by increasing efficiency and reducing fines; pollution prevention and achieving environmental excellence.

For now, we have only the experience of ISO 9000 and industry initiatives to indicate the extent to which firms are likely to take up ISO 14000 certification efforts (Heller, 1993: 32). *Chemical Week* magazine reported in 1993 that with NAFTA and

MercoSul that both Latin American firms and multinationals "are anxious to use ISO 9000 registration to prove their global equity" (April 28, *Chemical Week*, 1993: 52). By mid-1995, over 500 plants in Brazil had been ISO 9000 certified (Bittencourt, 1995). By July, 1995, seventy-five percent of the firms in the Brazilian chemical industry organization (Abiquim) had supported their version of the Responsible Care initiative (Wood and Salles, 1995). The program is building momentum in Mexico. U.S. Big Three automakers are reported to have included ISO 9000 methods in a first-ever common quality program, but U.S. multinationals such as Motorola and Hewlett-Packard are reported to be attempting to streamline ISO certifications so that they can get certified once instead of for each facility around the world (Zukerman, 1994; 1995).

It remains to be seen if the same will be true for the ISO 14000 environmental standards. Some experts at the September, 1995 conference on ISO 14000 in the chemical industry believed that the standards "may not be appropriate for every company" (Sissell, 1995). There has been heated debate about whether companies will be forced to release findings of "audits" of their environmental records (Heller, 1993; Fairley and Roberts, 1995). Some CEOs of the largest chemical companies in the USA are reportedly opponents of third-party auditing, on the grounds that these audits could become weapons of environmental groups and regulators. Expectations from the European Union for an "Eco-Management and Audit Scheme" (EMAS) may push audit schemes which "harness public participation as a tool to pressure industry" (Begley, 1995: 47). The British equivalent BS7750 standard requires that firms "look at the environmental effects of all their activities, decide which are most significant, and draw up objectives and targets for reducing those effects. Progress on the targets is regularly audited... the ISO standard does not have an effects register and thus has been criticized as toothless" (Roberts, 1995: 48). The E.U. has said it will probably make the EMAS arrangements "mandatory if companies do not adopt it voluntarily" (Roberts, 1995: 48). Many environmentalists have harshly critiqued environmental audit schemes as they are emerging in the U.S. because they often exempt firms from lawsuits on issues they divulge publicly and voluntarily (Williams, 1996; Cushman, 1996; Just Cause, 1996).

More basically, some businesses fear that going through the ISO certification might also increase costs and raise non-tariff barriers. Tibor and Feldman point out that small and medium enterprises account for 75-90% of the world's industry, and that ISO 14000 may be too burdensome for them. Since much of product innovation comes from small businesses, the American Ceramic Society Bulletin cites the potentially negative impacts of ISO certifications (ACSB, 1994). Firms in Third World nations are less likely to be able to get ISO certified, and officials of those nations are beginning to clamor that they these types of standards are "biased toward vertical integration" (Ominami, 1993). There also exist many uncertainties about how to apply the standards. For example, many standards call for the use of best available technology, but there is often not agreement on what constitutes "Best Available Technology."

What does adoption of these ISO standards really mean for actual production processes? How widely will these standards be adopted and how closely will they be conformed to? In developing nations, it appears that these standards will have the greatest initial impact on suppliers of raw materials and intermediate products such as minerals and chemicals to overseas manufacturers, especially in Europe. Small firms and the informal sector will probably continue to produce with little concern for environmental regulations. However, the linkages between informal producers and multinational export firms (Portes et al., 1989) suggest that quality control and "green labeling" may force some small-scale producers to pay closer attention to environmental effects. Second, as West points out (1995), many of these "ecolabeling" efforts have been co-opted by industry and mean very little improvement in process and production methods. Most companies and products are getting green labels without any change in their production techniques. And the comparison of products by rankings often excludes those which are radically better (such as cloth towels versus paper towels).

Company and Industry Environmental Programs

What about company- or industry-specific environmental campaigns? After the tragic accident in Bhopal, India which killed over 4,000 people at a Union Carbide plant, the chemical industry has become increasingly aware that the public image of each company is tied directly to the records not just of that company but of all others in the industry (Roberts and Hunter, 1995). They therefore have become more active in creating both better environmental records and in attempting to build their corporate images, both individually and collectively.

The major collective effort by the chemical industry is called the "Responsible Care" Initiative, a major push by industry organizations to standardize operations and to gain better public images based on improved safety and environmental records. Responsible care is beginning to take off in Latin America and around the "Third World." Actual environmental cleanups and emissions reductions are often complemented by individual firms setting up or supporting nature preserves or zoos near their factories, running or supporting environmental education efforts, and supporting cultural activities and universities in the cities of their headquarters and operations. Critics argue that these are merely "corporate greenwashing" efforts designed to silence potential critics and boost polluting firms' corporate image.

Sociologists have been placing greater emphasis on the social "embeddedness" of the economy (Granovetter, 1985; Kincaid and Portes, 1989) but little has been said about normative and status reasons for companies launching environmental campaigns. I would argue that big public relations projects become important elements of a firm's status in both the business community and the society at large. As even industry trade magazines reflect, pressure from environmentalists and public opinion may drive a "keeping up with the Joneses" effect whereby after one firm launches such a campaign the others must. Peter Pauwels of Kodak's Kirkby, U.K. factory says that adoption of health, safety and environment (HSE) elements in their ISO 9000 quality certification is an essential part of being "a prestige company and a good member of the community" (*Chemical Week*, September 30, 1992: 62). June Nash's study of General Electric in Pittsfield, Massachusetts provides important and supporting insights into firm/community relations issues (1989), as is the importance given to community and environmental participation expressed in ALCOA's public relations campaign in Brazil (ALCOA, 1993). That is, environmental campaigns and other community programs are part of efforts by large transnationals to actively manage their relations with local and global publics. Big companies have been seen to usually take a dual approach, supporting industry-wide public relations efforts while not abandoning their own corporate image-care.

Again, often only large firms can afford such efforts, and this serves to extend their advantage over small ones. Companies such as DuPont are making concerted efforts to get all their production sites (in their case all 225 of them around the world) certified in ISO 9000 and ISO 14000 (Mullin, 1995). DuPont's ISO 9000 coordinator Sue Jackson says that "it will be up to each site to determine if it is appropriate and if there is a business reason to implement [ISO 14000]. DuPont will not impose ISO 14000 in any shape or form at the site level" (Mullin, 1995: 45). However, it appears that DuPont is using social pressures on plant managers to force them into ISO 14000 compliance, thus proving the firm and industry don't need further regulations. Research is needed to weigh positions of local plant managers and directives coming from headquarters in determining environmental compliance and campaign investments.

It is difficult in this polarized debate to accurately assess the ability of these voluntary standards and green labeling programs: do they have the potential to improve environmental conditions by taking a proactive (not regulatory) approach, or are they are merely corporate "greenwashing," as critics would have it? Solid systematic field data is entirely lacking and needed on individual firm- and plant-level practices and on their relation to publicity campaigns. The debate over green labeling is critical for evaluating the realistic potential for sustainable development in Third World nations.

Concluding Remarks/Directions for Research

If the era of global environmental standards is indeed dawning, the implications for sustainability and economic growth in the Third World are striking. To summarize, global integration is, in fits and starts, bringing some level of international standardization of environmental regulations. This is occurring in five ways. First, in international treaties on the environment. Second, in side agreements for economic integration treaties such as NAFTA, the CBI and Mercosur. Future trade pacts (at least those which include the U.S.) will almost certainly incorporate environmental protection in the main treaty or a side agreement. In cases with imbalances in regulations, it is not certain whether environmental regulations will "harmonize" at core or peripheral levels, but in the case of NAFTA so far Mexico is having to do the most work to get "up to speed." Third, the very globalization of commerce and the demand for "green products" have forced many core-based firms to create standardized quality control guidelines which are now spreading around the world. These guidelines, which will most affect export-oriented firms and their suppliers in Latin America, are increasingly incorporating health, safety and environmental management systems at global levels. Together these three elements will increase global standardization, but it appears unlikely that they will reach more than 25-50% of the economy: the large-scale and export sectors. National industries and the informal sector are likely to avoid increasing environmental regulations as long as possible (which might be indefinitely).

The sword has two edges for developing societies: polluting industries in the region may begin in earnest to clean up their production processes, but firms may no longer seek to relocate there to flee stricter regulatory climates in the wealthier nations. However, because of their emphasis on incremental improvement by individual firms rather than enforcing specific limits on *levels* of pollution, and because they lack effective enforcement guidelines, critics see some international standards such as the ISO 14000 series as both vacuous and without teeth.

I believe the question must be asked explicitly and systematically: Are these emerging global environmental standards forcing firms to approach environmental protection differently?[5] Emerging global environmental standards have potentially profound environmental and economic implications and the moment of their institutionalization is upon us. Systematic and timely research, and rapid dissemination of the findings is critical at this time when such analyses could positively influence our understanding of these new international environmental institutions and perhaps the ISO adoption process itself. I would argue that the key actors' (business and governments) attention to environmental issues is likely to continue only as long as the pressure on politicians and the banks continues from core environmentalists (especially those in large consumer market nations). To understand the likelihood of the this dynamic continuing, I believe that we also need a solid understanding of both North and South environmental movements: their class roots and public support. Particularly important is the internationalization of environmental and social justice NGOs, which strengthens the movement in the short term but can mean risking local support when developing nation groups must bend to international desires (Roberts, 1996b; Christen et al., 1998). Some core environmentalists are realizing they must learn to care about the urban, human health and social justice-related environmental issues which inspire wider popular support in Latin America.

That was the positive side of the picture; now for the balance. Global integration overall is not conducive to environmental protection because cutthroat international competition can drive nations to neglect it, and because austerity programs and the economic crises of transition create a desperation which drives poor people to unsustainable use of their resources (see, e.g., Barkin, 1995; Serbin et al., 1993). To correct exchange rates, stabilize inflation and lower tariff barriers, global integration and export orientation have been linked with drastic programs of privatization and "state shrinking" in nations across the "South." As the state is shrunken, respect for the rule of law often weakens as does confidence in environmental protection agencies.[6] Even if those agencies are well funded in times of austerity by outside financing, to many people they will seem increasingly alien and irrelevant in times of desperate hardship. Desperate times tend to favor short-term thinking, not sustainable development. With the demise of government social programs and substantial state employment most researchers also envision greater income inequality and poverty throughout the region. An important question then will be whether income inequality leads to wasteful consumption with greater environmental damage without commensurate social gains (see Sanderson, 1993). The direct implication of this is that too rapid liberalization and "modernization" of the state risks dire environmental crisis.

Finally, if greater openness to trade brings economic growth to developing societies, it will provide the opportunity for greater spending on sanitation and urban air pollution control. However carbon dioxide emissions and many other pollutants are almost bound to increase with economic expansion (from new autos, factories, mines, agrochemicals, dumping, etc.).[7] The only force with the capacity to change the relation between economic growth and pollution in the South is strong pressure brought on governments, transnational *and* national firms through lobbying, boycotts, and direct action, all supported by cross-border links.

NOTES

1 Acknowledgments: Helpful comments on earlier drafts were provided by Jerry Speir, Francis Adeola, the editors, and anonymous reviewers of this journal. Portions of this research were funded by the Mellon Foundation and the National Science Foundation.
2 Others tend to improve steadily with income levels (e.g., percent of population with basic sanitation, water (Grossman and Krueger, 1995; World Bank, 1992)). Other types of pollution seem to be

worst for countries at middle levels of income as measured by GDP per capita (see Roberts and Grimes, 1997).

3   From the early 1960s' weapons testing to the current debate over the terms of the U.N. Framework Convention on Climate Change, a series of global agreements have been drafted, debated and signed. Dietz and Kalof (1991) compiled an index of "state environmentalism" based on which of the nine treaties nations had signed during the period 1963-1987. The treaties were the Nuclear Test Ban Treaty (1963), Wetlands (Ramsar) 1971, Biological and Toxic Weapons (1972), World Cultural and Natural Heritage (1972), Ocean Dumping (1972), Endangered Species (CITES, 1973), Ship Pollution (1978), Migratory Species (1979), Law of the Sea (1982), Ozone Layer Vienna (1985), CFC Control Montreal (1987), and Hazardous Waste Movement (1989) (Dietz and Kalof, 1992: 355).

4   This includes the Border Environmental Cooperation Commission (BECC), North American Development Bank (NADBank), the Border Ecology Project (BEP), university research centers, state government agencies and NGO groups (Ron Mader, *personal communication*).

5   I am currently examining the chemical industry since the sector is widely perceived as potentially one of the world's most dangerous and polluting, and because it has taken strides toward addressing public and health concerns. I believe in the analytical value of a carefully-designed comparative approach, and have sought to make it feasible by focusing on two strategically chosen petrochemical poles in three nations: the USA, Brazil and Mexico. My research involves collaborations with researchers focusing on the Mexican and U.S. cases.

6   However, through the late 1980s economic crisis Brazil was able to keep its environmental protection agency IBAMA growing, largely through funding from the World Bank and other external sources.

7   See note six.

REFERENCES

ALSOGARAY, María Julia
    1993   "International Trade and the Environment: A View from Argentina." In *Difficult Liaison: Trade and the Environment in the Americas*, Heraldo Muñoz and Robin Rosenberg (Eds.), pp. 153-158. New Brunswick, N.J.: Transaction.
BARKIN, David
    1995   "Wealth, Poverty, and Sustainable Development." Working Paper, Lincoln Institute, March 1995.
BAUMAN, Robert J.
    1995   "The Latin American Petrochemical Industry." *Chemistry and Industry* (2 October), 773-777.
BEGLEY, Ronald
    1995a "The Spirit of ISO 9000." *Chemical Week* (April 5), 5.
BEGLEY, Ronald
    1995b "Environmental ISO Standard Adds to Management Tasks." *Chemical Week* (April 5), 45-47.
BIGGS, Gonzalo
    1993   "The Interrelationship Between the Environment and International Trade in Latin America: The Legal and Institutional Framework." In *Difficult Liaison: Trade and the Environment in the Americas*, Heraldo Muñoz and Robin Rosenberg (Eds.), pp. 167-204. New Brunswick, N.J.: Transaction.

BITTENCOURT, Carlos Mariani
1995 "Brazil: an Expanding Industry." *Chemistry and Industry* (2 October), 789-791.

CARTWRIGHT, Graham
1992 "Lessons Learned about ISO 9000." *Journal of Quality and Participation* (September), 44-48.

CHASE-DUNN, Christopher and Peter E. GRIMES
1995 "World-Systems Analysis." *Annual Review of Sociology* 21, 387-417.

CHRISTEN, Catherine, Selene HERCULANO, Kathryn HOCHSTETLER, Renae PRELL, Marie PRICE, and J. Timmons ROBERTS
1998 "Latin American Environmentalism: Comparative Views." *Studies in Comparative International Development* (Fall), forthcoming.

COFIR/PÖLO
n.d. "Pensando no Global. Agindo no Local: Compromisso Pölo." Pamphlet, Comitê de Fomento Industrial de Camaçari/Pölo Petroquímico de Camaçari.

COVELLO, Vincent T. and R. Scott FREY
1990 "Technology-Based Environmental Health Risks in Developing Nations." *Technological Forecasting and Social Change* 37, 159-179.

DICKEN, Peter
1992 *Global Shift: The Internationalization of Economic Activity.* New York: Guilford Press.

DIETZ, Thomas and Linda KALOF
1992 "Environmentalism among Nation-states." *Social Indicators Research* 26, 353-366.

FAIRLEY, Peter and Michael ROBERTS
1995 "Pilot Projects and ISO 14000 Moving Forward." *Chemical Week* (July 5/12), 34-35.

FROBEL, Folker, Jurgen HEINRICHS, and Otto KREYE
1981 *The New International Division of Labor.* New York: Cambridge University Press.

GARCIA-JOHNSON, R.
1995 "Conforming with Emerging International Environmental Standards: External Demands for Progressive Environmental Polity and Developing Country Response—A Tentative Case Study of Brazil (1972-1994) and Preliminary Model." Paper presented at the International Studies Association Annual Conference, Chicago, IL (February 21-25).

GEREFFI, Gary and Miguel KORZENIEWICZ (Eds.)
1994 *Commodity Chains and Global Capitalism.* Westport, CT: Praeger.

GOULD, Kenneth
1994 "Transnational Trade Deregulation: A Collision Course with Sustainable Development?" St. Lawrence University, Department of Sociology. Paper presented the Conference on The Politics of Sustainable Development. University of Crete, Greece (21-23 October), 24.

GRANOVETTER, Mark
1985 "Economic Action and Social Structure: The Problem of Embeddedness." *American Journal of Sociology* 91, 481-510.

GREER, Jed and Kenny BRUNO
1997 *Greenwash: The Reality Behind Corporate Environmentalism.* Penang: Third World Network/Apex Press.

GRIMES, Peter E. and J. Timmons ROBERTS
1995 "Oscillations in Atmospheric Carbon Dioxide and Long Cycles of Production in the World Economy, 1790-1990." *American Sociological Association,* Annual Meetings (August), Washington, D.C.

GROSSMAN, Gene M. and Alan B. KRUEGER
  1995 "Economic Growth and the Environment." *Quarterly Journal of Economics* (May), 353-377.
HAMNER, Burt
  1996 "Pollution Prevention: The Cost-Effective Approach Towards ISO 14000 Compliance." Paper published on *Infoterra Electronic List* (Digest 669), 20 March 1996.
HAJEK, Ernest R.
  1991 *La situaciön ambiental en América Latina: Algunos estudios de casos.* Buenos Aires: CIEDLA (Centro Interdisciplinario de Estudios sobre Desarrollo Latinoamericano).
HELLER, Karen
  1993 "ISO 9000: Stepping-Stone on the Road to a Global Economy: Environmental Standards Take Center Stage." *Chemical Week* (February 10), 30-32.
HOFFMAN, Andrew J.
  1995 "Faces of Environmental Stewardship: How Other Programs Stack Up." *Chemical Week* (July 5/12), 63-64.
KARLINER, Joshua
  1994 "The Environment Industry Profiting from Pollution." *The Ecologist* 24 (2), 59-63.
KAZIS, Richard and Richard L. GROSSMAN
  1991 *Fear at Work: Job Blackmail, Labor and the Environment.* (New Edition) Philadelphia: New Society Publishers.
KINCAID, A. Douglas and Alejandro PORTES
  1994 "Sociology and Development in the 1990s: Critical Challenges and Empirical Trends." In *Comparative International Development*, Kincaid and Portes (Eds.), pp. 1-25. Chapel Hill: UNC Press.
KORZENIEWICZ, Roberto P. and William MARTIN
  1995 "The Global Distribution of Commodity Chains." In *Commodity Chains and Global Capitalism*, Gary Gereffi and Miguel Korzeniewicz (Eds.), pp. 67-92. Westport, CT: Praeger.
LEFF, Enrique
  1986 "Notas para un análisis sociolögico de los movimientos ambientalistas." In *Politica ambiental y desarrollo: Un debate para América Latina*, Marta Cárdenas (Ed.), pp. 115-126. Bogota: FESCOL/INDERENA.
LOW, Patrick and Alexander YEATS
  1992 "Do "Dirty" Industries Migrate?" In *International Trade and the Environment*, Patrick Low (Ed.), pp. 89-104. World Bank Discussion Papers. Washington, D.C.: International Bank for Reconstruction and Development/World Bank.
MARASH, Stanley A.
  1994 "Quality, Standards, and Free Trade." *Quality Progress* 27 (May), 27-30.
McMICHAEL, Philip
  1996 "Globalization: Myths and Realities." *Rural Sociology* 61 (19), 25-55.
METZGER, Jennifer
  1995 "Global Corporations and Ecological Imperatives: An Agenda for Research on the Environmental Impacts of Transnationals." Paper presented for the 1995 ISA Conference. Chicago, IL, 34 pp.
MILLER, Marian A.L.
  1995a "Globalization and Interdependence: The Third World in the Evolution of Environmental Regimes." International Studies Association Annual Meetings (February 21-26), Chicago, IL.

MILLER, Marian A.L.

1995b *The Third World in Global Environmental Politics*. Boulder, Colo.: Lynne Rienner.

MORRIS, Gregory D.L.

1995 "Responsibilidad Integral: Peso Plunge Plagues Purpose." *Chemical Week* (June 14), 24.

MULLIN, Rick

1995 "DuPont Charting Path to ISO 9000-ISO 14000 Integration." *Chemical Week* (April 5), 45.

NASH, June

1987 "Community and Corporations in the Restructuring of Industry." In *The Capitalist City: Global Restructuring and Community Politics*, Michel Peter Smith and Joe R. Feagin (Eds.), pp. 275-296. Cambridge, MA: Blackwell.

OLIVERA, A. and Manuel FELIPE

1995 *Responsibilidad Integral: La Forma Mas Moderna de Gestion Ambiental Empresarial.* ANDI: Asociacion Nacional de Industriales, Colombia. Xerox.

OMINAMI, Carlos

1993 "International Trade and the Environment: A View from Chile." In *Difficult Liaison: Trade and the Environment in the Americas*, Heraldo Muñoz and Robin Rosenberg (Eds.), pp. 147-151. New Brunswick, N.J.: Transaction.

PEARSON, Charles S. (Ed.)

1987 "Environmental Standards, Industrial Relocation, and Pollution Havens." In *Multinational Corporations, Environment, and the Third World: Business Matters*, Charles S. Pearson (Ed.), pp. 113-128. Durham: Duke University Press.

PERIN, Monica

1995 "Economic Realities Vex Environmental Aspirations. Cash Flow Crimps Progress [Mexico]." *Chemical Week* (June 14), 22-24.

PORTES, Alejandro, Manuel CASTELLS, and Lauren A. BENTON (Eds.)

1989 *The Informal Economy: Studies in Advanced and Less Developed Countries.* Baltimore: Johns Hopkins University Press.

ROBERTS, J. Timmons

1994 "Economic Crisis and Environmental Policy [Brazil]." *Hemisphere* 6 (1), 26-30.

ROBERTS, J. Timmons

1996a "Predicting Participation in Environmental Treaties: A World-System Analysis." *Sociological Inquiry* 66 (1), 38-57.

ROBERTS, J. Timmons

1996b "Global Restructuring and the Environment in Latin America." In *Latin America in the World Economy*, Roberto P. Korzeniewicz and William C. Smith (Eds.), pp. 187-210. Westport, CT: Greenwood Press.

ROBERTS, J. Timmons and Peter E. GRIMES

1997 "Carbon Intensity and Economic Development 1962-1991: A Brief Exploration of the Environmental Kuznets Curve." *World Development* 25 (2), 181-187.

ROBERTS, Michael

1995a "Starting Up Care Before Trouble Begins: Green Pressure is Growing." *Chemical Week* (July 5/12), 82-90.

ROBERTS, Michael

1995b "Deregulation: But First, Europe Needs Proof." *Chemical Week* (July 5/12), 91.

ROBERTS, Michael and David HUNTER

1995 "Building the Dream: Responsible Care Takes Off Worldwide." *Chemical Week* (July 5/12), 32-33.

RUBIN, Debra K.
  1994 "Firms Gear up to Think Globally, Link Locally, Focus on Environment." *Engineering News-Record* 232 (February 21), 42.
SANDERSON, Steven E.
  1993 "International Trade, Natural Resources, and Conservation of the Environment in Latin America." In *Difficult Liaison: Trade and the Environment in the Americas*, Heraldo Muñoz and Robin Rosenberg (Eds.), pp. 53-78. New Brunswick, N.J.: Transaction.
SAYRE, Don
  1996 *Inside ISO 14000: The Competitive Advantage of Environmental Management.* Delray Beach, FL: St. Lucie Press.
SCHWARTZMAN, Stephen
  1986 *Bankrolling Disasters: International Development Banks and the Global Environment.* Washington, D.C.: Sierra Club.
SERBIN, Andrés, Antonio De LISIO, and Eduardo ORTIZ
  1993 "The Environmental Impact of International Trade and Industry: Reflections on Latin America and the Caribbean." In *Difficult Liaison: Trade and the Environment in the Americas*, Heraldo Muñoz and Robin Rosenberg (Eds.), pp. 127-145. New Brunswick, N.J.: Transaction.
STERN, Paul C., Oran R. YOUNG, and Daniel DRUCKMAN (Eds.)
  1992 *Global Environmental Change: Understanding the Human Dimensions.* Washington: National Academy Press.
STEVENS, Candice
  1993 "Organization for Economic Cooperation and Development Framework for the Discussion of Trade and Environment Concerns." In *Difficult Liaison: Trade and the Environment in the Americas*, Heraldo Muñoz and Robin Rosenberg (Eds.), pp. 161-166. New Brunswick, N.J.: Transaction.
TIBOR, Tom and Ira FELDMAN
  1995 *ISO 14000. A Guide to the New Environmental Management Standards.* Irwin Professional Publishing, Burr Ridge, IL, 250 pp.
WEST, Karen
  1995 "Ecolabels. The Industrialization of Environmental Standards." *The Ecologist* 25, 16-20.
WOOD, Andrew and Flavio SALLES
  1995 "Care Programs Develop in South America." *Chemical Week* (July 5/12), 99-101.
WORLD BANK
  1992 *World Development Report 1992.* New York: Oxford University Press.
WORLD BANK
  1995 *World Development Report 1995.* New York: Oxford University Press.
YOUNG, Oran R.
  1982 *Resource Regimes: Natural Resources and Social Institutions.* Berkeley: University of California Press.
YOUNG, Oran R.
  1989 *International Cooperation: Building Regimes for Natural Resources and the Environment.* Ithaca: Cornell University Press.
YOUNG, Oran R.
  1994 *International Governance: Protecting the Environment in a Stateless Society.* Ithaca: Cornell University Press.

ZUCKERMAN, Amy
    1994 "Ford, Chrysler, and GM Introduce a Common Quality Standard." *New Steel* 10 (November), 22-25.
ZUCKERMAN, Amy
    1995 "New Walls: With International Borders Falling, Nontarriff Trade Barriers are on the Rise." *Industry Week* 244 (March 20), 11.

The Nationality and Globality of Social Science

The Issues of Globalizing Sociology in America

SHAHID M. SHAHIDULLAH*

ABSTRACT

Reforming social science at present is a global agenda. In all countries and regions of the world, demands from political leaders, business executives, and social science communities are growing for a social science relevant and competent to examine the nature and uncertainty of the emerging world arising from globalization. What should be done to reform social science? This paper argues that social science will need transformations both in its theoretical and practical missions. Globalization is creating a new trajectory of transcultural and transcivilizational issues which are time and space neutral. New theoretical categories to explain these issues need to be discovered. Social science will have to contribute to the designing of new social structures and cultural models as well. American sociology is traditionally local and pragmatic in nature, but it is also theoretically highly advanced. What is needed for the globalization of American sociology is a new theoretical framework which can create a bridge of thought between the issues of globality and locality in America. There is also a need for a mission for the construction of new social actors and structures such as new communities, cities, regions, and organizations, which will be essentially American in spirit but global in character. In all countries, social science and sociology are facing this challenge of change and transformation.

Introduction

Since the end of the Cold War in the middle of the 1980s, there has been growing a new movement for the globalization of social science in almost all countries of the world, particularly in the United States. In the wake of the end of the Cold War, almost all American institutions became seriously concerned with reforms in social science education and research. The demand came not only from social science and educational communities but also from political and business leaders. The 1983 Report of the National Commission of Excellence in Education *A Nation* at *Risk:*

*   Department of Sociology and Social Work, Virginia State University, Petersburg, Virginia 23806, U.S.A.

The Imperative For Educational Reform, the 1986 American Society For Engineering Education's Report *Quality of Engineering Education*, the 1986 Report of the Business-Higher Education Forum *An Action Agenda For American Competitiveness*, the 1988 MIT Commission's Report *Made in America: Regaining The Productive Edge*, the 1989 Report of the American Council on Education *International Studies and the Undergraduate*, the 1990 Report of the National Governor's Association's Task Force on International Education *America in Transition: The International Frontier* and many other recent reports and commission studies recommended that U.S. education must improve global and international studies to be able to effectively cope with contemporary global changes.

One survey conducted by the U.S. News and World Report in 1988 shows that about forty five percent of American adults can not correctly match the names of such countries as England and France with their locations. In an era when many see the "end of geography," American adults in their knowledge of geography, a recent Gallop survey shows, rank behind that of Sweden, Germany, France, Great Britain, Canada, and Japan. One in seven adults could not locate the United States on the world map; more than one half did not know, even roughly, the size of the nation's population. About fifty percent of the adults could not identify even one South American country; and only fifty five percent could locate New York—in fact thirty seven states were identified as New York (National Governor's Association, 1990). All these manifestations are there at a time when American economy and culture are becoming intensely global. It is in this context that the issue of reforming social science has been raised and discussed, and it is with this problem that this paper is concerned.

What does it mean to globalize social science? How is globalization and internationalization in social science defined and conceptualized? Why does social science need to be globalized? What are the problems of globalizing and internationalizing social science? And how should reform for globalization be pursued? This paper will explore and explain some of these questions, particularly in the context of the case of globalizing sociology in America.

Globalization and the Need for Reforming Sociology

The construction of a new social science and sociology will need serious understanding and scrutinization of the process of globalization. In contrast to the idea of many critics, globalization is not merely "a free market ideology" (Hirst and Thompson, 1995) or a process of "the McDonaldization of the world," it is a process sociologically far more fundamental in nature. It is fundamentally transforming the nature and the organization of the economy (Barnet and Cavanagh, 1994), politics (Petras and Morley, 1995; Mittleman, 1995), and culture (Basu, 1995; Ginsburg and Rapp, 1995) of the world societies. Many observers see it as the "end of the west" and the "end of geography," if not the "end of history" (Fukuyama, 1992). It is "a social process," as one sociologists puts it, "in which the constraints of geography on social and cultural arrangements recede and in which people become increasingly aware that they are receding" (Waters, 1995: 3). Globalization is not therefore a

> "mere hype or ideology. The international economy is rapidly restructuring. The burden on social scientists is therefore to present a suitable analytical framework" (Lie, 1996: 586).

Since the beginning of the 1970s, there has been a discourse growing in sociology for a more historical, comparative, and global perspective. One of the earliest approaches which has generated a large amount of literature is the world systems perspective (Wallerstein, 1991a; Chase-Dunn, 1995). The advocates of the world systems perspective argue that the unit of sociological analysis should not be an individual or a nation-state, but a historical system. At different stages of the growth of human civilizations, different nations, societies, and cultures have been governed by different historical systems. The modern historical system is the world capitalist system, and different modern nations and cultures are governed by the dynamics of its logic and necessities (Forte, 1996; Sahlins, 1994).

From the beginning of the 1980s, questions, however, began to be raised about the deterministic role of economics in the world systems approach. In response, many began to rather conceptualize the world in cultural terms (Featherstone, 1990). One of the cultural approaches suggests that the world is becoming a single social space of human action (Robertson, 1992). This thesis states that since the beginning of modernity, a global action frame of mind has been evolving and spreading across the world. Within this evolving frame of action, an evolving "imagined community" (Anderson, 1983), the nation-states, individuals, and humanity have been evolving new meanings and significance. Globalization is essentially an increasing expansion of this action frame of mind; "a consciousness of the world as a single space" (Robertson, 1992: 183).

Closely related to the idea of "imagined community," is the concept of world society which appears in many discourses on globalization in Europe (Heintz, 1992). The world society thesis claims that all over the world there is increasingly growing a holistic orientation to the world as a whole. "World society is a fact of life, i.e., people live with this fact, and in order to do so, they produce or simply adopt an image of the society as a means of orientation" (Heintz, 1992: 11). The world society is "the worldwide field of interaction whose smallest units are its individual members. It is therefore more comprehensive than the concept of an international or intergovernmental system, and than the sectoral concept of a world economy. It is more in the tradition of sociological thinking" (Heintz, 1992: 12). The task of global sociology is to understand the nature of the world society and its varying layers of world systems and subsystems, and the codes and principles that are articulated by different nations, cultures, and individuals.

The evolution of the European community is a significant event, not only in world politics and the economy, but also in the world of social science. German sociologist Bernd Hamm claims that the European community can be a model for sociological analysis of contemporary globalization. The European community "is indeed unique and deserves to be recognized as such by the social sciences" (Hamm, 1992). The European Community is a model of how a higher form of socio-political boundary can be deliberately constructed out of diverse cultures and nationalities, not only for trade and economics but also for designing a new civilizational structure and identity. It is a model for the construction of a transnational civilization on the basis of the ideology of globalism.

In modern science in general, there is a notion growing that a holistic perspective is needed to understand the complexities of nature, mind, body, and culture. The perspective of holism is recently becoming popular in social science as well (Appadurai, 1991; Forte, 1996). During the mid-1970s, a series of attempts were made for global modeling from holistic interpretations. Two of the important concepts which emerged from those attempts are "World Problematique" and "World Resolutique" (King, 1992). The World Problematique is "a model of the global situation which suggests that it is no longer possible to tackle individual problems one by one and sequentially, without taking into account the impacts that the proposed solution of one problem would have on many others" (King, 1992). The World Resolutique, on the other hand, is a model for problem-solving in a holistic way. It suggests that one part of a problematique can not be solved without solving the others which constitute the whole problematique. From the perspective of the world problematique model, global efforts are needed for solving such issues as global development, poverty, ecology, security, and human welfare. The policies and considerations for their resolution within the bounds of the nation-states are bound to be limited. The specific focus in this model is on the emergence of a series of global problematiques as a result of the advancement of modern industrial and technological civilization.

The purpose of this study is not to make a detailed critique of these and other existing approaches to the study of globalziation. The purpose rather is to explore some new analytical directions. The issue of reforming social science in the context of globalization is both theoretical and practical. Theoretically, the issue is that social science will have to be able to present a sound analysis of what globalization is, what the driving forces are, and what key parameters are to be used for the analysis of its growth and expansion. Practically, the issue of reforming social science is the issue of policy making and policy interventions.

In the United States, as in other countries, the policy-making communities are eagerly seeking knowledge from social science for innovative policy models and designs (Holzner, 1991; Shahidullah, 1997). The perspectives of the world system, global action framework, and the world society present many important theoretical insights, but they are limited in terms of policy interventions. The EC model and the concept of world problematique are policy-relevant, but are theoretically less rigorous.

Globalization is transforming the very core of the construction of social facts, and the formation of social discourses in all the world societies. It is driven by a complex set of economic, technological, and cultural actions and forces. What needs to be reexamined for a new sociology of globalization first and foremost, therefore, is the way in which the constitution and the construction of social facts, events, and, institutions are changing and being challenged. In the nineteenth century, when the industrial civilization was expanding, old social facts, institutions, and symbolisms were challenged. In the twentieth century, a new sociology of urban-industrial society emerged to explain the need for new cultural codes and institutions within the bounds of the nation-states. Today, the analytical categories of the industrial society of the twentieth century are becoming obsolete (Carrier, 1995; Said, 1978) and a new set of cultural codes and institutions, and new analytical frameworks are needed for understanding the nature of postindustrial global economics, politics, and culture. Reform in social science today should therefore proceed by discovering a new set of analytical categories which can explain new issues and problems of the emerging global society.

One of the key characteristics of the emerging social facts and symbolisms in the global society is that they are increasingly becoming space-neutral (Giddens, 1990; 1991; Wallerstein, 1996). What it means is that in every society people's actions, hopes, dreams, and expectations are being shaped by forces which lie outside their immediate social and physical space. These extra-societal and extra-regional forces include such facts as the spread of the global commodity market, expansion of global technology, the progress of multinational corporations, and the formation of new economic and political blocs. It is hard for common people to grapple with the significance of such forces, but they are sociologically understandable.

The general public in America sometimes does not see the rationality of why American companies, seeking access to foreign markets, are increasingly employing, even in higher management positions native-born candidates rather than U.S. expatriates. As one of the vice-presidents of Levi Strauss, an American multinational company, once said, "In the old days, each operating entity was autonomous. Now collaboration across national and divisional boundaries is what makes a company global." One survey shows that about 70% of American companies hope to expand their offshore locations, particularly in Asia and Europe, in the near future. The recent restructuring, reengineering, downsizing, and increasing joblessness in America are confusing for many, but they are sociologically explainable and comprehensible (Reich, 1991).

The emerging global facts and symbolisms are also becoming time-neutral. New social institutions and values are emerging because of the removal of time barriers. Human social interactions are time-dependent and time consuming. Time, like space, creates barriers between individuals, societies, and civilizations. Time constrains the diffusion and expansion of social ideas and events across space. A letter, which today takes less than a minute to travel from London to Calcutta, took six months two hundred years ago. One of the major triumphs in modern society is overcoming of time constraint. With the expansion of the information superhighway, digitalization of information, and the arrival of a multilingual global Internet system, the nature and intensity of inter-societal and inter-civilizational relations will reach a new stage of expansion in the twenty-first century. This will fundamentally alter the traditional meaning of "habitat" or "home." In the "global habitat," individuals from one society can live far away in another society butl can still keep and cultivate their primordial ties and kinship (Friedman, 1990). With the help of the information superhighway, individuals can live in one society and work for another. It is now possible for a Japanese person to catalogue-shop in America while sitting in Japan, as it is possible for an American sitting in Amercia to shop for a car in Japan.

An Indian living in New York can participate in a wedding in India, in a virtual way, and buy presents from a market of his or her choosing with the help of the India Internet. Kurds living in Frankfurt, Palestinians in New York, and the Chinese in Los Angeles can easily participate in their homeland's on-going freedom struggles because the constraints of time and distance have been removed. In the heart of New York, where there are people from almost all the world's nations, there is a resurgence of ethnic cults and cultures. The Chinese, Japanese, Koreans, Vietnamese, Thai, Indians, and Arabs have their own ethnic bazaars, restaurants, banks, media, temples, mosques, and doctors. Ethnic goods and products are regularly imported from their motherlands, and the ethnic media fosters their language and culture. The concept of "ethnomarketing" therefore has recently become a new paradigm in marketing science. The removal of time constraint is giving birth to a new sociology where the meanings of nationality, citizenship, and identity are becoming radically different. The conquest of time is leading to the conquest of space and distance, and this is adding new meanings to the constructed boundaries of different societies and civilizations.

Sociologists should also explore how emerging global social facts are becoming transcultural, transcivilizational, and transhistorical. With the advance of modernization and globalization, cultural and civilizational values, ethos, and preferences of one civilization are moving to another. There are many cultural habits and preferences in non-western societies which are explicitly western in nature, as there are many in the west which are explicitly non-western. Western movies and daytime television programs run with extreme popularity in almost all the capitals of the developing world.

Western-style malls are also swiftly globalizing in all regions. The enthusiasm of the people of Abidjan, the capital of Ivory Coast, and the self-proclaimed Paris of Africa, for the recent opening of L'Espace Latrille, a 10,000-square meter western mall, has been noticeable to all observers. A local social scientist, Dr. Frederic Torimiro, however, looked at it from a different category of thought. He noted that suburban malls have led to the decline of downtown shopping areas in the United States. The same could happen to Africa's traditional markets, but with wide ramifications. Similar artifacts from other cultures are also swiftly spreading across the west. The Restaurant magazines predict that the next trend in U.S. dining will have greater Asian influence.

Cultural diffusion and emulation are as old as civilization, but in no stage of development were they as intense and visible as they are today. Japan deliberately borrowed many ideas and institutions from the west after the Meji Restoration, and now many East Asian nations are borrowing from Japan, and there are explicit national policies described as "Look East." While America is trying to emulate the Quality Control Model of Japan and the School-to-Work Transition Model of Germany, the rest of the world is experimenting with the American model of constitutionalism and political democracy.

Many emerging cultural artifacts are also transsymbolic where symbols and meaning of different cultures are cross-fertilizing new cultural artifacts. Coca-Cola, while tempting American teens with the new caffeine drink "surge," is treating Taiwanese teens with a new drink named "Fei Yang." There are about ten million believers of the "New Age Movement" in America, and many of its key philosophical principles came from Hinduism and Buddhism. Chinese teens today observe Christmas with as much festivity as the Chinese New Year. The Rights Movement of the west is swiftly growing across non-western societies and creating new meanings and symbols of romanticism, sex, and the body.

Thousands of American teens are moving to the Asian nations in search of their "American Dream," and believe that the American dream does not have any national boundary. There are about 100,000 expatriates in Japan. In Hong Kong, Singapore, Thailand, Malaysia, China, and Vietnam, large colonies of America's "Generation X" are growing. One journalist made an interesting sociological observation about this growing American migration to Asia: "Americans, of course, have ventured in waves in the Orient many times before, usually bent on some form of conversion. By contrast, the new generation ventures abroad with a surprising sense of humility and open-mindedness, bent on reinventing themselves through immersion in local cultures. In the process, they are ultimately redefining the American frontier" (Lam, 1995: 1).

While transcultural and transsymbolic facts and issues manifest the growing of cultural homogeneity around the world, many transcivilizational facts and issues express deep diversity. Globalization is leading to the growth of a global culture, but it is also leading to a serious scrutinization of the values of one civilization by another. Different civilizations, in the wake of rising complexities in social, political, and cultural governance, are reflecting on their own time-honored institutions, values, and morality (Huntington, 1996).

All civilizations want to participate in the construction of a good and humane world society, but they also tend to assert their respective civilizational values and preferences. One of the major differences is that the west wants to see its liberal values and institutions engulf all other civilizations (Huntington, 1996). Other non-western civilizations such as the Chinese, Japanese, Hindus, Africans, and Moslems assert modernization from their own civilizational point of view. This was once beautifully expressed by the former Prime Minister of Japan, Nakasone Yasuhiro in the context of his deliberation on the internationalization of Japanese education: "It is my belief that educational reform should aim to preserve and further develop the traditional Japanese culture which we have inherited and to cultivate in children lofty ideals, sound physical strength, well-balanced personalities and creative power, as well as moral and behavioral standards as are universally accepted in human society, so that these future Japanese citizens may be able to contribute to the international community with a Japanese consciousness" (Lincicome, 1991: 2).

In a recent Economic Summit of 25 European and Asian leaders in Bangkok, the Asian leaders openly expressed their cultural differences to the west. Western style democracy, they said, is not applicable for East Asian nations. The only way is the "Asian Way," based on Confucianism which emphasizes learning, social harmony, family values, hierarchy, respect for the elderly, and loyalty to authority. In their views, western concepts of democracy, human right, and environment are not universal and necessary for modernization and economic growth. China has opened its door wide to western multinationals for economic investment, but only within the framework of Chinese values and cultural preference. Recently, the Canton city government has notified the local business community that foreign names for the streets and businesses in Canton, such as Manhattan Plaza, Monte Carlo Villas, Wall Street Financial Plaza, would be illegal, although the business and the "bazaar" of the Chinese in America and all over the west are named mostly in Chinese. The British-named Indian city of Bombay has recently been changed to Mumbai to reflect its local heritage, but this is happening in a nation which is also deeply committed to modernization and globalization.

In the Middle East and the Moslem nations of East and South Asia, there is now growing a strong movement for the expansion of the Islamic Bank, and it has spread as far as England. The bedrock of Islamic banking is the ban on interest payment. The total assets of the Islamic bank is about 70 billion dollars, and it is now in a process of globalization. Interest-free loans from the Islamic Banks will undoubtedly attract millions of American consumers and bring great competitive challenge, should it be allowed to undertake business in America. Civilizational differences are unlikely to produce any great world conflicts (Huntington, 1996), but will have many impacts on the unfolding of the future economy, politics and culture of the world societies. Sociology will have to be able to understand the nature and meaning of these emerging complexities of intercivilizational encounters (see Fig. 1).

Human social life has been organized since the beginning of civilization around families, communities, tribes, cities, nations, empires, and civilizations. The rise of nation-states, on the basis of citizenship, is a modern phenomenon less than two hundred years old. Over the course of the last two millenniums, there were many political transformations in the boundaries of nations, empires, and civilizations. But humans' primordial attachment to family, community, tribes, nations, and civilizations has remained practically unchanged. Michael Elliott, a Newsweek columnist, put this sociological discovery in the context of the recent Rwanda tragedy in a cogent way: "The churning mass of humanity around the great lakes of Central Africa this fall did more than remind the comfortable world how much of the planet remained unsafe and fearful place. It symbolized, rather, a human instinct as ancient as the hills, but still powerful-people belong somewhere. They have roots, traditions, myths, and cultures. They know who they are" (1996: 41).

Contemporary forces of globalization are not going to change those attachments in any fundamental way. It is highly unlikely that the present boundaries of the nation-states, many of whom are armed with highly sophisticated military machines, are going to be permanently dissolved in the conceivable future. Many of the "civilizational-states," such as the United States, Japan, China, India, and regional civilizations such as the European Community will rather be increasingly powerful both economically and politically. Different world societies and civilizations are not dissolving as a result of globalization. They are rather competing and cooperating with, and learning and emulating from each other. They are also becoming curious about their respective differences. Their intense intermingling is producing many new possibilities and constraints, creating new hopes and despair, and forming new groups and alliances (Commission on Global Governance, 1994).

Industrial society	Post-industrial global society
Time-bound	Time-neutral
Space-bound	Space-neutral
Monocultural	Transcultural
Monocivilizational	Transcivilizational
Historical	Transhistorical
Monosymbolic	Transsymbolic
Unidimensional	Multidimensional

Figure 1. The emerging nature of social phenomena.

Global social facts and institutions are now constructed in a way fundamentally different from any other periods of human history. Today, they are not constrained by time, space, distance, culture, and civilization. The understanding of the present world of turbulent change and transformations will need a qualitatively different set of sociological categories. The task of reforming sociology and social science for global studies is a task of discovering those new categories of analysis. The challenge of globalization to social science is not only a matter of including more studies on foreign cultures and language, a process described as internationalization, but it is rather to bring globalization into the core of theorizing, and this suggests the need for new conceptual apparatus and paradigm change. As British sociologist Margaret Archer points out: "The task of international sociology is to specify how global mechanisms combine with regional circumstances, in non-uniform fashion, to shape new trajectories and novel configurations. Globalization is not merely the effect of the 'new world on the old:' the two together make for a radically different world, which is the job of international sociology to capture—social theory is never intransitive" (1991: 131).

The Nationality and Globality in Social Science: Reform as a Global Agenda

Globalization has recently become a central theme in the reorganization of social science in almost all countries and regions of the world. The need for inter-societal understanding and learning has never been so central to social science discourses as it is at the present time. In 1996, the theme of the British Sociological Association's annual meeting was "Worlds of the Future: Ethnicity, Nationalism, and Globalization." The organizing theme of the annual meeting of the American Sociological Practice Association in 1996 was globalization and its impact on the emerging territories and profession of sociological practice. The theme of the 1997 annual meeting of the American Sociological Association held in Toronto was "Bridges for Sociology: International and Disciplinary." In Africa, Asia, and Latin American regions, social science meetings and seminars continuously focus on the theme of globalization.

Social science was not born to become a national intellectual enterprise of a particular country. Hobbes, Locke, Rousseau, Smith, Marx, Mills, Freud, Weber, and Durkheim of classical social science searched for universals in the understanding of human behavior and the organization of human society. But in the wake of the rise of social science in the nineteenth century, the old boundaries of empires crumbled, a process of decolonization began, and world societies began to be divided into nation-states. Social science's growth and expansion, then, began primarily as a part of national reconstruction and modernization in all the world societies in the twentieth century.

The historical predicament of the nationality of social science does not, however, mean the lack of universality in social science education and training (Deutsch, Markovits, and Platt, 1986; Luce, Smelser, and Gerstein, 1987). Students majoring in sociology in India or Singapore study the same theoretical traditions of Marx, Weber, Durkheim, Parsons, and Merton as studied by students majoring in sociology at Oxford or Princeton. It is only in few countries that students can probably major in psychology without studying Freud and Piaget, or major in management without studying Maslow's theory of the hierarchy of needs, or specialize in ethics without studying Rawls theory of justice.

The nationality of social science is expressed more in terms of social science's location within a cultural and national milieu. The dominant view here is that social science, along with its concerns for theoretical universality, will have to be able to advance the understanding of local needs and peculiarities of the nation-states (Kyvik, 1988). People and cultures of different nation-states share many basic similarities, but they are also different from one another in many fundamental ways. Social science, in contrast to physical and biological sciences, is characterized by this predicament, and it became particularly strong when the expansion of social science was politicized and seen as part of the movement for national reconstruction in the emerging industrial societies in the twentieth century. Since the beginning of the 1960s, a process of indigenization began in social science of all countries and nations of the world (Riggs, 1987; Smelser, 1989). This was a movement for locating social science within the program of national reconstruction, and the development of new categories of analysis compatible with indigenous cultural systems.

A process of indigenization, however, can be vital for the growth and use of social science. The importance of silence and stillness in Japanese nonverbal communication, or nonverbal communication and hierarchical relationship in Indian culture, for example, may not be clearly comprehended by western sociologists trained in a society with more verbal and formalistic social roles and relationships. It is increasingly recognized in the context of the rise of the post-positivistic movement and the growing acceptance of the constructivistic perspective in contemporary social science that human mind, morality, self, identity, cognition, and consciousness are historically and culturally embedded (Kitayama and Markus, 1992). The understanding of a society should be contextual. But what is happening theoretically is that this contextualist argument is becoming a universal tradition in social science.

The nationality of social science and its indigenization can not be harmful to the growth and expansion of social science as a global enterprise. A cross-cultural research on Piagetian theory of learning or Kohlberg's theory of moral development will not undermine, but rather enrich theorizing in modern psychology (Adler and Gielen, 1994). The scrutinization of the relevance of the Japanese organizational model of Quality Circle, or the German model of School-to-Work transition in America is a matter of examining the contextual relevance, and it does not undermine the pursuit of universality in American sociology. One of the continuing themes in Japanese sociology is about the relevance of the western concept of individualism. In exploring that theme, the Japanese sociologists may like to examine the ideas of Robert Nisbet, Robert Bellah, Amitai Etzioni and other American critics of individualism. This will not undermine but enrich the content of Japanese sociology.

Like indigenization, globalization is also becoming an integral part of the evolution of contemporary social science. Globalization is also a search for new categories of thought and frames of analysis, but those which can explain the emerging globality of local and indigenous social systems. The globalization of social science will not mean the abandonment of the search for local peculiarities, but will mean that bridges are being built between the contexts of locality and globality.

Globalization is leading to the development of a community of global social scientists who are interested in exploring new theories and categories of a transcultural nature. Social scientists of different countries and regions are increasingly collaborating in charting the nature and territory of a global social science. As a practical and policy interest, efforts for the globalization of social science, however, will remain primarily a national effort.

Many international research programs on transcivilizational issues, such as violence against women, human rights, ethnic revivalism, fundamentalism, global migration, and the cultural impact of technology, are now developing in social science. The UNESCO's "MOST Framework" (Management of Social Transformations), European Community's "FAST Program," and the European Institute of Human Sciences' "SOCO" (Social Cost of Economic Transformation in Central Europe) projects are some of the important examples of a new generation of transnational research programs in contemporary international social science.

At the level of global theorizing, the initiative of the Uppsala Theory Circle is also remarkable. Under the sponsorship of the Department of Sociology at Uppsala University in Sweden, an international collegium consisting of scholars (sociologists, economists, political scientists, ecologists, and mathematicians) from Europe and the United States, as well as Asia and Africa, has been established. The Circle, which meets on a regular basis, is a global social science forum on various emerging transcultural and transcivilizational issues.

Immanuel Wallerstein is also currently leading a global project for reforming social science. Under the sponsorship of the Calouste Gulbenkian Foundation of Portugal, Wallerstien is gathering some of the world's leading social scientists in a forum to think and reconceptualize the traditional nature and boundaries of social science (Wallerstein, 1991b). What Wallerstein and his group are considering, is what Japan is trying to materialize: a new curriculum innovation in the Nishi-Ikuta

University of Japan. In 1990, this university has set up a new Faculty of Inte-grated Arts and Social Sciences covering five disciplines: sociology, social welfare, psychology, humanities, and cultural studies, where scholars coming from different specialties and countries deliberate on the future of globalization in world societies, including Japan. While these kinds of global programs and initiatives will continue to increase at the international level, reforming social science for globalization is also a local challenge, and it will depend on the historical nature and traditions of social science in different nations (Genov, 1993).

The Nationality and Globality in American Sociology: The Directions for Reforms and Restructuring

The nationalization of American sociology has evolved in two stages. Sociology in America was imported from Europe in the late nineteenth century, and up until the end of the Second World War, the process of nationalization was a process of indigenization (Klausner and Lidz, 1986; Parsons, 1986). Sociology's dominant preoccupation at that time was to explain the problems of the emerging urban and industrial society and the growth of a national culture from of diverse constellation of migrated Europeans. In no nation has sociology faced the same predicament at the time of its birth as it faced in America. It was to explain and articulate the boundary of a new civilization destined to progress on the basis of cultural institutions which did not have any comparable experiments in Europe and precedence in world human history. American sociology before the war, therefore, was pragmatic and predominantly involved in national reconstruction.

After the Second World War, the nationalization of American sociology pro-ceeded in four directions. The first was the direction for the rise of scientific sociol-ogy. The dominant concern of scientific sociology was not national reconstruction, but theorizing and empirical research in the tradition of the natural sciences (Bryant, 1985). The referential reality of scientific sociology was primarily the evolving nature of modernity in America and the uniqueness of the American civilization. The second was the development of sociology as a policy science, particularly in the context of the construction of the "Great Society"—the governing ideology of the Roosevelt era. From the 1950s to 1960s, for almost a decade, sociology was intellectually close to political power in America.

Sociology's closeness to political power, however, began to be immediately chal-lenged by a section of the sociological community, particularly by the left radicals who emerged in the wake of the civil rights movement, anti-Vietnam protest, and the expansion of counter-culture. The rise of radical sociology, within the span of a decade, brought a radical separation between mainstream sociology and policy-making in America. American mainstream sociology from the beginning of the 1970s began to be practiced mostly within the walls of the universities (Bryant,

1985). Sociology's recent direction for globalization and contribution to policy-making for the emerging century did not grow until the end of the Cold War in the mid 1980s, and the discovery that America is losing in global economic and educational competitiveness.

From the beginning of its birth, American sociology has remained engaged in national reconstruction and the construction of its soul as a scientific enterprise. The study of the historical evolution of different societies and civilizations did not form any significant niche within the intellectual structure of the discipline. As K. Erikson said more than two decades ago, "Sociology in the US continues to lack historical focus. Most of what passes for sociological research in this country is not informed by much in the way of a historical perspective" (1971: 61).

During the Cold War, when knowledge of different countries and cultures was needed for policy-making, and when modernization was expanding in the Third World under the planned guidance of international assistance organizations, the use of social science in Area Studies and foreign affairs expanded. In that context, some interests for the study of other cultures were generated in American sociology (Almond and Coleman, 1960; Bellah, 1957; Inkles and Smith, 1974; Levy, 1972; Smelser, 1957). But because of sociology's classical notion of separation between traditional and modern societies, and the rise of the dependency paradigm in the mid 1970s as a critique of modernization, the movement for the study of other cultures did not gain a firm ground within the intellectual bounds of American sociology. During the Cold War, the American anthropologists (Geertz, 1963; 1983) and political scientists (Almond and Verba, 1963; Pye, 1985) were probably more involved than American sociologists in the study of foreign cultures. The growth of literature on comparative politics (Almond and Verba, 1963; Inglehart, 1981) and administration (Riggs, 1971; Waldo, 1976) was far more extensive than that of comparative sociology.

Some of the early presidents of the American Sociological Association, such as Graham Sumner, W.I. Thomas, E.A. Ross, and R.E. Park, advocated for a more historical and global orientation in American sociology. Between the 1930s and 1950s, there were twenty ASA presidents and "not one is known primarily or substantially for (cross-national) comparative work" (Kohn, 1996: 48). One survey of the articles published in the American Journal of Sociology from 1945 to 1985 shows that in 1945, about 45% of the articles published had historical and global directions. In 1985, there was none with historical and global content.

The recent rise of historical orientation in American sociology, particularly that which emerged through the writings of such authors as Charles Tilly and Theda Skocpol, is a new turn, but has remained primarily Euro-centric (Sztompka, 1986; Tilly, 1984; Skocpol, 1979). With the exception of the studies done by S.N. Eisenstadt on the evolution of political empires and urban civilizations in different world regions (1963; 1974), Benjamin Nelson on modernization and intercivilizational en-counters (1981), Edward Shils (1968; 1981) and Joseph Ben-David (1971) on the nature of traditions and science in different world societies, Immanuel Wallerstein on the perspective of the world systems (1974), and Richard Bendix on the decline of aristocracy and the rise of modern polity (1978), most of American sociology, until recently, has remained nationalistic and local in character (Gareau, 1984).

A considerable amount of literature on globalism, however, is now developing (Barber, 1995; Basu, 1995; Ginsburg and Rapp, 1995; Lie, 1995; Mittleman, 1995; Robertson, 1992; Richmond, 1995; Waters, 1995). But efforts for restructuring the discipline are still in infancy. In the early 1990's, the American Sociological Association set up a Task Force for the globalization of American Sociology, and various national and regional associations since have also made globalization an important agenda for future research and deliberations. These organizational efforts are making some impacts, but theoretical restructuring and efforts for conceptual innovations are still a big challenge. In most restructuring efforts, globalization is defined as internationalization—which means the infusion of more foreign language and cultures in the curriculum (Tirayakin, 1993). What is needed, however, is a movement for theoretical and conceptual change from below.

The perspective of globalization does not suggest an abandonment of concerns in American sociology for local and national issues. But it will require the recasting of such existing theoretical traditions as structuralism, exchange, rational choice, symbolic-interactionism, feminism, and culturalism in the context of the historical specificity of different cultures and civilizations. The increasing emergence and crys-tallization of intercultural and intercivilizational facts and events within the bounds of the American society has to be theorized in terms of new paradigms. Melvin Kohn rightly said that American sociology is at an "early stage in the development of appropriate methodologies for transnational research" (1996: 31).

One of the emerging perspectives in social science is evolutionism. In recent biology, cognitive psychology, archeology and philosophy of science, the notion of evolutionism has been emerging as a dominant theoretical perspective (Wukettis, 1984). In classical sociology, social evolution and the concepts of differentiation and integration were prominent in the writings of Auguste Comte, Herbert Spencer, and Emile Durkheim. In contemporary sociology, the evolutionary perspective was further advanced by Talcott Parsons (1977) and other theorists of modernization. But in the wake of the rise of empirical sociology and the crystallization of national traditions, the evolutionary perspective was by and large abandoned in sociology in general, and in American sociology in particular.

The perspective of evolutionism can bring the notions of competitiveness, growth and survival, cooperation and conflict, learning and adaptation, risk and uncertainty, and cultural retention and rejections into the core of theoretical understanding and explanations. The contemporary global social space, within which different nation-states exist, is space for increased inter-societal and intercivilization exchanges and competitions, learning and adaptations, and risks and uncertainties in the growth and survival of the nation-states. The global space is an arena for the evolution of new complexities (Arthur, 1994). Different nation-states, because of the rise of new constraints and possibilities, will evolve new institutional structures and designs through the retention and rejection of many of their own cultural traditions. The increased competition will create new areas of conflicts, new regions and structures of cooperation, and new domains of policy-making. The evolutionary perspective, combined with the theoretical models of structuralism, conflict sociology, symbolic-interactionism, exchange, and feminism can provide important analysis of the nature and peculiarities of the emerging change and transformations in the world societies. In organizational studies, institutional economics (Gilpin, 1996; Hodgson, 1996), politics (Modelski, 1996), and foreign affairs (Farkas, 1996), the evolutionary perspective is recently gaining a significant theoretical ground (Modelski and Poznanski, 1996).

There is also needed a futuristic vision for the globalization of social science. In the twentieth century, one of social science's practical missions was to provide scientific and moral justification for the construction of a liberal-industrial society—first in the west and then in the rest of the world on a global scale. In the twenty-first century, the liberal-industrial society—the American model of civilization, will be further globalized. The "American Dream" is no longer bounded by territory—it is becoming a global dream. But at the same time, there will emerge new tensions and territories of conflicts centering around the basic premises of a liberal-industrial society (Shahidullah, 1997). In America, the cultural war between tradition and modernity will further escalate. The globalization of the American economy and culture will enlarge the boundary of cultural clash. One of the recent court battles, with respect to a massive sexual harassment case against the Japanese company, Mitsubishi, in America, is a case in point. Many of the accepted norms of management in a Japanese company may be socially unacceptable in America.

Many contemporary directions in American sociology such as the rise of the communitarian perspective (Bellah, 1991; Etzioni, 1995) and the growth of a new movement for moral sociology (Etzioni, 1988), however, point to the possibility of a new bridge of thought between the fundamentals of the civilizations of the west and the non-west. American sociology in this context needs to be directed toward what James Coleman called the construction of purposive social structures (Coleman, 1990). The emerging forces of globalization in America will demand new structures of the social ecology of work, organizations, family, school, and governance. The physical ecology of communities, cities, and regions also have to be socially redesigned to meet with global economic challenges. In the construction of new social structures, intercultural and intercivilizational norms and issues have to be addressed and mediated. The challenge for the globalization of social science, and particularly sociology in America is, therefore, both theoretical and practical in nature.

Conclusions

The globalization of the world economy and cultures have been fundamentally transforming the constitution of the whole domain of human actions, beliefs, and values. New facts and forces are increasingly becoming time and space neutral, intercultural, and intercivilizational. New intercultural forces are creating a new world homogeneity in the design of social structures in different societies and in the dreams, aspirations, perceptions, and morality of their people. Different civilizational societies are also becoming intensely local and discovering their fundamental differences. A new series of intercivilizational issues such as human rights, equality for women, and the rights of children are impacting on the conduct of the world economy and politics.

Globalization is not merely a process of the expansion of trade and technology. It is rather a trajectory of new human possibilities, choice, and preferences which are fundamentally different from other periods of human history. Modernity in the nineteenth century created and engulfed the world with new social ideas and tensions fundamentally different from those of the middle ages. Similarly, globalization in the twentieth century has been creating ideas and tensions which are vastly different from those of the industrial society of the nineteenth century. It is in this context that the demand for reforming social science has become a global agenda.

The globalization of social science does not mean the abandonment of its concerns for local issues and problems. It should also not be defined as a matter of infusing in social science more studies of foreign cultures. The globalization of social science is rather a matter of evolving new categories of theoretical tools and new forms of social designs and cultural models for the mediation of transcultural and transcivilizational facts and forces. Evidence shows that efforts for the globalization of social science are growing in all world societies. The nature and the success of those efforts will probably depend on respective national traditions in social science.

Of all the social sciences in America, sociology traditionally lacks a genuine historical and comparative-civilizational orientation. But sociology is theoretically far more advanced, and what is needed for globalization is the enlargement of that tradition with new theoretical orientations. The pragmatic nature of American sociology can also be vital. There are concerns about the utilization of social science knowledge in America, but social science in America, in general, is much more pragmatic and practice-oriented. This pragmatism, now in the context of globalization, needs to be recast as efforts for sociology's engagement with policy for the construction of new actors and institutions. The challenge for the globalization of social science in the next century is, therefore, both theoretical and practical in nature. The world of social science needs a new paradigm and a new philosophy of praxis in the context of globalization.

REFERENCES

ADLER, L.L. and U.P. GIELEN

1994 *Cross-Cultural Topics in Psychology*. Westport, Conn: Praeger.

ALMOND, G. and S. VERBA

1963 *The Civic Culture: Political Attitudes and Democracy in Five Nations*. Princeton, NJ: Princeton University Press.

ALMOND, G. and J. COLEMAN (Eds.)

1960 *Politics of the Developing Areas*. Princeton, NJ: Princeton University Press.

ANDERSON, B.

1983 *Imagined Communities*. London: Verson.

APPADURAI, A.

1991 Global ethnoscapes: notes and queries for a transnational anthropology. In R.G. Fox (Ed.), *Recapturing Anthropology* (pp. 191-210). Santa Fe, NM: School of American Research Press.

ARCHER, M.S.

1991 Sociology for one world: unity and diversity. *International Sociology* 6, 131-147.

ARTHUR, B.W.

1994 *On the Evolution of Complexity [Research Report]*. Stanford: Santa Fe Institute, Stanford University.

BARBER, B.R.

1995 *Jihad vs. McWorld*. New York: Times Books.

BARNET, R.J. and J. CAVANAGH

1994 *Global Dreams: Imperial Corporation and the New World Order*. New York: Touchstone.

BASU, A. (Ed.)

1995 *The Challenge of Local Feminism: Women's Movement in Global Perspective*. Boulder, CO: Westview Press.

BELLAH, R.N.

1957 *Tokugawa Religion*. New York: Free Press.

BEN-DAVID, J.

1971 *The Scientist's Role in Society: A Comparative Study*. Englewood, NJ: Prentice-Hall.

BENDIX, R.

1978 *Kings or People: Power and Mandate to Rule*. Berkeley: California University Press.

BRYANT, G.A.C.

1985 *Positivism in Social Theory and Research*. New York: St. Martin Press.

CARRIER, J.G.

1995 *Occidentalism: Images of the West*. New York: Oxford University Press.

CHASE-DUNN, C. and P. GRIMES

1995 World-systems analysis. *Annual Review of Sociology* 21, 387-417.

COLEMAN, J.S.

1990 *Foundations of Social Theory*. Cambridge and London: The Belknap Press of Harvard University Press.

COMMISSION ON GLOBAL GOVERNANCE
    1995 *Our Global Neighborhood: The Report of the Commission on Global Governance.* Oxford: Oxford University Press.
DEUTSCH, K.W., A.S. MARKOVITS and J. PLATT
    1986 *Advances in the Social Sciences, 1900-1980.* New York: University Press of America.
EISENSTADT, S.M.
    1978 *Revolutions and the Transformation of Societies.* New York: Free Press.
EISENSTADT, S.M.
    1963 *The Political System of Empires.* New York: Free Press.
ELLIOTT, M.
    1996 Going home: People and nations have a sense of identity, which could fuel a growing resentment of America. *Newsweek* December 30, 40-42.
ERIKSON, K.T.
    1971 Sociology and the Historical Perspective. In W. Bell and J.A. May (Eds.), *The Sociology of the Future.* New York: Russell Sage Foundation.
ETZIONI, A.
    1988 *The Moral Dimension: Toward a New Economics.* New York: The Free Press.
ETZIONI, A. (Ed.)
    1995 *Rights and the Common Good: The Communitarian Perspective.* New York: St. Martin Press.
FARKAS, A.
    1996 Evolutionary models in foreign policy analysis. *International Studies Quarterly* 40, 343-361.
FEATHERSTONE, M. (Ed.)
    1990 *Global Culture: Nationalism, Globalization and Modernity.* London: Sage.
FORTE, M.
    1996 *Globalization and World-Systems Analysis: Toward a New Paradigm of a Geo-Historical Social Anthropology.* Research Paper 2. State University of New York, Binghampton.
FRIEDMAN, J.
    1994 *Cultural Identity and Global Process.* London: Sage.
FUKUYAMA, F.
    1992 *The End of History and the Last Man.* New York: Free Press.
GAREAU, F.H.
    1984 An empirical analysis of the international structure of American social science. *The Social Science Journal* 5, 23-35.
GEERTZ, C.
    1983 *Local Knowledge: Further Essays in Interpretive Anthropology.* New York: Basic Books.
GEERTZ, C.
    1963 *Old Societies and New States.* New York: Free Press.
GENOV, N.
    1993 National Sociological tradition and the internationalization of sociology. In N. Genov (Ed.), *National Traditions in Sociology.* Newbury Park: Sage.
GIDDENS, A.
    1991 *Modernity and Self-Identity.* Stanford: Stanford University Press.
GIDDENS, A.
    1990 *The Consequences of Modernity.* Stanford: Stanford University Press.
GILPIN, R.
    1996 Economic evolution of national systems. *International Studies Quarterly* 40, 411-431.

GINSBURG, F.D. and R. RAPP (Ed.)
  1995 *Conceiving the New World Order: The Global Politics of Reproduction*. Berkeley: University of California Press.
HAMM, B.
  1992 Europe: a challenge to the social sciences. *International Social Science Journal* 134.
HEINTZ, P.
  1992 *Introduction to the Sociological Code for the Description of World Society and Its Change*. (Mimeo), Sociological Institute, University of Zurich.
HIRST, P. and G. THOMPSON
  1995 *Globalization in Question: The International Economy and the Possibilities of Governance*. London: Polity Press.
HODGSON, G.
  1996 An evolutionary theory of long-term economic growth. *International Studies Quarterly* 40, 391-410.
HOLZNER, B.
  1991 Knowledge and action in the emerging world: social science, the shocks of global structural change, and policy. *Knowledge and Policy: The International Journal of Knowledge Transfer* 4 (1-2), 18-36.
HUNTINGTON, S.P.
  1996 *The Clash of Civilizations and the Remaking of World Order*. New York: Simon and Schuster.
INGLEHART, R.
  1990 *Culture Shift in Advanced Industrial Society*. Princeton, NJ: Princeton University Press.
INKLES, A. and D.H. SMITH
  1974 *Becoming Modern*. Cambridge: Harvard University Press.
KING, A.D.
  1992 The holistic path to a global society. *International Social Science Journal* 134.
KITAYAMA, S. and H.R. MARKUS
  1992 Construal of the self as a cultural frame: implications for internationalizing psychology. Paper Presented at *the Symposium on Internationalization and Higher Education*. Ann Arbor: University of Michigan, May, 6-8.
KLAUSNER, S.Z. and V.M. LIDZ
  1986 *The Nationalization of the Social Sciences*. Philadelphia: University of Pennsylvania Press.
KOHN, M.L.
  1996 Cross-national research as an analytical strategy: American Sociological Association, 1978 Presidential Address. In A. Inkles and M. Sasaki (Eds.), *Comparing Nations and Cultures* (pp. 28-54). Engelwood Cliffs, NJ: Prentice-Hall.
KYVIK, S.
  1988 Internationality of the social sciences: The Norwegian case. *International Journal of Social Science* 115, 163-172.
LAM, A.
  1995 Generation X in East Asia—Reinventing the self and redefining the frontier. *Pacific News Service* November (2).
LEVY, M.
  1972 *Modernization: Latecomers and Survivors*. New York: Basic Books.
LIE, J.
  1996 Globalization and its discontent. *Contemporary Sociology* 25, 585-587.

LIE, J.
 1995 American sociology in a transnational world. *Teaching Sociology* 25, 136-144.
LINCICOME, M.
 1991 *Ideology, Culture, and Politics in the Internationalization of Japanese Education.* Paper Presented at the Midwest Japan Seminar, DePauw University, March.
LUCE, R.D., N.J. SMELSER and D.R. GERSTEIN
 1987 *Leading Edges in Social and Behavioral Sciences.* New York: Russel sage Foundation.
MEYER, W.H.
 1989 Global news flows: dependency and neoimperialism. *Comparative Political Studies* 22, 243-260.
MITTLEMAN, J.H. (Ed.)
 1995 *Globalization: Critical Reflections.* Boulder, CO: Lynne Rienner Publication.
MODELSKI, G.
 1996 Evolutionary paradigm for global politics. *International Studies Quarterly* 40, 321-342.
MODELSKI, G. and K. POZNANSKI
 1996 Evolutionary paradigms in the social sciences. *International Studies Quarterly* 40, 315-319.
NATIONAL GOVERNORS ASSOCIATION
 1990 *America in Transition: The International Frontier.* Report of the Task Force on International Education. Washington DC: National Governor's Association.
NELSON, B.
 1981 *On the Roads to Modernity: Conscience, Science, and Civilizations*, T.E. Huff (Ed.). Totowa, NJ: Rowman and Littlefield.
PARSONS, T.
 1986 Social science: a basic national resouce. In S.Z. Klausner and V.M. Lidz (Eds.). *The Nationalization of the Social Sciences* (pp. 42-109). Philadelphia: The University of Pennsylvania Press.
PARSONS, T.
 1977 *The Evolution of Societies*, J. Toby (Ed.). Engelwood Cliffs, NJ: Prentice-Hall.
PETRAS, J. and M. MORELY
 1995 *Empire or Republic: American Global Power and Domestic Decay.* New York: Routledge.
PYE, L.W.
 1985 *Asian Power and Politics: The Cultural Dimensions of Authority.* Cambridge, Mass: Belknap Press of Harvard University Press.
REICH, R.B.
 1991 *The Work of Nations: Preparing Ourselves For the 21st Century Capitalism.* New York: Alfred A. Knopf.
RICHMOND, A.H.
 1995 *Global Apartheid: Refugees, Racism, and the New World Order.* New York: Oxford University Press.
RIGGS, F.W.
 1987 A conceptual encyclopedia for the social sciences. *International Social Science Journal* 111 (February), 111-124.
RIGGS, F.W. (Ed.)
 1971 *Frontiers of Development Administration.* Durham, NC: Duke University Press.
ROBERTSON, R.
 1992 *Globalization: Social Theory and Global Culture.* London: Sage

SAHLINS, M.
   1994 Cosmologies of capitalism: The trans-pacific sector of the world system. In N.B. Dirks, G. Eley, and S.B. Ortner (Eds.), *Culture, Power and History* (pp. 412-455). Princeton: Princeton University Press.

SAID, E.
   1978 *Orientalism.* New York: Vintage Books.

SHAHIDULLAH, S.M.
   1997 The manufacturing of knowledge for policy-making: The role of social science in the 21st Century. *Future Research Quarterly* 12, 5-34. Washington, DC: The World Future Society.

SHILS, E.
   1981 *Tradition.* Chicago: University of Chicago Press.

SHILS, E.
   1968 *Criteria For Scientific Development: Public Policy and National Goals.* Cambridge, Mass: The MIT Press.

SKOCPOL, T.
   1979 *State and Social Revolutions: A Comparative Analysis of France, Russia, and China.* Cambridge: Cambridge University Press.

SMELSER, N.J.
   1959 *Social Change in the Industrial Revolution.* London: Routledge.

SMELSER, N.J.
   1989 External influences on sociology. *International Sociology* 4, 419-429.

SZTOMPKA, P.
   1986 The renaissance of historical orientation in sociology. *International Sociology* 1, 321-337.

TILLY, C.
   1984 *Big Structures, Large Processes, Huge Comparisons.* New York: Russel Sage Foundation.

TIRYAKIAN, E.
   1993 Sociology's great leap forward:challenge of internationalization. In M. Albrow and E. King (Eds.), *Globalization, Knowledge, and Society: Readings from International Sociology* (pp. 63-78). London, Newbury Park: Delhi: Sage.

WALDO, D. (Ed.)
   1976 Comparative and development administration—a symposium. *Public Administration Review* November-December, 615-653.

WALLERSTEIN, I.
   1996 *The Time of Space and Space of Time: The Future of Social Science.* (Geographical Society lecture.) UK: University of Newcastle.

WALLERSTEIN, I.
   1991a *Geo-Politics and Geo-Culture: Essays on the Changing World System.* Cambride: Cambridge University Press.

WALLERSTEIN, I.
   1991b *Unthinking Social Science.* Cambridge: Polity Press.

WALLERSTEIN, I.
   1974 *The Modern World System.* New York: Academic Press.

WATERS, M.
   1995 *Globalization.* New York: Routledge.

WUKETTIS, F.M. (Ed.)
   1984 *Concepts and Approaches in Evolutionary Epistemology.* Dordrecht: D. Reidel Publishing Company.

CONTRIBUTORS

Alessandro Bonanno is Professor and Chair of the Department of Sociology at Sam Houston State University, Huntsville, Texas. He has researched, among other topics, economy and society, regional and international development and the state. He is the author of numerous journal articles and books in English and other major languages.

Stephen W.K. Chiu is Associate Professor of Sociology at the Chinese University of Hong Kong. His research interests are social movements, industrial sociology, and East Asia. He has recently co-authored *East Asia and the World Economy* (Sage, 1995), and *City States in the Global Economy: Industrial Restructuring in Hong Kong and Singapore* (Westview, 1996).

Douglas H. Constance is Research Assistant Professor of Rural Sociology at the University of Missouri-Columbia. His research interests include the globalization of economy and society, environmental sociology, and social movements. He has several articles and a book published in these areas.

Richard J. Estess is Professor of Social Work at the University of Pennsylvania where he chairs the graduate specialization in Social and Economic Development. His research interests include international and comparative social development and social welfare. His recent books include: *The Social Progress of Nations* (Praeger, 1984), *Trends in World Social Development* (Praeger, 1988), and *Internationalizing Social Work Education* (University of Pennsylvania, 1992).

R. Scott Frey received a Ph.D. in Sociology from Colorado State University and is currently Professor of Sociology at Kansas State University. He has also held appointments at George Washington University and the National Science Foundation. His work has appeared in various journals, including the American Journal of Sociology and the American Sociological Review.

Archibald O. Haller (Ph.D., University of Wisconsin) is Professor Emeritus of Rural Sociology and of Sociology at University of Wisconsin. He has made contributions to the theories of societal stratification structures, social mobility, and status stratification processes, as well as to the measurement of socio-econmic development.

George A. Miller is Professor of Sociology at the University of Utah. He received his B.A. degree from Eastern Washington University, and his M.A. and Ph.D. degrees from the University of Washington. His current research involves the cross-national comparison of organizational structures and the measurement of national development.

Proshanta K. Nandi is Professor of Sociology at the University of Illinois at Springfield. A Fulbright Scholar, he received his M.A. and Ph.D. degrees from the University of Minnesota. He has published numerous journal articles and a book in the areas of comparative education, quality of life, ethnicity, and conflict resolution.

Winifred R. Poster is a doctoral candidate in Sociology at Stanford University. She is currently working on her dissertation which examines the social construction of gender in high-tech companies in India and the United States. Her interests involve the cross-cultural dynamics of gender, class, race and ethnicity.

J. Timmons Roberts (Ph.D., Johns Hopkins University) is an Assistant Professor of Sociology and Latin American Studies at Tulane University in New Orleans. His research interests include study of psychosocial effects of environmental contaminations, and linkages between environmental organizations in Latin America and the wealthy nations.

Shahid M. Shahidullah (Ph.D., Pittsburgh) is Assistant Professor of Sociology at Virginia State University. His research interests include development and modernization, knowledge utilization in policy-making, and technology and crime policies. Author of a book on *Capacity-Building in Science and Technology in the Third World* (Westview), his research has been published in a number of edited books and journals.

Bam Dev Sharda is Professor of Sociology at the University of Utah. He received his B.A. and M.A. degrees from Punjab University, India, and his Ph.D. degree from the University of Wisconsin. His current research involves the analysis of social mobility in India and the effects of national development on stratification.

Alvin Y. So is Professor of Sociology at the University of Hawaii. His research interests are class analysis, development, and East Asia. His recent publications include *East Asia and the World Economy* (Co-author, Sage 1995), and *Hong-Kong Guangdong Link: Partnership in Flux* (Co-editor, Sharpe, 1995).

INDEX

INTERNATIONAL STUDIES
IN
SOCIOLOGY AND SOCIAL ANTHROPOLOGY

EDITED BY S. ISHWARAN

21. FUSÉ, T. (ed.). *Modernization and Stress in Japan.* 1975. ISBN 90 04 04344 6
22. SMITH, B.L. (ed.). *Religion and Social Conflict in South Asia.* 1976.
ISBN 90 04 04510 4
23. MAZRUI, A.A. (ed.). *The Warrior Tradition in Modern Africa.* 1977.
ISBN 90 04 05646 7
25. SMITH, B.L. (ed.). *Religion and the Legitimation of Power in South Asia.* 1978.
ISBN 90 04 05674 2
31. LELE, J. (ed.). *Tradition and Modernity in* Bhakti *Movements.* 1981.
ISBN 90 04 06370 6
32. ARMER, J.M. *Comparative Sociological Research in the 1960s and 1970s.* 1982.
ISBN 90 04 06487 7
33. GALATY, J.G. & P.C. SALZMAN (eds.). *Change and Development in Nomadic and Pastoral Societies.* 1981. ISBN 90 04 06587 3
34. LUPRI, E. (ed.). *The Changing Position of Women in Family and Society. A Cross-National Comparison.* 1983. ISBN 90 04 06845 7
35. IVERSON, N. (ed.). *Urbanism and Urbanization. Views, Aspects and Dimensions.* 1984.
ISBN 90 04 06920 8
36. MALIK, Y.K. *Politics, Technology, and Bureaucracy in South Asia.* 1983.
ISBN 90 04 07027 3
37. LENSKI, G. (ed.). *Current Issues and Research in Macrosociology.* 1984.
ISBN 90 04 07052 4
39. TIRYAKIAN, E.A. (ed.). *The Global Crisis. Sociological Analyses and Responses.* 1984.
ISBN 90 04 07284 5
40. LAWRENCE, B. (ed.). *Ibn Khaldun and Islamic Ideology.* 1984. ISBN 90 04 07567 4
41. HAJJAR, S.G. (ed.). *The Middle East: from Transition to Development.* 1985.
ISBN 90 04 07694 8
43. CARMAN, J.B. & F.A. MARGLIN (eds.). *Purity and Auspiciousness in Indian Society.* 1985. ISBN 90 04 07789 8
46. SMITH, B.L. & H.B. REYNOLDS (eds.). *The City as a Sacred Center. Essays on Six Asian Contexts.* 1987. ISBN 90 04 08471 1
47. MALIK, Y.K. & D.K. VAJPEYI (eds.). *India. The Years of Indira Ghandi.* 1988.
ISBN 90 04 08681 1
48. CLARK, C. & J. LEMCO (eds.). *State and Development.* 1988. ISBN 90 04 08833 4
49. GUTKIND, P.C.W. (ed.). *Third World Workers. Comparative International Labour Studies.* 1988. ISBN 90 04 08788 5
50. SELIGMAN, A.B. *Order and Transcendence. The Role of Utopias and the Dynamics of Civilization.* 1989. ISBN 90 04 08975 6
51. JABBRA, J.G. *Bureaucracy and Development in the Arab World.* 1989.
ISBN 90 04 09194 7

52. KAUTSKY, J.H. (ed.). *Karl Kautsky and the Social Science of Classical Marxism*. 1989. ISBN 90 04 09193 9
53. KAPUR, A. (ed.). *The Diplomatic Ideas and Practices of Asian States*. 1990. ISBN 90 04 09289 7
54. KIM, Q.-Y. (ed.). *Revolutions in the Third World*. 1991. ISBN 90 04 09355 9
55. KENNEDY, C.H. & D.J. LOUSCHER (eds.). *Civil Military Interaction in Asia and Africa*. 1991. ISBN 90 04 09359 1
56. RAGIN, C.C. (ed.). *Issues and Alternatives in Comparative Social Research*. 1991. ISBN 90 04 09360 5
57. CHOUDHRY, N.K. (ed.). *Canada and South Asian Development. Trade and Aid*. 1991. ISBN 90 04 09416 4
58. RAZIA AKTER BANU, U.A.B. (ed.). *Islam in Bangladesh*. 1992. ISBN 90 04 09497 0
61. AHMAD, A. (ed.). *Science and Technology Policy for Economic Development in Africa*. 1993. ISBN 90 04 09659 0
62. VAJPEYI, D.K. (ed.). *Modernizing China*. 1994. ISBN 90 04 10046 6
63. BRADSHAW, Y.W. (ed.). *Education in Comparative Perspective*. New Lessons from around the World. 1997. ISBN 90 04 10734 7
64. UDOGU, E.I. (ed.). *Democracy and Democratization in Africa*. Toward the 21st Century. 1997. ISBN 90 04 10733 9
65. BEHAR, J.E. & A.G. CUZÁN (eds.). *At the Crossroads of Development*. Transnational Challenges to Developed and Developing Societies. 1997. ISBN 90 04 10732 0
66. LAUDERDALE, P. & R. AMSTER (eds.). *Lives in the Balance*. Perspectives on Global Injustice and Inequality. 1997. ISBN 90 04 10875 0
67. LOVEJOY, P.E. & P.A.T. WILLIAMS (eds.). *Displacement and the Politics of Violence in Nigeria*. 1997. ISBN 90 04 10876 9
68. JABBRA, J.G. & JABBRA, N.W. (eds.). *Challenging Environmental Issues*. Middle Eastern Perspectives. 1997. ISBN 90 04 10877 7
69. SASAKI, M. (ed.). *Values and Attitudes Across Nations and Time*. 1998. ISBN 90 04 11219 7
70. SPERLING, J., Y. MALIK & D. LOUSCHER (eds.). *Zones of Amity, Zones of Enmity*. The Prospects for Economic and Military Security in Asia. 1998. ISBN 90 04 11218 9
71. NANDI, P.K. & S.M. SHAHIDULLAH (eds.). *Globalization and the Evolving World Society*. 1998. ISBN 90 04 11247 2